CHICAGO STUDIES IN THE HISTORY OF AMERICAN RELIGION

Editors

JERALD C. BRAUER
AND MARTIN E. MARTY

A CARLSON PUBLISHING SERIES

For a complete listing of the titles in this series,
please see the back of this book.

Can Two Walk Together Unless They Be Agreed?

AMERICAN RELIGIOUS SCHISMS IN THE 1970S

Bryan V. Hillis

PREFACE BY MARTIN E. MARTY

CARLSON
Publishing Inc

BROOKLYN, NEW YORK, 1991

Please see the end of this volume for a listing of all the titles in the Carlson Publishing Series *Chicago Studies in the History of American Religion*, edited by Jerald C. Brauer and Martin E. Marty, of which this is Volume 8.

BR
526
. H55
1991

Copyright © 1991 by Bryan V. Hillis

Library of Congress Cataloging-in-Publication Data

Hillis, Bryan V., 1956-
  Can two walk together unless they be agreed? : American religious
schisms in the 1970s / Bryan V. Hillis ; preface by Martin E. Marty.
      p.   cm. — (Chicago studies in the history of American
religion ; v. 8)
  Revision of thesis (Ph.D.—University of Chicago, 1988)
originally presented under title: Varieties of religious schism in
the seventies.
  Includes bibliographical references and index.
  ISBN 0-926019-45-7 (alk. paper)
  1. United States—Church history—20th century. 2. Church
controversies. 3. Lutheran Church—Missouri Synod. 4. Lutheran
Church—United States. 5. Episcopal Church. 6. Anglican Communion-
-United States. 7. Presbyterian Church in the U.S. 8. Presbyterian
Church—United States. 9. Christian sects—United States.
  I. Title. II. Series.
  BR526.H55   1991
  277.3'0827—dc20   91-25220

Typographic design: Julian Waters

Typeface: Bitstream ITC Galliard

Case design: Alison Lew

Index prepared by the author.

Printed on acid-free, 250-year-life paper.

Manufactured in the United States of America.

Contents

An Introduction to the Series xi

Preface by *Martin E. Marty* xv

Acknowledgments xvii

I. *Introduction* 1

II. *Schism in the Southern Presbyterian Church*
Establishing a 'Supernatural Institute' 5
From "Jure Divino" to Social Activist:
    Twentieth-Century Controversies 9
"Can Two Walk Together Unless They Be Agreed?":
    Polarization in the 1960s and 1970s 18
"Come out from Among Them and Be Ye Separate":
    From 1971 to the Schism 31

III. *Schism in the Lutheran Church-Missouri Synod*
Growing up in America 45
"Something's Burnin'. . .": Events Until 1973 48
"If You Can't Stand the Heat":
    Events Between 1973 and 1975 64
"Get out of the Kitchen":
    From Anaheim to the Schism 84

IV. *Schism in the Episcopal Church*
"A Branch Shall Grow" 99
"Other Seeds Fell on Good Ground . . .":
    Polarizing Issues of the 1960s and 1970s 101

". . . And They Sprang Up . . .":
Resolution of the Two Main Issues 104
". . . And Bare Fruit an Hundredfold":
The Schism Crystallizes and Splinters 118

V. *Conclusion: The Fuel of Schism*
Two Existing Sociological Models 127
Applying Wilson and Takayama 130
Coser's Propositions and Their Applications 133
Concluding Comments 138

Notes 139
Bibliography 205
Index 229

For Joanne

An Introduction
to the Series

The *Chicago Studies in the History of American Religion* is a series of books that deal with topics ranging from the time of Jonathan Edwards to the 1970s. Three or four deal with colonial topics and three or four treat the very recent past. About half of them focus on the decades just before and after 1900. One deals with blacks; two concentrate on women. Revivalists, fundamentalists, theologians, life in the suburbs and life in heaven and hell, the Beecher family of old and a monk of new times, Catholics adapting to America and Protestants fighting one another—all these subjects assure that the series has scope. People of every kind of taste and curiosity about American religion will find some books to suit them. Does anything serve to characterize the series as a whole? What does the stamp of "Chicago studies" mean?

Yale historian Sydney Ahlstrom in *A Religious History of the American People*, as influential as any twentieth-century work in its field, pays respect to the "Chicago School" of American religious historians. William Warren Sweet, the pioneer in such studies (beginning in 1927) at Chicago and, in many ways, in America at large represented the culmination of "the Protestant synthesis" in this field. Ahlstrom went on to name two later generations of Chicagoans, including the seminal Sidney E. Mead and major figures like Robert T. Handy and Winthrop Hudson and ending with the two editors of this series. He saw them as often "openly rebellious" in respect to Sweet and his synthesis.

If, as Ahlstrom says, "a disproportionate number" of historians have some connection with the Chicago School, it must be said that the new generation represented in these twenty-one books carries on both the lineage of Sweet and something of the "openly rebellious" character that scholars at Chicago are encouraged to pursue. This means, for one thing, that the "Protestant synthesis" does not characterize their work. These historians question the canon of historical writing produced in the Protestant era even as many of them continue to pursue themes shaped in a Protestant culture. Few of them concentrate on the old "frontier thesis" that marked the early years of the school. The shift for most has been toward the urban and pluralist scene. They call into question, not in devastating rage but in steady patterns of inquiry, the received wisdom about who matters, and why, in American religion.

So it is that this series of books focuses on blacks, women, dispensationalists, suburbanites, members of "marginal" denominations, "ethnics" and immigrants as readily as it does on white men of progressive urban bent in mainstream denominations and of long standing in America. The authors relish religious diversity and enjoy discovering the power of people once considered weak, the centrality to the American plot of those once regarded as peripheral, and the potency of losers who were once disdained by winners. Thus this series enhances an understanding of an America overlooked by the people of Sweet's era two-thirds of a century ago when it all, or most of it, began.

Rebellion for its own sake would not long hold interest; it might tell more about the psychology of rebels and revisers than about their subject matter. Revision, better than rebellion, characterizes the scholars. Re+vision: that's it. There was an original vision that characterized the Chicago School. This was the contention that in secular America and its universities religion mattered, as a theme in the national past and as a presence in the present. Second, it argued that the study of religious history belonged not only in the seminaries and archives of denominations, but also in the rough-and-tumble of the secular university, where no religious meanings were privileged and where each historian had to make a case for the value of his or her story.

Other assumptions from the earliest days pervade the books in this series. They are uncommonly alert to the environment in which expressions of faith occur. That is, they do not take for granted that religion comes protected in self-evidently important and hermetically sealed packages. Churches and denominations are porous, even when they would be sealed off; they cannot be understood apart from the ways the social environs effect them, but their power to effect change in the environment demands equal and truly unapologetic treatment. These writers do not shuffle and mumble and make excuses for their existence or for the choice of apparently arcane subject matter. They try to present their narrative in such ways that they compel attention.

A fourth characteristic that colors these works is a refusal in most cases to be typed in a fashionable slot labeled, variously, "intellectual" or "institutional" history, "cultural" or "social" history, or whatever. While those which concentrate on magisterial thinkers such as Jonathan Edwards are necessarily busy with and devoted to his intellectual achievement, most of the books deal with figures who cannot be understood only as exemplars in a sequence of studies of "the life of the mind." Instead, their biographies and circumstances come very much into play. On the other hand, none of these writers is a reductionist who sees religion as "nothing but" this or that—"nothing but" the working out of believers' Oedipal urges or expressing the economic and class interests of the subjects. Social history becomes in its way intellectual history, even if the intellects are focused on something other than the theologians in the traditions might like to see.

Some years ago *Look* magazine interviewed leaders in various denominations. One was asked if his fellow believers considered that theirs was the only true faith. Yes, he said, but they did not believe that they were the only ones who held it. The editors of this series of studies and the contributors to it do not believe that the "Chicago School," whenever and whatever it was, is the only true approach to American religious history. And, if they did, they would not hold that Chicagoans alone held it. To do so would imply a strange solipsistic or narcissistic impulse that would be the death of collegiality in the historical field. They have welcomed the chance to be in a climate where their inquiries are given such encouragement, where they find a company of fellow scholars in the Divinity School, the History Department, and the Committee on the History of Culture, whence these studies first emerged, and elsewhere in a university that provides a congenial home for massed and massive concentration of a special sort on American religious history.

While the undersigned have been consistently involved, most often together, in all twenty-one books, we want to single out a third person mentioned in so many acknowledgment sections, historian Arthur Mann. He has been a partner in two or three dozen religious history dissertation projects through the years and has been an influential and decisive contributor to the results. We stand in his debt.

Jerald C. Brauer
Martin E. Marty

Editor's Preface

In the eyes of many, religious schism should belong to an earlier time, an earlier place, than the 1970s. A casual American is likely to think that religion is so marginal and held to so apathetically that no one would have motive or passion to generate schism over it. Such a person is overlooking the devotion Americans give to faith and church, and Bryan Hillis's tale of motives and passions will be an eye-opener. An informed American who pays attention might be ready to talk about intense commitment to religion, but may be prepared to see such commitment devoted to private or civil religion, not to denominations. Hillis will help such a reader revise his or her views of the way power is located in American religion.

Far from being serene, boring, simply bureaucratized agencies remote from personal and congregational life, denominations survive with ever-changing functions. For most people they do not serve the historic role of defining doctrine, setting boundaries around creedal communities, or serving as bases for battle against other denominations. Yet they do represent "family," "tradition," "ways of life," and certain kinds of belief. When too much change occurs around them and when there is significant adaptation by "moderates" within them, "conservatives" react and battles royal begin.

Hillis, a Canadian, crosses a national border to bring a measure of distance to three controversies that disturbed the peace of millions of Americans within one decade. Alert to the fact that theology, doctrine, and liturgy remain ways of defining faith communities, he resists the notions that the scraps were only "about" personalities, social upheaval, and the search for power—though he does not slight such factors when they are manifestly present.

Instead, Hillis engages in a work of retrieval, by digging deeper into the sources of the controversy and having the courage to counter social scientific reductionism, the notion that religious controversy has to be "about" everything but religion. He allows the agents in the story to make their own case, and acts on the assumption that even angered partisans on both sides of denominational warfare have integrity and have to be taken at their word. He shows, convincingly, that whatever other factors were present, it was when profound religious issues surfaced that the battles became most scarring.

One does not have to be religious, Christian, or Protestant to find reasons to care about his three communions—the southern Presbyterians, the Missouri Lutherans, or the Episcopalians. Southern Presbyterianism has played an inordinate role in shaping American life, from before the War between the States, as the ancestors called it, down to the time when it produced the Woodrow Wilsons and any number of secretaries of state and senators. When this church fought over the inerrancy of the Bible, the standards of faith, foreign policy, and race relations, there was a bearing on national life.

Missouri Lutherans are a national body; Missouri is a misleading geographical designation. Chiefly midwestern, this denomination of 2.5 million represented a theological tradition of increasing weight in America. And the Episcopal Church, thinly spread everywhere in the nation, has been one sort of "national church." When it saw a schism over ordination of women and revisions in liturgy, it touched on many dimensions of cultural life.

The people Hillis quotes are so contentious, so lively, so ready for drama that his story would carry itself even if he only quoted. But he has a thesis, a provocative one, which stands a chance of leading to revision of theory, and he teases readers enough with this that there should be more motives than one to read this story of passion with passion.

Martin E. Marty

Acknowledgments

The list of people who deserve thanks for their contributions to this project is a long one. On the professional level, the Social Sciences and Humanities Research Council of Canada supported me with a doctoral fellowship. Pastor Marvin Janz of St. Luke's Lutheran Church in Willowdale, Ontario, saved me hours and expense by providing many of the documents for the Lutheran chapter. Most important, Dr. Martin E. Marty, whose knowledge and scholarly ability are well known, is revered by his students for his ability to direct, correct, and thereby bring many an undeveloped idea to maturity; his contribution was incalculable. To Dr. Jerald Brauer and Dr. Arthur Mann I extend my most hearty thanks for their cooperation, direction, and accessibility. I doubt I could have had a better committee.

Friends are important at any time but especially in a new country, a big city, and an intimidating university. Barb Kahn and Robert Bloch together with their friends and relatives, especially Mrs. Betty Kahn, were my Chicago family, without whom I could not have survived the "Chicago experience." My immediate family was far away in miles but always gave me reason to be confident of their unwavering support. Thanks Mom, Grandma, Margie, and Jim.

On June 14, 1986, a beautiful, beaming, and independent woman assumed the responsibility of supporting, in so many ways, this struggling student despite many forewarnings that it would be a difficult task. It belittles her contribution merely to dedicate this work to her, but I do; I must do at least that much. Thanks Joanne for always being there; thanks for permitting me to be your husband.

September 1989
Luther College
University of Regina

Can Two Walk Together Unless They Be Agreed?

ONE

Introduction

Thirty years ago, the topic of schism or formal division within a church body would have been a very unpopular topic. The ecclesiastical scene in the 1950s and 1960s was characterized by interdenominational coalitions, ecumenical movements, and denominational mergers.[1] The reasoning behind such movements was sound from a practical perspective and idealistic from a Christian one. A combined testimony was not only more efficient to administer but also was thought to be a more effective witness of the truth of the Christian message.

Such ecumenical drive was not nearly as evident in the 1970s. The kind of movement toward mergers that William Rusch indicated in *Ecumenism*[2] died amid growing apathy as reports were published but not implemented or the talks surrounding such movements simply dissolved. There are exceptions, of course,[3] but on the whole, K. Peter Takayama was justified in saying in 1980 that "these cooperative ventures have apparently now come to a halt."[4] For many observers, the pendulum seemed to swing in the opposite direction, with intradenominational conflicts not unheard of and schisms more apparent.

Three major denominations experienced schisms in the 1970s; none of them has had a detailed history recorded from a detached scholarly perspective.[5] This study tells the story of those three schisms as they occurred in the Lutheran Church—Missouri Synod, the Presbyterian Church in the United States, and the Protestant Episcopal Church in the U.S.A. (also called "The Episcopal Church" since 1967). In an effort to understand how and why each schism took place as it did, this work examines the social forces, ecclesiastical organization, leadership personalities, and religious warrants involved in each schismatic process.

Two sociological models of schism have been advanced to aid in understanding schismatic events.[6] Takayama says that the major conditions for organizational splits are a high degree of environmental permeability and ideological concern regarding the legitimacy of organizational authority and the behavior of the leadership, rather than the doctrinal purity per se. In his

1

model, schism takes place when "external environmental changes act as catalysts to internally generated and unresolved strains, producing crises." Religious denominations are particularly susceptible to cultural and moral aspects of environmental change, because "denominations have highly environmentally permeable boundaries."[7]

John Wilson's model is much more schematic, as he sees five determinants comprising the necessary and sufficient conditions for schism. The cornerstone of his scheme is structural strain or the "disjuncture between norms and values or between roles and norms." In the need to "get a fit" between norms and values, strain occurs and manifests itself in uneasiness, frustration, and an increasing inhibition to the social rules one is expected to follow. A schismatic group is a movement that alleges that the main group has departed from the values of the original movement. On the basis of economic or political reasons, this minority group decides to withdraw from the parent group. Despite his emphasis on the disputes over values and norms, Wilson does not give such disputes the determining place. Because a religious group has a "fund" of issues over which conflict "legitimately" could take place,

> . . . it is not sufficient . . . to point to the doctrinal disputes, or to the underlying social differences in cases of schism. We must look also at strains inherent in the movement which these other factors may only exacerbate.[8]

What is important here is that neither sociologist regards the disagreements concerning matters of religious belief and practice as critical to the schismatic event. This disparaging attitude towards the religious content of schismatic events is not confined to these two articles but receives expression also in periodicals and monographs with wider public appeal.[9]

This study demonstrates that schism occurred in these three major American denominations when a core religious issue of the tradition became the matter of central dispute. My hypothesis is that when a schism takes place, both sides in the dispute have to be able to argue that they alone are the ones remaining faithful to the religious content of the tradition by which they are named.[10] In a context where ecumenism is still highly regarded, a schismatic movement has to be justified and legitimized to the extent that schism is the only option for both the denomination and the dissenting group. Parties in the dispute can justify the schismatic action only when they can claim themselves as the true adherents to the original tradition. Remaining in fellowship with the other party then becomes an offence to the tradition or to the goals of the tradition, and the dissenting group leaves to pursue its vision of the tradition. In sociological terms, schism acts as a "tension-reducing agent."[11]

Finding the most appropriate terminology to signal the matters of central dispute in the denominations has been a difficult task. Theological differences may have been at the center of the Presbyterian dispute, but "theological" does not adequately describe the debated issues of the Episcopal schism where matters of "liturgical practice" were the foci of controversy. In the Lutheran Church—Missouri Synod debate, arguments concerning denominational practice and theology played supporting roles, but neither "theological" nor "liturgical practice" adequately describes the debate regarding "ecclesiological" definition that led to the schism.

Hence a term is needed that is broad enough to cover a wide range of meaning and specific enough to remain true to the thesis that explanations of schism demand some recognition of the debated issues. Only when the project was all but completed did it become clear that the most obvious term was also the most satisfactory. A "religious" matter is the object of dispute in each denomination. Without entering into the great scholarly debate regarding what makes a matter "religious," there is a certain common ground that the term encompasses and that easily applies to the debates studied in these schisms. Concerns of belief, doctrine, theology, ideology, ritual, practice, liturgy, textual interpretation, and ecclesiology are assumed under the rubric "religious." The term is broad enough to include all these categories and yet specific enough to distinguish the disputed aspects of the denominational splits all but ignored by previous observers of schism.

More important, "religious" carries with it the implication of something far more significant than the trivial pursuits of the everyday world. Religious matters are matters of great emotion; wars are declared, lives lost, and nations born as a result of religious debate. Religious matters are so central to a denominational identity that families fight, friendships dissolve, and new groups form. At issue in these religious debates are matters of sacred meaning, of inviolable principles, even of ultimate concern,[12] at least insofar as they relate to the identity of the group. In short, these religious matters are the fuel of the schismatic process without which the organizational splits would not have occurred; yet there is a sufficient diversity of issues involved in the three denominations that one can truly speak of a variety of religious schisms in the past decade.

None of this is meant to suggest that sociological factors are of no effect in the schisms of ecclesiastical bodies. Rather, the interdependence of sociological factors and religious concerns in a schism is indicated.[13]

The denominational schisms chosen were the major ones of the 1970s in terms of the number of people involved. Different types of ecclesiastical organization and confessional bases are represented. Even more relevant is the fact that each denomination utilizes different dispute settlement mechanisms. What actually happened in the schismatic processes also varies enough to test the thesis; in two of the schisms, the more conservative party left the denomination, while in the third, a more moderate faction left. In short, the schisms are major enough to be the subject of a historical study and representative enough to test the thesis.

TWO

Schism in the Southern Presbyterian Church

Establishing a "Supernatural Institute"

The history of the Presbyterian Church in the United States (PCUS), or southern Presbyterian church, as it is more commonly called, helps explain its character as a regional church of distinctive theological emphases. Only thirteen years after four presbyteries organized themselves into The General Synod in 1716, the threat of rationalism compelled the fledgling denomination to declare its confessional standards in the Adopting Act of 1729.[1] Conservatives were satisfied that subscription to the Westminster Standards was required of all ordained clergy, while liberals took comfort in the provision that a candidate for ordination could harbor reservations about the confessional standards and still be ordained with integrity provided he received the sanction of his presbytery. Hence an inexact pattern of doctrinal subscription was established.[2]

In 1801, Presbyterians and Congregationalists agreed to combine their efforts in the vast missionary fields of the West by signing the Plan of Union. This agreement escalated existing disputes between Old School Presbyterians with their stricter Calvinistic theology and New School Presbyterians of congregationalist leanings.[3] By 1837, the Old School Presbyterians decided they could no longer live with the New School people, and two separate denominations of the same name (The Presbyterian Church in the United States of America) maintained separate organizational structures until 1869.[4]

Between 1837 and 1869, the Old School consolidated its membership and power in the southern United States. Under the leadership of James Henry Thornwell (1812-1862), southern Old School Presbyterians emphasized the spiritual mission of the church; as a corporate entity, the church should not be involved in political and social affairs. Thornwell's doctrine of the

5

spirituality of the church was captured in the succinct and oft-repeated "the State looks to the visible and outward, the Church is to be concerned for the invisible and inward."[5]

In 1861, with the Civil War well underway, Gardiner Spring of New York introduced the following resolution to the General Assembly of the Old School.

> Resolved, that this General Assembly, in the Spirit of that Christian patriotism which the Scriptures enjoin, and which has always characterized this Church, do hereby acknowledge and declare our obligation to promote and perpetuate, so far as in us lies, the integrity of these United States, and to strengthen, uphold and encourage the Federal government in the exercise of all its functions, under our noble Constitution; and to this Constitution, in all its provisions, requirements, and principles, we profess our unabated loyalty.[6]

Southern Old School Presbyterians were outraged, not just because the southern church was being asked to commit itself in a matter of politics but because they felt they were being asked to submit to the government of the North. Since the Civil War prevented any kind of meaningful dialogue between the northern and southern churches anyway, the Old School southerners decided they could no longer remain in fellowship with the increasingly political northern church. In August of 1861 southern Presbyterians convened an advisory convention in Atlanta. This convention called for a constituting General Assembly in Augusta, Georgia, in December. At this first General Assembly, the Presbyterian Church in the Confederate States was formed, which at the conclusion of the war became The Presbyterian Church in the United States.[7] For its constitution the new denomination adopted the Westminster Confession of Faith, the Larger and Shorter Catechisms, the Form of Government, the Book of Discipline, and the Directory of Worship.[8]

In the "Address by the General Assembly, 1861 To all the Churches of Jesus Christ throughout the Earth, Unanimously Adopted at Their Sessions in Augusta, Georgia," the distinctive theological content of the new southern denomination was proclaimed.

> The provinces of Church and State are perfectly distinct, and the one has no right to usurp the jurisdiction of the other. The State is a natural institute, founded in the constitution of man as moral and social, and designed to realize the idea of justice. It is the society of rights. The Church is supernatural institute, founded in the facts of redemption, and is designed to realize the idea

of grace. It is the society of the redeemed. The State aims at social order, the Church at spiritual holiness.[9]

In addition to this distinctive characteristic of spirituality, Morton Smith identifies two other important denominational "distinctives" in the address:

A full acceptance of the authority of the Bible alone as its [the PCUS's] infallible rule of faith and practice.
The recognition of the Church as visibly organized to be the divinely ordained society called to carry out the work of the Lord.[10]

To describe the schism of this generation simply in terms of religious content would be a serious distortion of the historical reality. As the new southern church freely admitted, "There is one difference which . . . radically and fundamentally distinguishes the North and the South," namely the attitude toward slavery.[11] In pious tones, the "Address to the Churches" stated that on those matters which the Scriptures had not spoken clearly, southern Presbyterians could not pass judgment.[12] Slavery fell into this category because it "is expressly mentioned and treated as a lawful relation" in the Scriptures.[13] As further evidence, southern Presbyterians called attention to what they perceived to be the benevolence of the institution of slavery.

. . . the general operation of the system is kindly and benevolent; it is a real and effective discipline, and without it, we are profoundly persuaded that the African race in the midst of us can never be elevated in the scale of being. As long as that race, in its comparative degradation, co-exists, side by side, with the white, bondage is its normal condition.[14]

After the Civil War finally ended and southerners were forced to give up slavery, the chasm between the northern and southern Old School did not narrow; in fact the gap widened with the union of the northern Old and New School in 1869.[15] Though the union was to have granted latitude to both parties in the practice of their polity and theology, the New School quickly dominated the northern church, especially as more conservative Old School synods like Missouri and Kentucky left the northern denomination for the southern church.[16] As a result, the northern church increasingly declared itself on social issues, while in the south

no subject received more attention than the spiritual nature and function of the church. . . . This testimony by word and life to the spirituality of the church, it

7

was believed, was the reason why, in the providence of God, the Southern Church had been raised up.[17]

Thus when the northern church made overtures to the southern PCUS regarding reunion in 1870, the southern church declined on the basis of the political involvement of the northern church and its extensive doctrinal latitude.[18]

To guard against any liberal influence and to ensure that compromising confessional amendments would not slip into the governance of the southern church, Old School leaders persuaded the PCUS General Assembly of 1894 to adopt a measure requiring any confessional amendments to be approved by three-quarters of the presbyteries.[19] In 1914, the same three-quarters requirement was applied to unions with other churches, thereby ensuring that future unions would be very difficult to forge without overwhelming support.[20]

In the early 1900s both northern and southern churches debated the "inspiration" of Scriptures. The north settled on a permissive position that limited scriptural inspiration to moral and religious truths and acknowledged difficulties with a strictly literal interpretation. On the other hand, the southern church "extended the plenary and verbal inspiration of Scriptures beyond moral and religious truths to all statements of facts, whether scientific, historical or geographical."[21]

What is most significant about these and other PCUS decisions was that a consistency of doctrinal standards within the denomination was maintained of which PCUS authorities were proud.

> It is a fact . . . that while religious error, in many plausible and dangerous forms, pervades our country, it has not yet succeeded in making its way into our ministry and churches.[22]

There is no question that at least part of this consistency was due to the uniformity characteristic of a regional church.[23] Kenneth K. Bailey characterizes all of southern religion as full of "piety and tradition," having "a preoccupation with individual repentance, a dogged insistence on Biblical inerrancy, a tendency toward overt expression of intense religious emotions."[24] However, even amid the uniformity of southern religion, southern Presbyterianism was unique in its lack of diversity at the end of the nineteenth century. Ernest Trice Thompson, a leading historian of Presbyterianism, characterized the PCUS of this era:

At the end of the nineteenth century, the southern Presbyterian Church seemed solidly conservative, strongly Calvinistic, distinctly sectional and remarkably homogeneous in outlook and belief.[25]

As this remarkable homogeneity was eroded by exposure to an increasingly secular environment, theological differences were bound to occur.

From "Jure Divino" to Social Activist: Twentieth-Century Controversies

The PCUS schism of 1974 was viewed by many commentators as the result of conflict between groups separated by geography, social class, and race.[26] However, such simplistic generalizations ignore the theological tensions developing within the southern denomination from the turn of the century. Despite assertions to the contrary,[27] the schism of 1974 cannot be understood apart from the religious issues involved, which this section will outline.

As the twentieth century began, traces of a definite polarization became evident within the PCUS.[28] For example, some southern Presbyterians, affirming that the reformed tradition was the purest expression of biblical doctrine, refused to consider any changes to the Westminster Confession of Faith, while others chafed at the severity of the confession's election doctrine.[29] Despite the PCUS official stance that the church should not concern itself with secular matters, general assemblies early in this century made pronouncements on many social items, including Sabbath desecration, dancing, cardplaying, gambling, and liquor.[30] Some were very vocal with their challenge to the traditional southern view of the church with its spiritual mission.[31]

Though Thompson characterized the southern church prior to the beginning of the twentieth century as "remarkably homogeneous," he was not alone in his assessment that

> by the 1940's there were now two clearly defined groups in the church, two wings, two divergent points of view, two extremes, some would claim both equally sincere, one holding that newer points of view threatened the very existence of the faith, the other that they were essential if the faith was to remain viable for modern man.[32]

This polarization that began around the turn of the century developed into open conflict between the mid-1930s and 1970. It revolved around three issues: subscription to the historic confessions, the degree of the church's spirituality, and ecumenical relations.

A. Confessional Subscription

Conservatives in the PCUS constantly appealed to the confessional nature of the southern Presbyterian church as established in the Adopting Act of 1729:

> Although the Synod do not claim or pretend to any authority of imposing our faith upon other men's consciences . . . yet we are undoubtedly obliged to take care that the faith once delivered to the saints be kept pure and uncorruptible among us, and so hand it down to our posterity; and do therefore agree that all the Ministers of this Synod, or that shall hereafter be admitted into this Synod, shall declare their agreement in, and approbation of, the Confession of Faith, with the Larger and Shorter Catechisms of the Assembly of Divines of Westminster, as being in all the essential and necessary articles, good forms of sound words and systems of Christian doctrine, and do also adopt the said Confession and Catechisms as the confession of our faith. And we do also agree, that all the Presbyteries within our bounds shall take care not to admit any candidates of the ministry into the exercise of the sacred function but what declares his agreement in opinion with all the essential and necessary articles of said Confession, either by subscribing the said Confession of Faith and Catechisms, or by a verbal declaration of their assent thereto, as such Ministers or candidate shall think best.[33]

Determining a ministerial candidate's adherence to these confessional standards was accomplished by asking three questions, commonly called the ordination vows:

> 1) Do you believe the Scriptures of the Old and New Testaments to be the Word of God, the only infallible rule of faith and practice?
> 2) Do you sincerely receive and adopt the confession of Faith and the Catechisms of this Church, as containing the system of doctrine taught in the Holy Scriptures? . . .
> 3) Do you approve of the government and discipline of the Presbyterian Church in the United States?[34]

The first vow received little debate within the PCUS until well into the twentieth century.[35] However, by the early 1940s, Presbyterian teachers like

Dr. Sam Cartledge of Columbia Seminary taught openly the usefulness of biblical criticism, arguing that the historical critical method was a gift to be used to God's glory.[36] Such proponents of the new methods did not go unchallenged; in 1942, Rev. H. B. Dendy established the *Southern Presbyterian Journal* to battle modern trends like biblical criticism.[37] The *Journal* perspective continued through the 1960s and 1970s under the leadership of men like L. Nelson Bell and G. Aiken Taylor, who wrote editorials insisting that the liberal unrest was caused by the church "having been cut loose from the Bible as the basis of ultimate authority."[38] By 1966, opposition to historical criticism had coalesced into a group that felt confident enough to establish the Reformed Theological Seminary (RTS) in Jackson, Mississippi. Their advertisement campaign trumpeted that among those things "for which it stood," the "verbally inspired, inerrant Word of God" was *the* priority.[39]

For these and other conservatives, the "advancing low view of the Bible" was at the root of all liberal unrest in the PCUS, including the church's confessional apostasy, illicit ecumenical relations, and the loss of spiritual mission.[40] This thesis is very difficult to prove because even conservative writers cannot cite an official change in PCUS doctrine regarding the scriptures until 1972, when a paper entitled "The Meaning of Doctrinal Loyalty in the Ordination Vows" was introduced to the General Assembly.[41]

Conservatives argued that in the second ordination vow southern Presbyterians had distinguished themselves in 1837 from New School Presbyterians by upholding a policy of strict subscription to the Westminster Confessional Standards as "containing the system of doctrine" found in the Scriptures. This strict subscriptionism was not easily accomplished, since the term "system of doctrine" was a source of continuing controversy. In 1898, the General Assembly adopted the policy that "system of doctrine . . . precludes the idea of necessary acceptance of every statement in the Standards by the subscriber but involves the acceptance of so much as is vital to the system as a whole."[42] The 1934 and 1939 Assemblies attempted to define the term more specifically with the 1939 meeting actually designating a set of specific doctrines as essential to the Presbyterian faith.[43] However, the 1947 assembly declined to sanction this definition, saying only that it was "merely an 'in thesi' deliverance, interpreting a part of the content of the ordination vows without any intention of changing the whole substance of them."[44] Further developments in the denomination's policy of formal confessional subscription did not occur until the 1972 General Assembly.

Major changes in the confessions themselves were made in 1942 with the addition of chapters on the Holy Spirit and the Gospel. Since the chapters were almost identical to those added by the northern Presbyterians in 1903, conservatives were immediately suspicious.[45] Conservatives decried the suggestion of the Holy Spirit chapter that humanity has unaided ability to accept the Gospel. They also condemned the additions for not mentioning and even contradicting the doctrine of election; the chapter on the Gospel contained a statement regarding God's universal love, which conservatives said was so ambiguous it implied universalism.[46]

The concern with the doctrine of election continued through the 1950s. In 1958, a liberal attempt to change the doctrinal standards on this point failed, but the attempt did result in the adoption of a report by the Committee on the Study of the Confession, which stated that "the Confession is not an adequate statement of Christian faith, because it implies, regardless of the intention of the authors, an eternal negative decree." The adoption of this report was protested by conservatives, but to no avail.[47] In 1961, the General Assembly adopted another statement, which repeated the sentiments of the 1958 report; this "Brief Statement" spoke of God's "purpose for his world, which embraces the free and responsible choices of man."[48]

There were other changes that offended conservatives even further. The 1959 General Assembly approved divorces for causes other than adultery and desertion.[49] With the approval of the presbyteries, the 1963 and 1964 General Assemblies adopted changes that approved the ordination of women.[50] In 1966, the assembly went on record "favoring the discontinuance of the use of capital punishment" even though it acknowledged that the confessions and catechisms advocated the practice.[51] The 1968 General Assembly adopted a report that concluded

> that the true relation between the evolutionary theory and the Bible is that of non-contradiction and that the positions stated by the General Assemblies of 1886, 1888, 1889 and 1924 were in error and no longer represents the mind of the church.[52]

All of these confessional changes were opposed by conservative spokesmen who argued that both the confessional and doctrinal standards were being abrogated by these actions.

Changes in church government such as the establishing of a Commission on the Minister and His Work (1937) and the switch from denominational committees to church boards (1949) were regarded by conservatives as major departures from the Book of Church Order because these actions increasingly centralized power in the hands of a few.[53] When the denomination failed to exercise discipline upon men like E. T. Thompson, who encouraged the PCUS to take action on social issues,[54] conservatives saw this as another clear indication that the southern church was not willing to defend its spirituality position or use the provisions of the Book of Order to exercise appropriate discipline. Finally, in 1969, the General Assembly initiated the process by which a new Confession of Faith and Book of Confessions were to be drafted;[55] conservatives saw the move as the culmination of decades of increasingly relaxed subscription to the historic confessions, their content, and the ecclesiastical discipline inherent in them.[56]

B. Spirituality of the Church

The declared doctrine of the spirituality of the church prevented the PCUS from any sort of social involvement during the first few decades of this century. Liberals made efforts as early as the 1890s to have the denomination speak out on social issues such as child labor,[57] but not until the Depression, when there were three times as many people on relief in the south as in other areas of the country, did the church make any corporate statement that hinted of a social policy.[58] At the behest of the presbyteries the General Assembly established the Committee on Moral and Social Welfare in 1934. To preserve the spiritual mission of the church, even the founding of this permanent committee was justified by the reasoning that the individual, not the church, must act.

> The PCUS must stimulate its members to realize the ideals of Christ in their individual lives, in the life of each group of which they are participants and in the total life of the nation.[59]

Whatever the justification for the committee, conservatives were soon disturbed by the increasing number of social pronouncements and actions initiated by the PCUS.

One of the most obvious areas in which the PCUS needed to act was race relations. As noted, in the 1860s the southern church "hesitated not to affirm that it is the peculiar mission of the Southern Church to conserve the institution of slavery."[60] As late as 1910, when southern blacks were effectively disfranchised by a poll tax, the PCUS offered no comment, thereby giving its implicit consent to the action. Not until 1944 did the PCUS admit with official pronouncements its disgraceful handling of blacks.[61] Black commissioners were finally given all the rights of whites at the General Assembly of 1950, and in 1953 an attempt was made to desegregate the denominational schools. However, this action was not approved until 1954, when support for public school desegregation was also declared, just two weeks before the landmark Supreme Court ruling.[62] Even so, the PCUS decision was far from unanimous. Guy T. Gillespie, former president of PCUS conservative stronghold Belhaven College, said segregation was one of nature's "universal laws" and a "well-considered and time-tested American policy," and the increasingly influential *Presbyterian Journal* published a condemnation of integration.[63] As recently as 1973, one of the most outspoken conservative writers, Morton Smith, questioned whether the church should be leading in the matter of integration because he finds no scriptural justification for supporting integration; in fact, Smith implied that Scriptures support segregation.[64] When the denominational Board of Christian Education asked its members to consider the merits of the Black Manifesto in 1969, conservative reaction was predictable: conservative cries of socialism, black racism, and confessional infidelity condemned the document.[65]

The secular involvement of the PCUS increased dramatically in the 1960s. In 1963, capital punishment was deplored. A report of the Permanent Committee on Christian Relations was adopted in 1965 that commended peaceful demonstrations, sit-ins, and civil disobedience as a possible means of gaining one's civil rights.[66] In 1966, the Board of Church Extension received a name change; as the new Board of National Ministries it was authorized to experiment with new ministries (1966), to organize its own Project Equality in areas where such programs did not exist (1967),[67] to work with the National Council of Churches on its "Crisis in the Cities" program (1968), to experiment with new worship forms (1968),[68] and to facilitate abortions (1971).[69]

In another area, the Board for World Missions changed its seasonal emphases from more traditional (and conservative) themes like the study of a particular mission field to more worldly concerns like "race" in 1966 and "poverty" in 1967.[70] Conservatives were horrified that even the traditional-sounding study themes of *The Presbyterian Survey*, like "Christ and the Faiths of Men," turned out to be studies regarding technology, materialism, and modernism rather than a contrast of Christianity with other world faiths.

When faith comparisons were made in study books commissioned by the Board for World Missions, the happy coexistence of the world faiths was endorsed. All of these actions and many more like them indicated to conservatives just how secular and nonspiritual the PCUS was becoming.[71]

The worst fears of spiritually minded conservatives were realized in 1966 with the issuing of a paper by the Committee on Christian Relations entitled "The Theological Basis for Christian Social Action." The paper began innocently enough: "The Christian community as a whole and its individual members are called first of all and primarily to the task of evangelism and missions." However, its intention was revealed in the explanation of this "call." "This commission inevitably and inescapably means that the church and individual Christians will be concerned with the political, social, economic and cultural life of the world."[72] Liberals such as Thompson applauded the document and proudly declared that the "purely spiritual character [of the PCUS] was now completely transformed." Conservatives such as Morton Smith agreed that the church had lost its spiritual character and explained this loss in terms of a confusion of sin with sociopolitical ills where rational, not biblical, principles were the main criteria.[73]

C. Ecumenical Relations

Developments in relationships with other churches led to further polarization in the PCUS. Conservatives within the denomination cited an 1862 General Assembly statement as the only basis for pursuing unions with other denominations: "The General Assembly need scarcely reassert its earnest desire to cultivate friendly relations with Churches professing the same doctrine and practicing the same polity." These same conservatives were also proud of the denomination's record where union overtures from the Protestant Episcopalians were declined in 1887; further examples were available from 1920, 1929, and 1932.[74]

In the early decades of this century, Presbyterian liberals did not work for organic union but for cooperative relationships with other denominations; even these modest efforts annoyed conservatives. PCUS membership in the Federal Council of Churches (FCC) provides evidence of this. In 1909, liberal ecumenists succeeded in persuading the PCUS to join the FCC. When the FCC began addressing specific social issues like the steel strike in Pennsylvania in 1911, the conservatives gathered enough votes to force the denomination to withdraw. Under liberal influence the PCUS returned to the FCC in 1912 with conservatives formally requesting withdrawal from the organization almost annually after that. Liberals in the FCC and PCUS repeatedly explained that the actions and pronouncements of the FCC were not necessarily binding upon its members, but conservatives did not accept this explanation. After years of voicing displeasure with the FCC, the conservatives finally rallied enough support for a PCUS withdrawal over the issue of birth control in 1931. In 1941, the PCUS again renewed its membership in the FCC; thereafter overtures were presented annually at the General Assemblies protesting membership in this organization and its successor after 1950, the National Council of Churches (NCC).[75] Almost the same pattern can be found in the General Assembly Minutes regarding PCUS membership in the World Council of Churches, of which the PCUS was a founding member in 1948.[76]

Efforts at organic union with the northern Presbyterian church in the first half of the twentieth century were easily refuted by southern conservatives with an appeal to the spirituality of the southern church. Conservatives also justified their opposition to northern union by charging that the northern church was doctrinally lax; as proof of this laxity, conservatives cited the fact that the northern church had adopted the Auburn Affirmations, which stated that there are no essential doctrines one must confess in order to be a Presbyterian. Conservative influence in church relations was strengthened in 1914 with a constitutional amendment that required three-quarters of the presbyteries to approve any union actions.[77]

A good example of conservative power to block proposed unions is the attempt of 1954 when, after seventeen years of negotiations and approval by the General Assemblies of both denominations, union between the northern and southern churches was blocked by presbytery vote. Conservatives justified their opposition to the union by citing the liberal doctrines of the northern church, the fact that they had women as elders, and that the northern church had a much lower rate of financial giving than the southern church.[78] The fact that those presbyteries opposing union were most numerous in the Deep South where the antiblack feelings were most intense has led some commentators to insist that the racial question was still very much a part of the issue. Whereas the northern church had openly opposed segregation, the southern church had been much more hesitant.[79] Further evidence is found in the *Southern Presbyterian Journal*, which warned that the north would agitate on the race question; the periodical also clearly indicated which side of the race question it advocated.[80]

Though vindicated by the 1954 decision, conservatives soon had greater cause for protest. In 1961, the General Assembly adopted a brief report regarding the unity of the church. Though this document acknowledged that "unity [should occur] on the basis of theological terms . . . [it] does not define those terms as being distinctly Reformed." When the 1964 General Assembly adopted a paper written by the Permanent Theological Committee entitled "The Presbyterian Church in the United States and Church Unity," conservatives interpreted the document as advocating "union with non-Reformed churches" on the basis of "essential doctrines of our evangelical (not Reformed) standards."[81] The only bases for union conservatives accepted were the standards issued by the 1862 General Assembly, namely reformed doctrine and Presbyterian polity, and these were being ignored.

In 1963, the PCUS was invited to join the Consultation on Church Union (COCU), an effort by several mainline denominations to work toward organic union. PCUS liberals maintained that COCU was only a consultation and did not commit anybody to union, but they were not able to convince the General Assembly until 1966 to accept the invitation. Conservative overtures to the General Assembly in the following years claimed that COCU participation was unconstitutional because union should be considered only on the basis of the reformed confessional standards.[82] Headlines in the *Presbyterian Journal* in 1968 fired conservative fears that COCU plans were resulting in a unification process: "De Facto COCU Union said Progressing," "COCU Plans to Aid Local Merger Efforts," and "COCU Directs: Draft Plan [of union] Immediately."[83] PCUS moderator Marshall Dendy did little to ease conservative concerns when he chided southern Presbyterians for being "bound by dogma" and encouraged Presbyterians to give up some beliefs and traditions in order to participate in church unions.[84]

Conservative southern Presbyterians soon realized that in a far more subtle way southern Presbyterian liberals were attaining their ecumenical goals with northern Presbyterians. In 1960, the General Assembly approved union churches, which were combined PCUS/UPUSA (United Presbyterian Church USA) congregations with full membership in both denominations and full voting rights at each General Assembly. At the 1968 General Assembly, union proponents advanced the idea of union presbyteries and union synods; in 1969 the idea was accepted and later passed by a narrow majority in the presbyteries. In addition to the constitutional questions involved here, the conservative concern was that UPUSA elders and ministers, who did not subscribe to the PCUS position, were able to vote in PCUS assemblies and therefore had undue influence.[85]

With the exception of these "backdoor" union strategies, PCUS liberals were relatively ineffective in attaining organic union with other denominations. Even when conservatives were convinced of the orthodoxy of the union partner, liberal union efforts often failed, as the 1968 union attempt with the Reformed Church in America demonstrated.[86] Still, union proponents did not give up the search for partners in ecumenical unions.

These three debates concerning confessional subscription, ecclesial spirituality, and ecumenical relations were significant factors not only in the deterioration of PCUS homogeneity but also in the formal organization of various lobby groups within the denomination. Out of those organizations, schismatic movement originated.

"Can Two Walk Together Unless They Be Agreed?": Polarization in the 1960s and 1970s

Thus far the polarization in the PCUS has been identified simply by the terms "conservative" and "liberal" because this was the terminology used by the participants. As this account draws closer to the time of the schism, it is necessary to distinguish some of the major players and groups within each of these broad categories.

A. Dissenting Organizations

The founding of the conservative *Southern Presbyterian Journal* in 1942 by Reverend Henry B. Dendy with the support of L. Nelson Bell, former medical missionary to China, has been noted.[87] Under the title "Why the *Journal* at This Time?," the editor declared the sole aim of the supporters of the new periodical:

> to call our Southern Presbyterian Church back to her original position, a position unequivocally loyal to the Word of God and the Standards of our Church. . . . It [*PJ*] understands that these standards . . . teach the full inspiration of the Scriptures . . . the Virgin Birth of Christ . . . His substitutionary atonement; his bodily resurrection . . . his ascension into heaven;

and that this same Christ is coming again to judge the quick and the dead. The *Southern Presbyterian Journal* believes that the mission of the Church is spiritual and redemptive; and that it should not be used to promote the political, economic and social teachings of any group or extra-church organization.[88]

This weekly periodical continued to rally the conservative troops from the 1950s through the 1970s under the editorialships of Dendy, L. Nelson Bell, and G. Aiken Taylor. Every August, the *Journal* sponsored Journal Day in Weaverville, North Carolina, the event acting as a forum for conservatives to express their views on the preceding Assembly and the direction of the PCUS.[89] The *Journal's* credentials as the conservative mouthpiece are evidenced by the fact that PCUS liberals read it and responded to it, their letters to the editors often published in its pages.

In response to the nonactivist spirituality promoted by *Journal* editors, a group of liberals organized the Fellowship of Concern in 1963.[90] This group of young, liberal, socially committed PCUS ministers numbered around six hundred by 1967. They are best described as a civil rights action coalition that successfully lobbied denominational officials through the 1960s for liberal, socially progressive policies such as an integrated denominational school system and the elimination of "blacks only" congregations.[91] At the urging of moderator Marshall C. Dendy, who pleaded for a united church with a minimum of para-ecclesiastical organizations, the group disbanded in 1968, promising to seek the same liberal objectives by using more decentralized, unstructured methods within the denomination.[92]

In 1964, the conservative lay group Concerned Presbyterians, Inc. was founded in direct response to the liberal threat that the Fellowship of Concern posed.[93] Under the leadership of well-known Florida real estate executive Kenneth Keyes, the stated purpose of Concerned Presbyterians (CP) was outlined: "to return the church to its primary mission—winning people to Jesus Christ and nurturing them in the faith."[94] As events demonstrated, the faith of which the CP spoke was a faith in the verbal inerrancy of the Bible and a strict adherence to the standards of the Westminster Confessions. As well as propagating their views through *The Presbyterian Journal*, CP published *The Concerned Presbyterian*. Dendy also asked CP to disband in 1967, but unlike the liberal Fellowship of Concern, the CP decided to continue their efforts and were instrumental in the ensuing schism.[95]

Since 1958 the Presbyterian Evangelistic Fellowship (PEF) existed under the leadership of Reverend William E. Hill Jr., a well-known conservative

19

evangelist. The PEF was a group of more than a dozen evangelists who emphasized that the evangelical mission of the church meant a spiritual mission of converting individuals to faith in Christ as their Savior, with little or no emphasis on the social ramifications of the Gospel.[96] Until PEF leader Hill called for a separation from the PCUS in 1969, the PEF was endorsed by the PCUS administration. Well-known evangelists preached messages stressing individual salvation at PEF's revivalistic annual August meetings held at Montreat, North Carolina. The PEF was also the parent body to the Executive Commission on Overseas Evangelism (ECOE).[97]

The seminary to which the conservative groups looked for most of their theological leadership was the Reformed Theological Seminary of Jackson, Mississippi, which had its genesis in 1964 with the aeronautical travels of Morton H. Smith, formerly of Westminster Seminary, Philadelphia.[98] Not officially affiliated with any denomination, RTS listed among its "distinctives" a commitment to the "plenary, verbal inspiration" of the Bible and "its absolute inerrancy as the divinely revealed and authoritative Word of God." Also listed as "distinctives" were commitments to the "sovereignty of God as a central tenet of Biblical faith, along with the related doctrine of absolute predestination and unconditional election." RTS also professed a "strict creedal subscription to the whole Reformed faith" of the Westminster Confession and Catechisms as originally adopted by the PCUS. By 1969 the seminary had graduated eleven men, with sixty-five students enrolled in the 1969-70 academic year.[99]

B. Divisive 1969 General Assembly Decisions

Through most of the 1960s, these conservative groups struggled, often successfully, to enact their perspectives as church law, but the General Assembly of 1969 was pivotal in prompting the conservative groups to begin calls for a new "continuing" church. Liberals dominated the 1969 Assembly not only by electing the liberal Rev. R. Matthew Lynn as moderator but also by obtaining the adoption of far-reaching liberal resolutions.[100] One such resolution amended the constitutional document, the Form of Government, to allow synod and presbytery boundary lines to be "restructured" or redrawn. Conservatives claimed that this restructuring was a poorly concealed liberal effort at gerrymandering so that conservative voting strength would be diluted and liberal voting blocks favored.[101] Even more upsetting for conservatives was the 1969 Assembly resolution that amended the Book of Church Order, making union presbyteries a constitutional possibility.[102] In earlier Assemblies, conservatives had argued that, on the basis of previous denominational judgments, such an amendment required a three-quarters majority in the presbyteries.[103] However, under the guidance of the newly elected liberal moderator, the 1969 General Assembly ignored this advice and adopted the decision of the 1968 General Assembly, which resolved that only the approval of a majority of the presbyteries was required.[104]

Approval of union presbyteries would probably have been enough to goad conservatives into calling for a continuing Presbyterian church, but two other actions of this Assembly confirmed conservative strategists in their resolve. The first action authorized a new committee that would be responsible for drafting a "new Confession of Faith together with a Book of Confessions."[105] The second was the establishment of a committee to explore union with the northern Presbyterian church, at this time known as the United Presbyterian Church USA.[106] For conservatives, both actions endangered the historic confessional position of the PCUS, the first for obvious reasons and the second because of the Confession of 1967, adopted by the UPUSA as its confessional statement.[107]

The Confession of 1967 had been censured in *The Presbyterian Journal* long before the 1969 assembly.[108] Originally commissioned in 1958, the Confession of 1967 was a radical departure from the Westminster Confession at least in its emphasis; whereas the Westminster Confession had often been regarded as a system of doctrines derived from Scripture, this document emphasized its use as a guide for action in the church.[109] The theme of the Confession of 1967 was reconciliation first between God and humanity and second among humans.[110] God's love in Christ was emphasized, not just for the redemptive rewards associated with individual salvation but also for the social, political, and ethical responsibilities such love demands of the church in this world. This was blasphemous enough for conservative PCUS ears, always sensitive to attacks on the spirituality of the church's mission, but to make matters worse, conservatives judged the Confession of 1967 weak on historic Christian doctrines like the incarnation, the virgin birth, the bodily resurrection, original sin, and the authority of Scriptures.[111] Its inclusivistic descriptions of the relation of the Christian faith to other world religions were regarded by liberals as a step forward for ecumenical relations while conservatives regarded such rhetoric as heresy. With the Confession of 1967 the UPUSA had also adopted new ordination vows that asked ministerial candidates to accept the Scriptures

21

merely as a "unique and authoritative witness to Jesus Christ"[112] and the performance of ministerial duties as only "under the continuing instruction and guidance of the Confessions of this church."[113] Simply put, for conservatives, the Confession of 1967 with its new ordination vows violated every one of the distinctives that southern conservatives regarded so highly.

C. Conservative Coalition "Declares"

Conservatives regarded any ecclesiastical relationship with a church that had adopted such an unreformed document as unconstitutional. They were also upset that some PCUS congregations could be united unwillingly with UPUSA congregations in previously prohibited union presbyteries. The fact that the PCUS was considering adoption of another confessional standard confirmed conservative opinion that the PCUS was abandoning its confessional heritage for nonreformed, liberal foundations.[114] To think that the whole church would "explore" organic union with the UPUSA under the guidance of a committee dominated by liberals was the last straw for conservatives; they felt obligated to contemplate separation from the PCUS.[115]

Almost immediately, a group of conservative PCUS clergymen[116] drafted a Declaration of Commitment, protesting what they saw as their denomination's deviation from its official confessional position. They declared their conviction that only through faith in Christ is there "genuine reconciliation," "that the Holy Scriptures are the infallible Word of God,"[117] that the church is committed to "a mission whose primary end is the salvation and nurture of souls," that they "must strive to preserve a confessional Church, thoroughly Reformed and Presbyterian," that they "must oppose all efforts to change in substance or otherwise debase [their] historic doctrinal commitment," and that they "oppose the effort to take [their] Church into the massive organization envisioned by COCU."[118] In its concluding comment, the declaration gives one of the first public warnings that schism is a very real possibility for those conservatives unhappy with the liberal direction the PCUS was assuming:

> Should the basic theology or polity of the Church be altered or diluted, we shall be prepared to take such actions as may be necessary to fulfill the obligations imposed by our ordination vows to maintain our Presbyterian faith.[119]

By October of 1969 over five hundred clergymen or approximately 25 percent of PCUS ordained clergymen had signed the declaration.[120] This show of support prompted some of the signers to reorganize August 28-29, 1969 as Presbyterian Churchmen United (PCU), with Donald Patterson as chairman.[121] Among their purposes, the PCU pledged

1. To glorify the triune God.

2. To continually profess the Scriptures of the Old and New Testaments to be the Word of God written, the only infallible rule of faith and practice.

3. To defend, support and teach the Reformed Faith as set forth in the Westminster Confession of Faith and Catechisms, as the system of doctrine taught in Holy Scriptures. . . .[122]

6. To fervently support those within the Church who preach the Biblical Gospel in particular obedience to the Great Commission, at home and overseas. . . .

8. To hold conferences, consultations, and rallies wherever and whenever feasible, to further the educational aims of the organization. . . .

10. Being devoid of desire or power to threaten, we do solemnly declare to the people of the Presbyterian Church US our promise henceforth to do whatever may be necessary to maintain our Reformed faith and Presbyterian polity.[123]

On December 5 and 6, 1969, the PCU held its first rally in Atlanta with over fifteen hundred attending, the common bond between clergy and laity at this rally being the declaration.[124] The speeches were much more blatantly schismatic. For example, Rev. Frank M. Barker of Birmingham in a speech entitled "The Road Ahead" cautioned that evangelicals can expect "rough travelling on an uncharted road." Referring to the temptation to succumb to compromises in areas of polity and belief, he said: "There may well be a fork in the road ahead. But if so, it will not be we who are departing. We will continue straight ahead. And we will invite men from all over the nation to join us, if and when the time comes."[125]

This marked escalation in schismatic rhetoric prompted yet another group to organize. Several PCUS conservatives published "An Open Letter to the Church" in 1967. In it they complained of the polarization of the PCUS between "two dedicated and active groups, each well organized."[126] They also warned that "our Church seems to be headed toward some sort of division or fragmentation." Consistent with their aim of unity, they promised not to form any new organization, but to work through the courts of the church.[127] But by 1969, many of these same people realized that such relatively passive resistance was not very effective, so on January 12-13, 1970, they met in Atlanta to launch the Covenant Fellowship of Presbyterians (CFOP) with Rev. Dr. William M. Elliot president and Rev. Andrew Jumper executive vice president. Claiming they were "moderates" or "middle-of-the-roaders," the CFOP warned of the ever-widening gulf between liberals and conservatives within the PCUS and called on "the silent majority" to bridge the gap.[128] As independent as the CFOP claimed to be, a subsequent position paper indicated that on most issues it sympathized with the CP, PEF, and PCU, or what *The Presbyterian Outlook* called the "Conservative Coalition."[129]

The organization of a series of rallies by CP in 1970 gave further evidence of a developing "coalition." For example, in addition to the regular speakers at a CP rally held in Charlotte, North Carolina, representatives from PEF (Rev. William E. Hill Jr., president), Reformed Theological Seminary (Morton H. Smith, dean), the *Presbyterian Journal* (G. Aiken Taylor, editor), and PCU (John E. Richards, executive secretary) gave key speeches, explaining their organizations and their place in the PCUS.[130] As the year progressed, these groups increasingly coordinated their efforts, especially as rumors and statements circulated that de facto unions between the PCUS and the UPUSA[131] and even between the PCUS and other participants in COCU[132] had already taken place at the agency, congregational, and presbyterial level.

As ecumenical optimism increased, conservatives became even more blunt about their schismatic intentions. For example, the title page on *The Presbyterian Journal* changed on May 6, 1970 from "*The Presbyterian Journal* The Circulation leader among Independent Publications in the Presbyterian Reformed World" to "*The Presbyterian Journal* Advocating Continuation of a Presbyterian Church Loyal to Scripture and the Reformed Faith."[133] Keyes of the CP and Richards of PCU made presentations to the Joint Committee of 24 on January 26, 1970. Both men pleaded for a more conservative content to the union plan but, conceding that this was unlikely to occur, they suggested a method for making the union plan acceptable even to the conservatives.

> If a plan of union is to win the respect of the lay constituencies it must deal with the question of Church property in an honest, fair, and loving way. If the proposed union produces more divisions than it eliminates, those who divide should be permitted to go their way as brethren, taking their possessions with them and without resorting to civil courts.[134]

D. Aftermath of the 1970 General Assembly

The events of the 1970 PCUS General Assembly did little to mollify the increasingly militant conservative coalition. An avowed liberal and former chairman of COCU, William A. Benfield, was elected moderator.[135] Union discussions with the UPUSA were to continue, with a presentation scheduled for the General Assembly in 1971.[136] A proposal that congregations not wishing to enter the proposed union church be entitled to enter a provisional synod created strictly for that purpose did not receive action but was only referred to the negotiating committees.[137] The decision scheduled for this assembly regarding the restructuring of presbyterial and synodical boundary lines was referred back to the originating committee for further comment from the church membership.[138] Conservatives alleged that the magazine *Colloquy*, designed for leaders of young people and published jointly by the PCUS, UPUSA, and the United Church of Christ, was "blasphemous," "profane," and "immoral," but the Assembly refused to condemn the magazine.[139] The 1970 Assembly decided that a woman's decision to abort "may on occasion be morally justifiable"; listed as possible justifying circumstances were "medical indications of physical or mental deformity, conception as a result of rape or incest, conditions under which the physical or mental health of either mother or child would be gravely threatened or the socio-economic condition of the family."[140] Previous to the 1970 Assembly, abstinence from alcoholic beverages had been the official stance of the PCUS, but this convention decided that the individual could decide "whether, where, when and under what circumstances drinking is appropriate or inappropriate."[141]

At the conclusion of this Assembly, many conservatives were convinced that the PCUS was "beyond the point of no recovery."[142] Liberals had so controlled the convention that the major controversies (such as regarding *Colloquy*) seemed to be between liberals and ultraliberals.[143] When a "continuing church" was promised at Journal Day in August, those assembled gave a rousing cheer.[144] W. Jack Williamson, secretary of CP and an acknowledged conservative leader, spoke not of whether there should be a separation but when that separation should take place. Using the words of St. Paul as a directive for future action, Williamson urged his listeners to pray for preservation, fight against liquidation, and prepare for separation.[145] He referred to the restructuring plan as a way for denominational authorities to deny presbyteries the option of leaving the denomination. For that reason he warned his listeners to prepare especially well for the 1971 General Assembly,

25

where not only the restructuring plan was to be presented but also the first draft of a plan of union with the UPUSA, the first draft of the new confession, and a recommendation on church property.[146]

Williamson's speech had its effect, as ten of the more than seventy PCUS presbyteries "prepared" for the convention by adopting resolutions based on a working model developed by the conservative coalition. In this prototypical resolution the presbyteries "covenanted together to stand for the historic doctrine and form of government of the Presbyterian Church US."[147] More specifically, the resolution said that the presbyteries involved "would not consent to organic union with the UPUSA which union would inevitably result in the disappearance of the distinctive witness of the Presbyterian Church US." The presbyteries also covenanted to reject any "dilution of the Confession of Faith," "any demeaning of our [Westminster] Confession by including it in a book of Confessions,"[148] or any change in the ordination vows. Any amendments to the Book of Church Order "which would take control of local church property from congregations and vest it in the presbytery" would not be tolerated, nor would any "surrender" to "any united, combined or restructured body if such surrender, in the judgment of this presbytery, would constitute a threat to the spiritual and moral principles" of the historic confessions. Also censured by most of these presbyteries was "union by the back door" (i.e., union presbyteries), the ordination of women,[149] fully privileged youth delegates at General Assemblies,[150] the approval of civil disobedience,[151] and even consideration of a proposed plan of union from COCU.[152]

A desperate reconciliation effort was attempted in January 1971, when a summit meeting of pro- and antiunion representatives was convened.[153] Little was resolved. Moderator Benfield, who presided over the meeting, described the polarization within the denomination as the most serious in its history. He accused CP of trying to create a rift between clergy and laity;[154] he also attacked what he called the "conservative myth" that if one favors social action, one opposes the Word of God. For antiunion conservatives this meeting provided a forum wherein their resolve was galvanized and published. They were also able to present their conditions for supporting a union plan, among which were the following: 1) the plan would have to contain a "conscience clause" whereby a congregation or presbytery could vote for the plan without agreeing with everything in it; 2) the plan would have to provide for a continuing association or provisional synod to which nonunited synods could be assigned;[155] and 3) only a majority of the presbyteries would have to approve the plan.[156] Prounion representatives promised to take these conservative concerns to the Committee of 24.

The executive committees of the CP, PCU, and *The Presbyterian Journal* were not content to wait for a denominational committee on union to decide their fate for them. In April 1971 they issued a "Call for Realignment of American Presbyterianism." In it, they reaffirmed their commitment to the constitution of the PCUS and their opposition to plans for union with the UPUSA or the proposed Church of Christ Uniting. More important, they articulated their vision for the future of American Presbyterianism.

> Recognizing the doctrinal divergences within the Presbyterian Church in the United States and other denominations holding the Reformed faith, we would pray and work toward the realignment of present church structures to the ultimate end that for those who desire it, there will be in America, a fervently evangelistic church, faithful to the Bible, the Reformed faith, and Presbyterian polity.
>
> Therefore, we seek an open, complete and constitutional realignment of those denominations willing to participate either under a plan of union embodying necessary changes in the present plan, or under some special commission appointed by the General Assembly to accomplish this objective [true realignment], through proper constitutional process.[157]

In fact, efforts at such a realignment were already in progress. The National Presbyterian and Reformed Fellowship (NPRF) was formed late in 1970 by representatives from the major American reformed denominations.[158] The NPRF described its function as a "receiving body" for those "displaced" congregations and denominations that "professed the system of doctrine contained in the classic Reformed confessions" and "functioned under a presbyterian form of government." The NPRF statement of purpose implied a limited ecumenism defined by conservative guidelines. "Reformed doctrine and presbyterial church government furnish the basis for and the thrust toward a Scriptural ecumenism that is both contemporaneous and dynamic."[159] At the NPRF constituting convention in April, G. Aiken Taylor of *The Presbyterian Journal* was elected president.[160] By December of 1971, NPRF had hired a full-time executive director to facilitate the rallies they intended to organize.[161] The existence of the NPRF is significant because this group, though heavily dependent on the PCUS for its leadership, drew its members from all Presbyterian denominations and was not limited by geography, racial inclination, or social class. Rather, a conservative theological consensus bonded its members together.

27

E. Mission Problems

Another area of increasing tension in 1971 was that of missions. Since 1962, the PCUS Board for World Missions (BWM) had pursued a missions policy based on a commitment to the ecumenical movement and particularly to cooperation with the NCC and World Council of Churches.[162] Though the initiation of such policies had been gradual, the resignations of L. Nelson Bell, Peter Branton, and Walter Shephard in the late 1960s signaled that conservatives on the mission board and in the field were unhappy with board policies.[163] In May of 1969, the PCUS BWM acknowledged the widening gap between overseas PCUS churches and itself and asked that missionaries no longer defer decisions to the national churches but only to the BWM.[164] As well, BWM admitted severe financial difficulties necessitating spending restraint and even cutbacks. In any other denomination such action merely would have been a sign of the times, but in the PCUS, long noted for its generous support of overseas missionary endeavors, fiscal problems indicated discontent at the grass roots.[165]

The cause of this fiscal stinginess was the PCUS's equalization policy, which became effective in 1966. Equalization meant that any donations received directly by the BWM had to be reported to denominational headquarters, who in turn would make an appropriate reduction in the benevolence funds normally allotted to the BWM.[166] In effect, this meant that conservatives wishing to support overseas missions by direct donations were also indirectly supporting social programs like abortion clinics and racial integration programs. Conservatives protested this equalization policy vigorously at the 1969 General Assembly but the structure was upheld.[167] Finally, with denominational agencies facing projected receipts of only 85 percent of budgeted benevolence income in 1969, the PCUS General Council decided to relax its equalization policy by allowing "more designated giving to Assembly projects and agencies in which congregations have a particular interest." These "over and above" gifts would not be subject to equalization.[168]

Even with this effort to pacify the conservatives, the BWM continued to experience real financial difficulties; in 1970, the BWM found it necessary to recall some missionary personnel despite pleas for more help from the mission fields. Conservatives complained that only the evangelical missionaries they favored were being recalled and that conservative favorites remaining were being discriminated against financially. Conservatives also complained that the increasing centralization of power by the BWM meant that any funds received by the conservative missionaries in the field were already earmarked by the BWM.[169]

Despairing of continued efforts through the BWM, conservatives, under the leadership of the PEF, established the Executive Commission on Overseas Evangelism in 1970 in order to channel their financial support more effectively to conservative missionaries. Liberals soon charged the ECOE with giving funds to missionaries on the condition that the missionary not report such funds to the BWM and intentionally diverting funds from regular denominational budgets. ECOE authorities replied that their organization had been established simply to facilitate designated gift-giving, which was a perfectly legitimate activity since the General Council ruling in late 1969. When BWM found it necessary to adopt yet another reduced budget for 1970, ECOE officials offered to support the BWM overseas program if 1) ECOE was allowed "to support certain projects and specific personnel whose concept of evangelism agreed with that of the Presbyterian Evangelistic Fellowship"; 2) no ECOE funds "could be used either through or for the National Council of Churches or the World Council of Churches"; and 3) no ECOE funds "could be subject to equalization." The denominational General Council declined ECOE's proposition, saying it could not allow blanket approval to unequalized gifts.[170]

Though the Executive Committee of PCUS's General Council was authorized to investigate the ECOE in 1970, little was done by denominational authorities until February of 1971, when the ECOE announced that it would start supporting its own missionaries overseas.[171] The General Council held closed meetings to discuss the move, which would almost certainly deplete denominational funds. In March, the General Council released a report labeling ECOE a "serious threat to the peace and unity of the church" and recommending that the General Assembly voice its disapproval of ECOE and reaffirm part of a 1941 Assembly-approved statement on extra-denominational agencies that condemned activities in competition with the work of the denomination.[172] Yet another issue awaited the deliberations of the 1971 General Assembly.

F. Indecision and Despair at the 1971 General Assembly

The 1971 General Assembly was not the landmark convention it was expected to be. Rev. Albert C. Winn, chairman of the committee responsible for drafting the new confession, was able to offer only an outline of a proposed confession. The plan for union with the UPUSA, released in February and full of conservative compromises including an escape clause, a conscience clause, and a provision that would facilitate division of property in dispute cases,[173] was referred for further study with no Assembly vote expected until the summer of 1973.[174] The 1971 General Assembly also received and adopted the Permanent Judicial Committee report on church property, which recommended no change in the constitutional regulations.[175] The conclusions of this property report were not very helpful because they did not address the real problem for congregations wishing to secede, namely who held title to the property in those situations where a minority was willing to fight to keep the property with the PCUS.[176]

What was noteworthy about this Assembly was its decision to proceed with the plan of restructuring despite great conservative opposition. The 1971 Assembly decided that the denomination's fifteen synods would be realigned to become seven by July 1, 1973, with presbytery boundaries redrawn sometime after that. Conservatives protested that this meant that the new alignment of presbyteries would decide the UPUSA union issue. Past moderator Benfield replied that if he had considered this restructuring proposal linked to the union plan, he would not have voted for the restructuring since he thought the present alignment was more favorable to union.[177]

The 1971 Assembly also alienated conservatives with the decision to condemn ECOE as

> a grave departure from orderly processes of the Church. . . . The possible temporary gain for parts of the overseas mission that might be realized by money given through ECOE, as it is presently operating is far outweighed by the likelihood of grievous harm to the life and health of the Church by solicitations or offers of support that are made in a divisive or irregular manner.[178]

Conservatives were also upset that despite spirited organizational efforts to sway votes their way,[179] the Assembly's five study papers full of social action programs were accepted,[180] attempts to have the PCUS withdraw from the NCC, WCC, and COCU were quashed,[181] the abortion policy remained unchanged; yet another liberal moderator was elected;[182] and despite efforts by conservatives to elect sone of their own to positions on important denominational boards and agencies, they were unsuccessful in electing even one.[183]

The one concession to conservatives that had extensive ramifications was the resolution stating that the lower courts (sessions, presbyteries, synods) were not tied to the decisions of the higher court of the General Assembly.[184] Another obvious goodwill gesture was the decision to enlarge the Committee of 24 to a Committee of 26 with the addition of two churchmen, one from each denomination, who were "not happy with the union plan."[185]

In "The Assembly Tried to be Gentle," Taylor of *The Presbyterian Journal* reviewed the events of the Assembly and, distressed particularly by the decision to restructure the denomination, expressed the resignation of conservatives: "In short, to all practical purposes, the show is over. . . . The hopes of many for better days have been taken away. Gently."[186]

"Come Out from Among Them and Be Ye Separate": From 1971 to the Schism

A. The Steering Committee and the "Escape Clause"

Following the disappointing 1971 General Assembly, the conservative coalition wasted no time in organizing their "continuing Presbyterian church." At the August 11 Journal Day meeting, W. Jack Williamson of the CP delivered a key speech in which he spoke of the "apparent inevitability of division of the Presbyterian Church in the United States, a division caused by the radical ecumenists." In Williamson's view, "radical ecumenists" have had a disproportionately negative effect on the PCUS:

> We see today the clear teachings of the Gospel being muted in favor of humanism, universalism and syncretism. We see a constant and progressive lowering of moral and spiritual values in some of the pronouncements of our Church.

Maintaining that the "right administration of Church discipline" had been neglected, Williamson called his "beloved Church . . . both de facto and de jure apostate."

> It is simply a false statement to assert that the Church, under the umbrella principle of "unity in diversity," should be allowed to remain a conglomeration of believers and unbelievers.[187]

Immediately following Williamson's speech, PCU chairman Patterson announced the formation of a new Steering Committee for a Continuing Presbyterian Church. As chairman of the twelve-man committee, Patterson introduced its members, who represented the CP, PCU, PEF, and *Presbyterian Journal.*[188] Then he outlined their common ground.

> These groups have reached a consensus to accept the apparent inevitability of division in the Presbyterian Church US caused by the program of the radical ecumenists, and to move now toward a continuing body of congregations and presbyteries loyal to the Scriptures and the Westminster Standards.
>
> This steering committee has been charged with the responsibility of developing and implementing a plan for a continuation of a Presbyterian Church loyal to the Scriptures and Reformed faith. . . . This is truly a historic day for all of us. We resolutely set our faces in a new direction. We shall, with God's help, preserve for future generations the witness of our historic faith, that faith once delivered to the saints.[189]

In a document released in early 1972, the Steering Committee detailed their "Faith and Purpose" by interspersing quotations from the Westminster Standards with their own explanations.

Scripture
We believe the Scriptures of the Old and New Testaments to be the Word of God written, the only infallible rule of faith and practice, and that the entire sixty-six books of the Bible were verbally inspired by God. (C.O.F. 1)

Reformed Faith
We believe and accept the Westminster Confession of Faith and Catechisms as *containing the system of doctrine* taught in the Holy Scriptures, and that these standards are the most acceptable expression of the Reformed Faith.

Mission of the Church
We believe "The sole functions (mission) of the Church are to proclaim, to administer, and to enforce the law of Christ revealed in Scripture." (B.C.O. 1-3) . . .

Church Union
We believe the Presbyterian Church in the U.S. may lawfully unite only with such "other ecclesiastical bodies whose organization is conformed to the doctrines and order of this church" (B.C.O. 18-6 (17)). The United Presbyterian USA and the Church of Christ Uniting *with their doctrinal inclusiveness* could not constitutionally unite with the Presbyterian Church U.S.

Apostasy

. . . We believe that many of the individuals, institutions, boards, and agencies, of the church are apostate, and we see no sign of repentance and revival among them. . . .

Reconciliation

To all Christians, we would be reconciled in love, through our one Faith in Christ, as Lord and Savior. To all who accept the Bible as the Word of God written, we would be reconciled in love through our one obedience to the Sole Authority of Scripture. To all for whom the Scriptures interpret themselves as teaching the true Reformed faith, we would be reconciled in love through our aim to *reestablish a church of pure doctrine* to the Glory of Our Lord Jesus Christ. We would be neighbors and friends to all men, calling them to be reconciled to God in Jesus Christ.[190]

Beginning in the autumn of 1971, representatives of the Steering Committee visited congregational meetings asking sessions to reconsider their membership in the PCUS.[191] Rather than allowing the continuing church movement to fragment with the departure of individual congregations, Steering Committee representatives urged congregations to wait for the provisions of the proposed plan of union when a mass departure would be constitutionally legitimated by the escape clause. Such a planned, group exodus would enable congregations to retain their property in departing, and would also establish and preserve a Presbyterian form of government.[192] Until that plan of union with its escape clause was ratified, conservative organizers encouraged congregations to sign a "Declaration of Intent" that condemned Assembly programs "contrary to the clear teaching of God's Word"[193] and, like the "Faith and Purpose" document, declared a determination to maintain the "purity of the church."[194]

> We believe that the time has come to take a definite stand against the continuing erosion of Presbyterian doctrine and polity which is taking place in the Presbyterian Church in the United States. . . .
> We stand ready to enter into fellowship with other like-minded congregations in preparing for a continuing church which will be faithful to God's Word, loyal to historic Presbyterian doctrine and polity, and obedient to the Great Commission.[195]

There were more cautious conservatives who doubted whether it was necessary to form a new church, especially since the official doctrine of the PCUS had not changed. Representative of these more cautious conservatives was L. Nelson Bell, who resigned his post as executive editor of the *Presbyterian Journal* immediately after the Steering Committee's announcement. Part of his resignation statement read: "It is, it seems to me, a calculated plan to schism prior to an issue which involves basic doctrine. In effect it calls for a battle without a cause and a concession of defeat before the battle is joined."[196] To counter this stinging criticism from men of similar doctrinal backgrounds, the Steering Committee made some effort to justify that though the official doctrine of the PCUS had not changed, the denomination had become apostate in practice, particularly in the activities of its boards and agencies.[197]

When it became apparent that this attempted justification might not be enough for some, the capable Steering Committee took steps to ensure that the denomination would have an opportunity to demonstrate its apostasy in doctrine also. First Presbyterian Church, Macon, Georgia, home parish for seventeen years of Rev. John E. Richards (now administrator of the Steering Committee), gave the denomination that opportunity by requesting that the 1972 General Assembly reaffirm

> . . . that Chapter I of the Confession of Faith on the Holy Scripture along with the parallel sections of the Shorter and Larger Catechisms do indeed teach the plenary verbal inspiration of Holy Scripture . . .
> . . . that "the infallible rule of interpretation of Scripture, is Scripture itself"; and that the Scriptures, being self-attesting, are not subject to the criticism or preconceptions of man . . .
> . . . that the Bible is the verbalized communication of God to men (the Word of God written); and that the Assembly, therefore, reject as inadequate, the so-called "Witness and Instrument" theory of Scripture.
> . . . that all Assembly boards, agencies, programs, literature and personnel shall be only those that willingly accept and follow the doctrine of the plenary verbal inspiration of Scripture.[198]

The 1972 General Assembly defeated this overture,[199] signaling to some cautious conservatives that the PCUS had indeed contradicted the Westminster Confession and therefore was apostate. The Steering Committee had secured its legitimating cause.

Conservatives were encouraged in the 1972 Assembly by the election of former *Presbyterian Journal* editor L. Nelson Bell as moderator; he immediately pleaded that the union proposal be voted upon as quickly as possible and that the legitimate complaints of the conservatives be heeded.[200] However, other Assembly events gave the Steering Committee reason to despair of any sympathetic hearing. Under the restructuring plan, a provisional General Executive Board (GEB) with great transitional powers regarding the restructuring of agencies was elected; conservatives were disappointed that of the sixty-five elected to this board, only a small proportion were conservative.[201] A new Confession of Faith was proposed for study by the denomination with final approval scheduled for the 1975 General Assembly.[202] Conservatives condemned the new poetic confession as weak in, if not lacking entirely, some important Christian doctrines (notably the virgin birth and resurrection)[203] and so full of compromises that it was confusing.[204] Efforts to condemn universalistic theology on the basis that it was contrary to the Westminster Standards were stymied by parliamentary debate; conservatives maintained that the denominational position remained as vague as before.[205] Though attempts were made to break the ecumenical alliances with COCU,[206] NCC, and the WCC, none was successful.[207] Various social pronouncements, including one that reaffirmed the 1970 position on abortion, demonstrated to conservatives the liberal activist role of the denomination.[208] As a result of these actions, conservatives felt they had little reason to attempt any kind of dialogue with the liberal authorities.

After the 1972 Assembly, the conservative coalition voiced their disappointment and their conviction that the PCUS apostasy was irreversible.[209] W. Jack Williamson, secretary of the CP and conservative representative on the Committee of 32,[210] pressed demands for the inclusion of an escape and conscience clause in the union proposal. He challenged "radical ecumenists" to show their good faith to the conservatives by bringing the proposed plan of union to a vote at the 1973 PCUS General Assembly and by postponing until after the union vote the establishing of new synod and presbytery boundaries.[211]

To cautious conservatives, Williamson lectured on the feasibility of creating a continuing Presbyterian church "through the election not to enter" (escape clause) in the union proposal. He argued that waiting for the escape clause would enable a greater number of churches to join the Continuing Church because of the psychological advantage involved in moving together at the same time. Williamson also reasoned that such group movement meant ministers would not have to break their ordination vows of obedience to the Presbyterian Church US because they would still be able to claim that they were obeying the Continuing Presbyterian Church.[212] Most important, Williamson said that waiting for the escape clause "is a guaranteed constitutional method for a local church to elect not to enter the union and still keep its local church property."[213] Williamson outlined a timetable in which the General Assemblies would vote on the proposal in 1973, with congregations and ministers having the option to utilize the escape clause between February and June 1974. Ideally, Williamson and the Steering Committee thought that the "new Church and the Continuing Church" would begin their new and separate lives at the conclusion of that sorting period.[214]

Though the Steering Committee and its member organizations were united in their resolve to wait until the 1973 General Assemblies of both the PCUS and UPUSA, when the first vote would be taken on the union proposal and its escape clause, conservative skeptics speculated that the liberal majority would try to delay the vote past July 1, 1973, the effective date for the geographical restructuring of synods.[215] Since most conservatives were convinced that the "political gerrymandering" resulting from restructuring would change the voting majorities in many presbyteries from conservative to liberal, waiting until after the restructuring was extremely risky. Not only would the union proposal with its escape clause be endangered by the new liberal majorities but the possibility that an individual conservative congregation could receive permission to be dismissed from its presbytery would also be threatened.[216]

Approximately ten congregations, influenced heavily by this conservative skepticism and convinced they could not withstand the pressures of restructuring, organized the independent Vanguard Presbytery on September 7, 1972.[217] Seven ministers and nine elders from six states[218] adopted the Westminster Confession of Faith and Catechisms as doctrinal standards and the PCUS Book of Church Order as it existed before 1935 for their church government.[219] Rev. Todd Allen, newly elected moderator of Vanguard and pastor of a Savannah church that left the PCUS, released a statement admitting that independence was not a desired status for any Presbyterian church. Allen said the reason his and other congregations did not join another denomination like the Orthodox Presbyterian Church or the Reformed Presbyterian Church (Evangelical Synod) was that they hoped to wait for PCUS conservatives to "reconstitute" themselves as a southern Presbyterian church.[220]

> We throw open the door to all ministers and churches who desire to separate from the Presbyterian Church, U.S. and who want a haven—a presbytery home. We are not seeking to persuade any minister or church to come out of the PCUS. However if they are already out, or plan to leave, we stand ready to welcome them into our fellowship.

> We are prepared to help any church that faces legal action. . . . We believe
> that we have something to offer churches in the legal expertise gained in our
> long court battle.[221]

Though there were strong objections to a motion that Allen act as Vanguard's representative on the Steering Committee, the motion was adopted.[222] At the Constituting Assembly of Vanguard Presbytery on November 14, 1972, members of the Steering Committee were present and cooperation with the new presbytery continued throughout the life of Vanguard.[223]

The suspicions of the Vanguard skeptics were confirmed at the February meeting of the Committee of 32 in Dallas. In a debate that began with the logistics of how a congregation would utilize the escape clause,[224] E. Dowey, a UPUSA opponent of any form of escape clause, insisted that such a clause was unconstitutional and that he would take the matter to the civil courts. Since the opinions of Dowey were already well known, this threat was no surprise; what was surprising was the response of the PCUS delegation, which recommended that the entire plan required revision.[225] With that, a resolution was adopted "to revise the plan and present the revision to the joint meeting of the two General Assemblies in Louisville in 1974 for study only."[226] W. Jack Williamson called the action of the committee "dishonest" and a "betrayal" of negotiations conducted in good faith.[227] Williamson's was not the only dissenting vote on the Committee of 32; William P. Thompson, stated clerk of the UPUSA and well-known liberal, had opposed the escape clause from the beginning but consented to it as a matter of expediency. As he told the PCUS delegates at the meeting

> I have always believed that politics is the art of the possible. You insisted that
> an escape clause was necessary in order to secure a favorable vote. You have
> now betrayed brethren who trusted your integrity. I now have no further
> commitment to the escape clause and I now declare that I will never consent to
> the inclusion of such a clause in a plan of union.[228]

Reaction from conservative ranks was immediate. Twenty small congregations in Alabama totaling approximately fifteen hundred members withdrew to form their own Warrior Presbytery.[229] They had been persuaded by the Steering Committee not to withdraw earlier but took matters into their own hands with the announcement of the union vote delay. The Steering Committee also acted quickly by voting unanimously to establish a continuing church in 1973.[230] Later, *The Presbyterian Journal* announced an organizational meeting for the continuing church in Atlanta May 18, 1973.[231]

Before that organizational meeting the Steering Committee adopted unanimously a document originally drafted by its chief administrator, John E. Richards. In topical format the "Reaffirmations of 1973" stated the position of the Steering Committee under the rubric "The Church Reborn" and contrasted that with the position of the PCUS as represented by the rubric "The Church Today." The Reaffirmation topics covered included Scripture, reformed doctrine, relations to the NCC and WCC, the church mission, the constitution of the church, church education, the spirituality of the church, church union, ethics, church discipline, union presbyteries, centralization of power, restructuring of synods/presbyteries, and property rights.[232] At the end of "Reaffirmations," a summary statement of "The Church Reborn" was given.

> Believing that unless two be agreed they cannot walk together, the Steering Committee, with profound sorrow and many tears, has concluded that there is a separation of those holding different ideologies within the PCUS. We commit ourselves to the rebirth and continuation of a Presbyterian Church in the United States in accord with these reaffirmations, praying our Lord Jesus Christ by the Holy Spirit to be our leader and helper. We believe that acknowledgment of the separation and the inevitable rebirth cannot and should not be delayed, and therefore call for the establishment during 1973 of a Continuing Presbyterian Church, loyal to Scripture, the Reformed Faith, and committed to the spiritual mission of the Church as Christ commanded in the Great Commission.[233]

B. Founding the "Continuing Presbyterian Church"

Acting on the advice of G. Aiken Taylor, the Steering Committee decided that the organizational meeting of those interested in establishing a continuing church would be a Convocation of Sessions followed by an Advisory Convention and finally the Constituting Assembly. This would follow the pattern established by PCUS fathers who organized the first General Assembly in 1861.[234]

Over 450 voting delegates representing 261 churches constituting a cumulative membership of 70,000 attended the initial Convocation of Sessions in Atlanta on May 18-19, 1973. The keynote address was given by Rev. William E. Hill, former leader of the PEF, who said that compromise cannot be afforded in the preaching of the Gospel.[235] W. Jack Williamson was even more blunt regarding the need for schism; claimed that his vows of ordination as a ruling elder actually required him to separate from his beloved church.[236] Relying on the evidence that Morton H. Smith of Reformed Theological Seminary had provided in his speech on PCUS departures from historic doctrine, Williamson argued that the separation had been delayed until 1973 in the hopes of utilizing the escape clause of the union proposal. However, since that method "has been taken away by the liberals for this decade, at least, and perhaps forever," the time to initiate the schism had arrived.

> We have always maintained that we who agree in principle should move together. We are convinced that if we wait longer, major fragmentation will occur. In order to maintain the significant corporate witness of a Church loyal to Scripture and the Reformed Faith, we must move now in 1973.[237]

With the elimination of the escape clause, Williamson suggested that the best option available to conservative congregations was withdrawal from their presbyteries, litigation in the civil courts for the rights to their property, and then joining the new Continuing Church. Such corporate action would decrease the possibility of civil lawsuits.[238] Williamson also chided those conservatives who wanted to wait for the revised Plan of Union in the hopes it would contain an acceptable escape clause.[239]

By the time Williamson was finished, the Convocation was ready to adopt unanimously, with only one dissenter, the "Reaffirmations of 1973." This action in turn paved the way for almost unanimous adoption of a resolution calling for a new church.

> Believing that unless two be agreed they cannot walk together, with profound sorrow and many tears we have concluded that there is a separation of those holding different ideologies within the Presbyterian Church US. We commit ourselves to the rebirth and continuation of a Presbyterian Church in the United States in accord with these reaffirmations praying our Lord Jesus Christ by the Holy Spirit to be our leader and helper.
>
> We believe that acknowledgment of the separation and the inevitable rebirth cannot and should not be delayed, and therefore call for the establishment during 1973 of a Continuing Presbyterian Church, loyal to Scripture, the Reformed Faith, and committed to the spiritual mission of the Church as Christ commanded in the Great Commission.[240]

To facilitate this rebirth, an organizing Committee of 40 was elected, with Morton Smith secretary of the committee and clerk protem of the

Convocation; Williamson was elected Convocation chairman protem.[241] The Committee of 40 was commissioned to organize an Advisory Convention scheduled for Ashville, North Carolina, August 7-9, 1973. The purpose of this Advisory Convention was to gather "duly elected commissioners from local congregations, who will plan and call later in 1973 a formal constituting Assembly for the Church."[242]

This flurry of conservative schismatic activity had a moderating effect on the 1973 PCUS General Assembly though few actions were taken to deal seriously with conservative doctrinal concerns, probably because few conservatives attended.[243] An Assembly resolution expressed "grief over the separation of our brethren . . . and called synods, presbyteries and individual churches to special prayer and a time of . . . repentance for sin in the life of us all."[244] A Committee on Unhappiness and Division in the Church was established by a resolution that also pleaded for conservatives to accept doctrinal differences within the denomination.[245] These were the only two resolutions that attempted to deal directly with the impending threat of schism.

Other motions were much more ambivalent regarding the impending schism. Acknowledging that eighty-six congregations had already withdrawn, the General Assembly virtually washed its hands of the problem by ruling that only the lower courts of the presbyteries and local church sessions had primary responsibility and jurisdiction regarding the separated churches. Though authorizing the appointment of an advisory Committee on Church Property, the Assembly's directive to the committee was to advise courts of "actions which might be taken to conserve property held by any of the congregations and judicatories of the church."[246] Other Assembly actions were even less conciliatory. The new liberal moderator Charles Kraemer made the inflammatory assertion that the division was due to the fact that the dissidents had moved away from the historic positions of the church to a type of congregationalism where local autonomy was more important than presbyterial strength.[247] Adopted resolutions reaffirming the restructuring procedures, the existence of union presbyteries, and the liberal stance on abortion and other social issues were not intended to console conservatives. The appointment of a denominational lobbyist in Washington, D.C., confirmed conservative fears that the denomination was determined to be as socially active as possible.[248]

A consolidation of the Continuing Church was evident at Asheville on August 7-9, when over 1,700 delegates representing nearly 200 churches registered for the Advisory Convention.[249] The most important resolution passed by this convention read in part:

1. . . . we call to convene in holy assembly the duly elected representatives of sessions and ministers who subscribe to the text and commitment to the Reaffirmations of 1973 and who meet such other credential requirements as are established by this Convention.[250]

2. This Assembly is hereby called to convene at Briarwood Presbyterian Church, Birmingham, Alabama on December 4, 1973 at 7:00 p.m.

3. The purpose of this Assembly shall be: a) to worship Almighty God . . . b) to petition God the Father, that, by His Spirit this people be constituted under His Son at a reborn Presbyterian Church, and that the representatives there assembled be constituted the first General Assembly of this reborn Church.[251]

The Advisory Convention recommended to the Constituting Assembly that the constitutional documents consist of the Westminster Confession of Faith, the unamended versions of the Larger and Shorter Catechisms, and the PCUS Book of Church Order of 1933.[252] W. Jack Williamson was elected chairman and Morton H. Smith secretary of the temporary Continuing Presbyterian Church. Four General Assembly committees of twelve members each were also recommended, including a Committee on Administration, a Committee on the Mission to the World,[253] a Committee on the Mission to the U.S., and a Committee on Christian Education and Publications. Each committee was to be staffed by one full-time employee but all other hints of centralization were avoided.[254]

The Advisory Convention also recommended that congregations be given absolute ownership over their local property and that women's ordination not be allowed. The decision-making process was to be slowed and assured of almost total unanimity as a three-quarters majority on an Assembly resolution affecting the constitution would be required not only in the presbyteries but also in the Assembly itself. Least surprising was the policy on interchurch relations. The Continuing Church

. . . will be a separate and distinct Presbyterian denomination. It is not likely to commit itself to organic union with other denominations in the near future. . . . [but] shall encourage fellowship with all evangelicals who believe the entire Bible to be the verbally inspired and inerrant Word of God . . . [and] fraternal relations and associations with those who adhere to the distinctives of the Reformed Faith.[255]

These recommendations were adopted by the Constituting General Assembly held December 4-7, 1973. Williamson and Smith retained their leadership positions in the new church as moderator and stated clerk. After three ballots, National Presbyterian Church (NPC) was chosen as the new name for the approximately 55,000 members in over 250 congregations and 16 presbyteries who had indicated their intention to join.[256] The Book of Church Order then monopolized debate. Since there was not enough time to discuss all the items in the Book, it was decided to omit any reference to a process for amending the adopted constitution so that further amendments could be made by simple majority vote of the Second General Assembly.[257]

Perhaps the single most important document adopted and released by this Constituting Assembly was the five-page "Message to All Churches of Jesus Christ Throughout the World."[258] Its first task was to declare that the new denomination was necessary to maintain the purity of the church:

> In much prayer and with great sorrow and mourning we have concluded that to practice the principle of purity in the Church visible, we must pay the price of separation.[259] We desire to elaborate upon those principles and convictions that have brought us to that decision.
>
> We are convinced that our former denomination as a whole, and in its leadership, no longer holds those views regarding the nature and mission of the Church, which we accept as both true and essential. When we judged that there was no human remedy for this situation, and in the absence of evidence that God would intervene, we were compelled to raise a new banner bearing the historic, Scriptural faith of our forefathers.[260]

There followed the doctrinal foundations of the denomination upon which all future ecumenical dialogues were to be based.

> First we declare the basis of the authority for the Church. According to the Christian faith, the Bible is the Word of God written and carries the authority of its divine Author. . . . We declare, therefore, that the Bible is the very Word of God, so inspired in the whole and in all its parts, as in the original autographs, to be the inerrant word of God. It is therefore, the only infallible and all-sufficient rule of faith and practice. . . .[261]
>
> We declare also that we believe the system of doctrine found in God's Word to be the system known as the Reformed Faith. We are committed without reservation to the Reformed Faith as set forth in the Westminster Confession and Catechisms. It is our conviction that the Reformed faith is not sectarian, but an authentic and valid expression of Biblical Christianity. We believe it is our duty to seek fellowship and unity with all who profess this faith.[262] We particularly wish to labor with other Christians committed to this theology.[263]

A description of the "spiritual" nature of the church followed with "the great end of our organization" defined in terms of the Great Commission of Matthew 28: 19-20.[264]

With these "distinctives," conservative southern Presbyterians set out to preserve their "historic witness" within the context of a "doctrinally pure reborn church."[265] The emergence of this new denomination from the schismatic process cannot be described merely in terms of geographical, sociological, and demographic factors with the theological or religious issues relegated to the category of "excuses" for a new organization.[266] Indeed, those nontheological factors were almost certainly involved, but without the religious differences and controversies, the story of schism in the PCUS in 1974 would be sadly deficient.[267] Further, the theological warrants cited by the conservatives were more than just "ideological weapons [used by] the conservative coalition to attack alleged violations of constitutional norms and departure from historic Presbyterian doctrine of the PCUS." Rather, the "critical factors in the split" involved not only "social changes"[268] but also religious concerns about which a conservative group felt strongly enough to initiate a structural change that would protect those cherished theological traditions in a new denominational body of independent congregations.[269]

THREE

Schism in the Lutheran Church-Missouri Synod

Growing Up in America

The early history of the Lutheran Church-Missouri Synod (LC-MS) exemplifies the growth of an ethnic denomination led by a small number of influential charismatic leaders, each of whom left his own theological imprint on the denomination. As this denomination struggled with its entry into the American religious mainstream, the effect of those theological legacies would be realized.

In the early 1840s a group of Saxon Lutherans immigrated to Missouri in pursuit of religious freedom and economic benefit. By forming a new church in a new land they were avoiding the influence of the Prussian King Frederick Wilhelm III (1797-1840), who was trying to combine Reformed and Lutheran congregations in their native land. They were also able to worship in a church with the kind of *"reine Lehre"* or pure doctrine not thought possible in Frederick's new hybrid church.[1]

They were led by the charismatic Martin Stefan. Shortly after their arrival, it was discovered that Stefan had embezzled the group's funds and solicited sexual favors from many of the young women who had made the journey.[2] As betrayed as the Saxons were, their problems really began with the banishment of Stefan from their midst. Without his leadership, which was thought to be divinely guided, there was some doubt as to whether the new church they were establishing had God's sanction.[3]

In a formal debate in 1841, Carl Ferdinand Walther assumed the leadership of the fledgling colony by convincing the pilgrims that their overseas colony was a real church. Though a young, sickly pastor, Walther was gifted with a theological insight, preaching style, and organizational skill that unified the German Lutherans in the Midwest. The theological reasoning came relatively easy to Walther; Christ's church existed wherever believers, justified by a true faith, came together to worship. However, the organization of such a church in America took much diplomatic skill. With the memory of the trusted Bishop Stefan fresh in their minds, the Saxon Lutherans were wary of giving their clergy too much power. Therefore, a movement began under Walther's watchful eye that would concentrate authority in the local congregation. When the Evangelical Lutheran Church of Missouri, Ohio and other States was founded in 1847, Article VII stated that the local congregation was not subject to the jurisdiction of any other local congregation or any other ecclesiastical body.[4]

Walther's leadership permeated the whole of the young denomination when the constitution he wrote for Trinity Church in St. Louis became the synodical model. The unifying and unalterable confessional base of the Synod was described in Article II:

> 1. The Scriptures of the Old and the New Testament as the written Word of God and the only rule and norm of faith and of practice;
> 2. All the Symbolical Books of the Evangelical Lutheran Church as a true and unadulterated statement and exposition of the Word of God, to wit: the three Ecumenical Creeds (the Apostles' Creed, the Nicene Creed, the Athanasian Creed), the Unaltered Augsburg Confession, the Apology of the Augsburg Confession, the Smalcald Articles, the Large Catechism of Luther, the Small Catechism of Luther, and the Formula of Concord.[5]

The controversy of 1925 illustrates tensions developing within the Missouri Synod. In that year, the Union Committee of the Missouri Synod recommended fellowship with selected other Lutheran bodies on the basis of a set of theses whose core is known as the Chicago theses.[6] This recommendation was defeated at the 1929 convention in River Forest, Illinois, largely on the basis of arguments from Francis Pieper, who, like Walther, had been a synodical president renowned for his theological insights. To support his position, Pieper issued "A Brief Statement of the Doctrinal position of the Evangelical Lutheran Synod of Missouri, Ohio and other States" in 1931. Adopted at the 1932 convention, the "Statement" articulated a verbal inspiration of the Scriptures wherein the Bible was deemed inerrant in all matters, even history and science.[7] Pieper also made a distinction in this document between the orthodox and heterodox church. On the basis of Romans 16:17 he urged the orthodox Missourians to refrain from worshiping with the heterodox even if there was no one else with whom to worship. How did Pieper identify the heterodox? They do not share the "inerrant" reading of the Scriptures with the Missourians.[8]

Under the leadership of Walter Maier, opposition united against those of Pieper's mindset, which was caricatured as "justification by correct doctrine."[9] At the synodical convention in 1938 differences regarding the resurrection of the martyrs and the interpretation of Revelation 20 were regarded as nonfundamental doctrines by Maier's group. They convinced the convention that these issues should not impede progress toward union with other Lutheran bodies.[10] Those opposing Maier's unitive movements organized and soon published *The Confessional Lutheran*. This pugnacious periodical provoked a group of forty-four more moderate pastors and professors to issue in 1945 "A Statement"(commonly called "Statement of 44"). In it they argued that many scriptural passages were not entirely clear and that the mission goals of the church were far too important to be held back by disagreement over inconsequential doctrines. The 1947 convention forced this group to withdraw the "Statement" because such a position would have opened the doors to fellowship with other denominations.[11]

The moderates continued to agitate, however, and in 1950, a "Common Confession of Faith" was worked out with the American Lutheran Church. Though the "Common Confession" met strong objections from within the Missouri Synod and also from its colleagues in the Synodical Conference, it did manage to survive the 1950s relatively intact.[12]

By the 1950s, the Synod was feeling the pressures of American culture. German was no longer the first language of the majority of Missourians after the Second World War. Professors and clergy were increasingly trained by those who had received their higher education in other than Missouri institutions. Under the pressure of modernization and increased funding needs, the parochial school system was no longer as comprehensive as it once had been.[13] Usury, life insurance, dancing, scouting, and unions—once outlawed as sinfully secular—were at first ignored and eventually condoned. In short, the Missouri Synod of the 1950s was no longer an exclusive immigrant German sect; it was becoming a more settled American denomination.[14]

The organization of the Missouri Synod reflected this. The Synod was divided into geographical districts that met in years that the synodical convention did not convene. Each district elected a president who represented them at more frequent meetings of the Council of Presidents (COP), which also included the synodical president and vice presidents. Most questions not requiring a decision of the synodical convention were decided by the COP or the Board of Directors, which was elected directly by the synodical convention. Committees and commissions could be established by either body to study important questions. In all matters, though, the convention had ultimate authority. Delegates to this biennial event were chosen by the districts.[15]

The relationship between Synod and congregation was a confusing one. According to the constitution, relatively unchanged since the Synod's founding, the relationship was more a "walking together" as the word "synod" implied.

> Synod is not an ecclesiastical government exercising legislative or coercive powers, and with respect to the individual congregation's right of self-government it is but an advisory body.

However, according to the more modern bylaws, authority was centralized.

> The Synod expects every member congregation to respect its resolutions and to consider them of binding force if they are in accordance with the Word of God and if they appear expedient as far as the condition of the congregation is concerned. The Synod, being an advisory body, recognizes the right of the congregation to be the judge of the expediency of the resolution as applied to its local condition. However, in exercising such judgment, a congregation must not act arbitrarily but in accordance with the principles of Christian love and charity.[16]

This discrepancy, like the controversies, was symptomatic of the entry of a relatively isolated church into the American mainstream. Also like the controversies, this discrepancy would be the germ for much more disruptive religious debate.

"Something's Burnin' . . .": Events Until 1973

The continued Americanization of the Missouri Synod, especially during the 1960s, threatened to disrupt the tranquility of what was often described as the "homogeneous family" atmosphere of the denomination.[17] Herman Frincke, a spokesman for the moderates and district president of the Eastern District, argued that a major factor in the controversy was the growing heterogeneity of the population.[18] As well, certain conservatives said that the destiny of their denomination increasingly was determined by an educated elite at the showcase Concordia Seminary in St. Louis whose theological sentiments did not correspond with those of the grass roots in the denomination.[19] John Montgomery summarized the sentiments of many observers when he spoke of Missourians overreacting to the "ghetto-like ingrownness of the synod" by searching for theological relevance at any cost.[20] Though these characterizations have a certain validity, they do not account for the passion of the debate that eventually led to the schism. For that passion one must look at the religious controversies involved.

A. Modern Disputes

In 1958, Martin Scharlemann, a professor of exegesis at Concordia Seminary in St. Louis, received support from his fellow faculty for a paper that proposed to "defend the paradox that the Book of God's truth contains error." With the help of *The Lutheran News*, conservatives rallied enough support at the synodical convention in 1959 to pass a resolution stating that all teachers were "bound to teach in harmony with 'A Brief Statement of Francis Pieper.' " Scharlemann finally retracted in 1962, but he apologized only for the tensions he had caused within the Synod and not for what he had said in his paper. In fact, it appears he was vindicated by the adoption of a resolution in 1962 that declared the 1959 resolution unconstitutional because it added to the confessional base of Article II.[21]

Despite the founding of the conservative group "Faith Forward—First Concerns" (FF-FC) in April 1965 and the adoption of resolutions reaffirming the Bible as "the verbally inspired and infallible written Word of God,"[22] the Detroit convention of 1965 was a victory for the liberal, or what is more properly termed the moderate, forces. Delegates voted to apply for membership in a new Lutheran council, which would involve cooperating with Lutheran synods not in fellowship with Missouri. The principle of giving women the vote was adopted as long as they did not have authority over men (that is, they could not preach).[23] Calls for an investigation into Concordia Seminary in St. Louis were turned aside by synodical president Oliver Harms, who promised that the newly established Commission on Theology and Church Relations (CTCR) would study the issues.[24] Though no motion was actually adopted approving altar and pulpit fellowship with the American Lutheran Church, there was movement in that direction.[25]

Most damaging to the conservative cause was the adoption of the "Mission Affirmations." These spoke of approaching men of other faiths in humility and love, ministering to the total human being with all the social and political ramifications that entailed. They also affirmed the place of the Lutheran Church as a "confessional movement within the total body of Christ rather than as a denomination emphasizing institutional barriers of separation." Conservatives were offended by the implications that the Synod was relinquishing its exclusive rights to doctrinal truth. This rhetoric, which spoke of a "common humanity" and a "universal redemption," smacked of unionistic intentions and universalistic theology.[26]

The primary concern of FF-FC after the 1965 convention was the theology being taught at Concordia Seminary, St. Louis. Despite the fact that President Harms was unsuccessful in answering FF-FC's concerns regarding the type of biblical exegesis being done in St. Louis,[27] the FF-FC was encouraged by the election of conservatives to important positions at the synodical convention in New York in 1967.[28]

B. Election of Jacob Preus

In anticipation of more significant victories at the next synodical convention in 1969 in Denver, the highly efficient United Planning Council (UPC) met every two months in Chicago after the 1967 convention. Regulars at the meetings included Waldo Werning, Edwin Weber, Karl Barth, and Jacob Preus.[29] In 1968, members of this group together with Robert Preus, Jacob's brother, launched Balance, Inc. Balance was dedicated to the preservation of the "traditional" values of the LC-MS, including the strict inerrancy of the Bible. Jacob Preus was chosen as the organization's nominee for the synodical presidency[30] and was directed to reverse the tendency of ecumenically minded Missourians who, in the opinion of Balance members, were ignoring the confessional base of Lutheranism in the process of seeking fellowship with the American Lutheran Church (ALC).[31]

The election of the synodical president is usually the first item at a synodical convention. With only one exception, the previous incumbents had been reelected easily.[32] However, before the Denver convention, there had been doubts that the incumbent, Oliver Harms, would be reelected. The question of ALC fellowship had become a real issue for the Synod;[33] Harms's well-known profellowship stance was bound to alienate many delegates. His investigation of the St. Louis faculty had proved inconclusive. Charges were made that Harms was acting in concert with the faculty to protect his supporters in the fellowship cause. There were rumors regarding his poor health. What really sealed Harms's fate, however, was the success of the UPC forces in lobbying the convention delegates to their cause.[34] Preus was elected synodical president on the third ballot.[35]

Assuming his position for the rest of the convention, Preus encouraged the delegates to vote according to their conscience on the issue of fellowship with the ALC. The resolution to pursue ALC fellowship was adopted. Perhaps the delegates voted for Harms's platform of fellowship because they felt some guilt about expelling the grandfatherly incumbent from office.[36] However, it is much more likely that the sentiment favoring ALC fellowship in the conventions preceding this one found its fulfillment in Denver with this affirmative vote. This may have been an instance in which the moderates, striving for a dialogue with the mainstream of American denominationalism, influenced successfully a convention decision.[37]

In any event, Preus left the convention with a directive from his Synod to pursue a policy with which he did not agree; he promised to follow the wishes of the convention. However, Preus's closing remarks to the convention indicated the lines along which he intended to direct the debate. The real issue was not fellowship but "the proper understanding of and adherence to the doctrine of inspiration and inerrancy of Scripture."[38]

C. Conflict at Concordia Seminary, St. Louis

There had been indications that trouble was brewing at Concordia Seminary in St. Louis[39] well before 1973. When John Behnken retired from the synodical presidency in 1962, he claimed that in his investigation of charges of liberal doctrine at the seminary he had been misled by the faculty.[40] In response to pressure from Balance, Harms had asked for a statement from the faculty of their confessional position in 1965 and received only a vague assertion of faith.[41]

As the questioning of their teaching and accusations by the editors of *Affirm* and *Christian News*[42] increased, the Concordia faculty grew anxious. Since they played a critical role in the election of the seminary president,[43] they wanted someone who sympathized with their position. In May of 1969, just two months before the Denver convention, they elected John Tietjen. He was a graduate of Concordia, had received his doctorate at Union Theological Seminary, and had pastored in New Jersey. Tietjen had also served as public

51

relations director for the Lutheran Council in the United States of America; this last position and the publication of his book, *Which Way to Lutheran Unity?*, indicate the ecumenical leanings of the man chosen to lead the troubled seminary. Not nearly as easy to demonstrate is the seriousness and self-determination Tietjen brought to every problem, characteristics that eventually led to confrontation with the equally determined leader of the conservatives, Jacob Preus.[44]

When Richard Jungkuntz, a moderate of the St. Louis faculty, was not reappointed executive secretary of the increasingly powerful Commission on Theology and Church Relations, a critical point was reached in the relationship between the synodical administration and the faculty. The majority of the faculty responded by signing "A Call to Openness and Trust" in January 1970. "We speak for freedom; diversity in unity" was the message. The document maintained that differences concerning the manner of creation, authorship of disputed books of the Bible, the manner of the presence of Christ in the Lord's Supper, and the amount of factual error in the Scriptures were open questions that should not be straitjacketed by synodical resolutions.

> We believe that faith in God is experienced by the quality of our relationship to people even more than by formulating precise doctrines about God and man. We resist the temptation in our own church body which would hold men to complete agreement in formal and informal doctrinal propositions or would make the doctrines rather than God himself the object of faith.[45]

Since rumors of schism already circulated, "Openness" also made a point of rejecting the notion that the faculty wanted to form a new church body. Rather, their goal was

> to increase freedom and responsibility in the church in which our Lord has placed us. To that end we ask only that our conscience not be bound, except by God, and that our freedom to speak, write or act not be arbitrarily curtailed.[46]

After the publication of "A Call to Openness," its condemnation by the CTCR,[47] and the ensuing open bickering among the faculty,[48] synodical president Preus announced the formation of a Fact Finding Committee (FFC) that would be directly responsible to him. Though initially there was great resistance, the FFC conducted taped interviews of the faculty between December 11, 1970 and March 6, 1971. Transcripts of the interviews were sent to Tietjen, the professor involved, and members of the FFC. At various times during the investigation, the faculty majority condemned the interviews as "unscriptural, unethical, divisive, disruptive and detrimental" and agreed to continue "only under protest." On June 13, 1971 the FFC submitted its report to Preus, just in time for it to be acted upon by the synodical convention of 1971, held in Milwaukee.[49]

In his presidential report to the Milwaukee convention, Preus quoted Carl Ferdinand Wilhelm Walther's address of 1868, "The False Arguments for the Modern Theory of Open Questions," where Walther asserted that the church is expected to interpret the faith of Scripture and can expect its members to hold to it.[50] Preus continued by saying that Article II "compels us to adopt such (doctrinal) statements as the course of events and the needs of the church develop." With these words of their past and present leader ringing in their ears, the convention resolved (Resolution 2-21) that doctrinal statements could be adopted not to establish doctrine, but to confess what is contained in Scripture. "To honor and uphold" synodical resolutions in this resolution meant not only "to examine and study them but to support, act and teach in accordance with them until they have been shown to be contrary to God's word."[51]

To accomplish this uniform observance of synodical statements the Milwaukee convention established a Board of Doctrinal Review.[52] With Resolution 5-13 the convention adopted the report of the Commission on Constitutional Matters entitled "Opinion Regarding Dissenting Groups," wherein organization of groups opposed to synodical statements was banned.[53] The power of the president's office was preserved with only one resolution adopted, calling merely for a study of the concept of collegiality or shared authority.[54] Further centralization of power was evident in that those responsible for "Openness" were to assure the Synod through the president that "they are faithful to the Confessional stance of the Synod." "Openness" was repudiated in Resolution 2-50.[55]

Preus also noted that copies of the FFC report had been given to the seminary's Board of Control and to Tietjen.[56] In Resolution 2-28 the convention recommended that the

> 1) Synod direct the Board of Control to take appropriate action on the basis of the report, commending or correcting where necessary
> 2) Board of Control report progress directly to the President of the Synod and the Board for Higher Education and
> 3) President of the Synod report to the Synod on the progress of the Board of Control within one year.[57]

Another crisis for faculty/Synod relations occurred in December 1971. Concordia's Board of Control refused to renew the four-year contract of Dr. Arlis Ehlen, assistant professor of Old Testament, because, they said, he did not believe in angels or devils. By February 1972, this decision had been reversed and the Board offered Ehlen a one-year contract.[58] Preus was not happy with this reversal,[59] but as it was the direct responsibility of the Board of Control to determine who was teaching false doctrine, all Preus could do was "offer a set of theological principles or guidelines which the Board of Control could use as it carries out its duties." Preus called these guidelines "A Statement of Scriptural and Confessional Principles" and said they were

> not to serve as a new standard of orthodoxy, but rather to assist the Board of Control in identifying areas which need further attention in terms of the Synod's doctrinal position. The Board of Control may well request the faculty members of the St. Louis seminary to indicate their stance towards these guidelines.[60]

More than half of this ten-page document contained the dominating emphasis of Preus's statement. Entitled "Holy Scripture," this section spoke of the Bible's inspiration,[61] its canonicity,[62] and its infallibility.[63] The most controversial assertion was that the Christian interpreter of Scripture

> cannot adopt critically the presuppositions and canons of the secular historian, but . . . he will be guided in his use of historical techniques by the presuppositions of his faith in the Lord of history.[64]

By this and other assertions in the document, the historical critical method was categorically banned from the study of Scripture and all scientific and historical assertions of the Bible were accepted as factual.

The faculty argued that the positions rejected in Preus's "Statement" were not at all descriptive of their teaching and that the "Statement" was invalid "as an assessment and as a solution to the problems at the Seminary." As a statement of doctrine for the Synod, the faculty found the "Statement" just as reprehensible because it made binding dogma out of "mere theological opinion." Even if Preus had followed correct procedure in having the document approved as a synodical statement of doctrine, the faculty argued that it was unnecessary because the constitution gave the Missouri Synod all it needed in terms of a confessional platform. The faculty also stated that they found the "Statement" inadequate theologically and that it had a "spirit alien to Lutheran confessional theology" because it "introduced a sectarian principle of tradition" that summarily rejected views and people. Instead the faculty stressed the positive aspects of a confessional theology that builds a "common faith" among Christians.[65]

Preus's response to these accusations was evasive. In "From the Desk of the President: Brother to Brother" of April 24, 1972 he argued that the antitheses of his "Statement" were not meant to describe the faculty position.[66] Preus also argued that the professors were avoiding the issues by not discussing the theological points he raised.[67]

Preus had either missed the central concerns of the faculty or did not want to deal with them. While Preus advocated a one and only proper understanding of Scripture, the faculty argued that on those issues not covered by the Scriptures or the Confessions (i.e., methods of scriptural interpretation), there was to be tolerance. In this lay the chief and increasingly obvious difference between the moderate and conservative parties: did the definition of "church" imply a toleration of diverse doctrines or did ecclesiastical definition require complete doctrinal conformity?

In compliance with Resolution 2-28 of the Milwaukee convention, Preus released his report regarding the FFC findings on September 1, 1972 in what is commonly called the "Blue Book" because of its blue cover. Preus readily admitted that there was no false doctrine among the faculty concerning the important doctrines like the trinity, the incarnation, justification, or the sacraments. However, there were a number of items that "are a matter of grave concern to the Synod." First, Preus reported a false view of Scripture among the faculty. Although allegiance to the Scriptures was proclaimed, it was not in fact practiced because the historical critical method of interpretation was used heavily. With the method's use, the concept of inspiration was watered down and the Scriptures lost their authoritative status.[68] Undoubtedly, Preus felt this was the most condemning of the accusations he hurled against the faculty. In fact, however, it was only part of a larger accusation, much more obvious in his next "finding."

In Preus's opinion, the faculty was much too permissive in doctrinal matters. The faculty would not condemn positions that Preus judged obviously in contradiction with Scripture. "While they themselves professed a doctrinal stance in harmony with the Scriptures and the Lutheran confessions, they were reluctant to condemn deviating positions."[69] Preus exhibited the same type of intolerance regarding the Lutheran Confessions, where he found the faculty's commitment "limited and abridged." What Preus considered intolerable was the faculty's position regarding the Synod's doctrinal stance.

The majority hold . . . that they have no responsibility to teach in accord with a doctrinal statement adopted by the Lutheran Church Missouri Synod unless they as individuals judge it to be in agreement with the Scriptures and Lutheran Confessions. . . . In effect they are saying that the church can never speak definitively on doctrine again. They are saying that the Lutheran Confessions of the sixteenth century are the last our church dare formulate and insist on, regardless of contemporary issues that divide the church.[70]

Finally, Preus alerted all readers to the uniformity that he and his conservative colleagues expected:

The president of the Synod is calling upon the Board of Control . . . to direct the faculty that, beginning with classes in the school year 1972-73 no faculty member shall in any way, shape, or form . . . use any method of interpretation which casts doubt on the divine authority of the Scriptures . . . *nor in any other way departs from the doctrinal position of the Synod* as set forth in Article II of the Constitution. . . . The world and the church do not need more questions or more debates. We need answers.[71]

Within a week, Tietjen published his reply to the "Blue Book." Not surprisingly, the "Tietjen Report," as it was called, rejected Preus's description of the "doctrinal position of the seminary faculty" and, calling for a return to fraternal relations, affirmed the doctrinal fidelity of the faculty. To the very stinging Preusian charge that he and his faculty had only complained of the procedural inadequacies in the preparation of the reports and not dealt with the theological questions raised, Tietjen argued that the procedural issues were also doctrinal issues because they were involved in the understanding of the nature of the Gospel and the church. Rather than publishing reports about one another, Tietjen reported that the faculty wanted to face their accusers and work out the doctrinal differences. What they did not want was a doctrinal position imposed on the Synod through the publishing of official reports.[72]

Though Tietjen used some of his report to show the inadequacies of the FFC's view of Scriptures,[73] what would ultimately lead to the schism was the question of how much diversity was to be tolerated within the Synod. As Tietjen said in his concluding remarks, the real issue was the degree of diversity the Preusian administration would allow in the Synod.

The issue that emerges is whether a professor who is practicing commitment to the Scriptures and the Confessions must be presumed to have departed from that commitment because his method of doing exegesis is different from that of his interrogators.[74]

With correspondence between the parties obviously becoming hostile, the Council of Presidents discussed the situation September 18-21. Preus and Tietjen attended on September 20 to air their differences, but their only accomplishment was a bland statement of the need for a "full and frank discussion" of the theological issues involved.[75]

Only three days after the COP met, the faculty issued "A Declaration by the Faculty of Concordia Seminary in Response to the 'Report of the Synodical President.' " They rejected Preus's report for its distortions and because Preus had not met with any of the faculty prior to publication. They reasoned that all attempts to enforce unity by pressure should be abandoned and that it would be much better to "nourish a fraternal respect for God-given convictions of brothers and sisters in the Church under the guidance of the Holy Spirit." Finally, they pledged to continue in their roles as servants and teachers of the church.[76]

In early January 1973 the faculty responded more fully to the COP's request for a full statement of their position with "Faithful to our Calling—Faithful to our Lord." The faculty opened with the assertion that there is no supplement to the Gospel; "the issue is not academic freedom but the freedom of the Gospel." They also discussed in some detail the issues that Preus had raised in his "Statement." On all the controverted issues the faculty maintained that the important thing about the Christian doctrines was not their foundation in historical fact but their purpose in conveying to the reader the message of the Gospel. The method one uses to get to that message is inconsequential. "In and of itself the so-called 'historical critical' methodology is neutral" because the choice of teaching methods is not determined by Scripture but by the circumstances.[77]

On January 15, 1973 the Board of Control handed down its ruling: on the basis of the FFC report all forty-four seminary professors were to be "commended." Though the Board was split on many of the questions, with dissenting votes usually numbering close to 45 percent on any one decision, not one of the faculty was to be "corrected."[78]

Preus reluctantly accepted the Board's decision, but his "Brother-to-Brother" letter of April 27, 1973 indicated that he thought the issue was far from dead. He argued that there was too much dissent within the Synod, since both the majority and minority could not be right. There was only one way to determine the right decision and that was to get the "highest authority," the synodical convention, to decide.[79]

D. New Orleans, 1973

The convention at New Orleans in July 1973 was billed by the Synod's official periodical as the "confrontation convention."[80] Herman Otten, editor of the ultraconservative *Christian News*, distributed *A Christian Handbook of Vital Issues* at the convention, which was intended to show the growing "liberal-ness" of the Lutheran churches. The *Handbook*'s tone was hostile and the accusations often slanderous. The last few pages emphasized the need to "separate from your [Missouri] denomination when it no longer preaches God's word and when it tolerates the anti-Christian views of modern theological liberalism."[81]

Though it is probably incorrect to say that Otten was representative of a large faction of the delegates at New Orleans, his presence was certainly evident if for no other reason than his bright red, 850-page *Handbook* received wide distribution. There is also no question that many of his extreme views found their way into the official convention workbook distributed to the delegates.[82] What is even more significant, however, about Otten and those who thought like him, was that this vocal, extremely conservative faction was politically organized and demanded answers, answers that could not always be easily obtained in a convention setting.

It was no surprise when Jacob Preus was reelected to the synodical presidency on the first ballot.[83] Just as important, though less obvious, were the elections for the Board of Control for Concordia Seminary and the Board for Higher Education (BHE), both resulting in conservative majorities.[84] This would prove decisive in the months to come; whereas the faculty at Concordia had been able to hope for the support of their Board of Control prior to New Orleans, and failing that, an appeal to the BHE, their only defense now was a public appeal to the synodical membership through the media.

Synodical legislation was similarly affected. Convention floor committees were instrumental in deciding which resolutions would come to the attention of the convention. Traditionally, the synodical president selected the floor committees. For this convention, Jacob Preus put known moderates on the committees dealing with relatively uncontroversial issues (Stewardship and Finance, Evangelism, Special and Sundry Matters) while staunch conservatives were assigned to committees controlling the controversial issues (Theology and Church Relations, Higher Education, Seminary Issues). By stacking the committees in this way, Preus effectively controlled what resolutions the convention considered.[85]

In session four, Resolution 2-12 was introduced proposing that Article II of the constitution be understood as requiring the formulation and adoption of synodical doctrinal statements on controversial issues. The justifications given for the resolution were that such statements had been adopted before, that the statements had to be in accord with the established "pattern of doctrine," and that the purpose of a vote in synodical convention was to determine how many agree with the doctrinal statements, not to determine whether the statement was right or wrong.[86]

> . . . WHEREAS, The very concept of a synod ("walking together") precludes individualism which allows every man to interpret Synod's confessional position according to his own subjective preference; and . . .
>   . . . WHEREAS, The Synod at the same (Milwaukee) convention has asked the church to "honor and uphold" such doctrinal statements and has interpreted "honor and uphold" as meaning . . . to support, act and teach in accordance with them unless they have been shown to be contrary to the God's Word (Milwaukee Proceedings, Res. 2-21); therefore be it
>   . . . RESOLVED, That the Synod understand Article II of its Constitution as permitting, and at times even requiring the formulation and adoption of doctrinal statements . . . and be it further
>   . . . RESOLVED, That the Synod reaffirm its position . . . that such statements . . . are, pursuant to Article II of the Synod's constitution, binding upon all its members.[87]

The "confrontation convention" adopted this resolution only after much haggling. Amendments were proposed that would have given the congregations rather than the convention the authority to decide such issues, but these were declined. Parliamentary stalling tactics were used to no avail by the moderates. After three sessions of discussion, the resolution was adopted by a vote of 653-381.[88]

The adoption of 2-12 cleared the path for the introduction of Resolution 3-01, which proposed to declare Preus's "Statement"

> in all parts scriptural and in accord with Lutheran confessions . . . and thereby expresses the Synod's position on current doctrinal issues.[89]

By the time this motion was introduced the convention was well behind schedule. Since this was obviously a controversial resolution, there were various motions put forward that would have limited debate; they all failed. The moderates tried to have the matter referred to the district presidents; that motion was also declined. The extreme right-wing delegates tried to amend the resolution so that the "Statement" could be used to judge "the fitness of any official, minister, teacher or confirmed lay member"; the conservative floor committee chairman denied this amendment, arguing that it went beyond anything the floor committee had envisioned in proposing the resolution. After the chairman closed debate based on a standing rule that had been adopted earlier in the day, the resolution was adopted by a vote of 562-455 or a 55 percent majority.[90]

Moderates protested dramatically. On a point of privilege, district president Rev. Herman Neunaber of the Southern Illinois District asked that his concerns regarding the resolution be entered into the record. Rev. Sam Roth made the same request and also asked those who agreed with him to proceed to the secretary's desk to register their disapproval, singing the first stanza of "The Church's One Foundation."[91]

In the following session, Resolution 3-09, "To Declare Faculty Majority Position in Violation of Article II of the Constitution," was proposed with a five-and-one-half-page introduction outlining St. Louis faculty errors.

> . . . WHEREAS, the theological doctrinal stance of the faculty majority of Concordia Seminary, St. Louis, has been shown to be in violation of Art. II of the Synod's Constitution . . . and
> . . . WHEREAS, The Board of Control of Concordia Seminary, St. Louis, has failed to recognize the validity of the charges contained in Pres. Preus's *Report* (Sept. 1, 1972) as based on the Fact Finding Committee's report; and
> . . . WHEREAS, It is in keeping with our Lutheran heritage, specifically our commitment to and under the Lutheran Confessions "that the opinion of the party in error cannot be tolerated in the church of God, much less be excused and defended" (Formula of Concord, SD, Preface, 9); therefore be it . . .
> . . . RESOLVED, (thirdly) That the Synod recognize that the theological position defended by the faculty majority of Concordia Seminary, St. Louis, Mo., is in fact false doctrine running counter to the Holy Scriptures, the Lutheran Confessions, and the synodical stance and for that reason "cannot be tolerated in the church of God, much less be excused and defended." (FC, SD, Preface, 9)[92]

On a point of privilege, John Tietjen spoke in defence of the Concordia faculty, rejecting charges of "Gospel reductionism," the denial of miracles, and the rejection of the third use of the law. Eugene Klug of the Springfield seminary replied for the floor committee, saying that after many hours of study the committee was convinced of the resolution's accuracy. Further discussion was postponed as time ran out in the session.[93]

When discussion resumed the next day, session chairman Roland Wiederaenders thought it necessary to remind the convention delegates of their kinship in Christ, gave permission for all faculty to speak though only three were official representatives, and allowed Tietjen and Preus speaking privileges equal to those of the floor committee.[94] The discussions lasted about seven hours.

Finally the floor committee made an effort to compromise by amending the critical third resolve listed above to read

> ... RESOLVED, That the Synod recognize that the matters referred to in the second resolved[95] are in fact false doctrine ...

and adding the fourth

> ... RESOLVED, That these matters be turned over to the Board of Control of Concordia Seminary, St. Louis.

After more discussion, the resolution as amended was adopted by a vote of 574-451.[96]

With these amendments, the faculty was not directly identified with the false doctrine listed in the second resolved. However, when one considers the fact that the introductory "Whereas" section remained in the resolution, there was no question as to whom the resolution was referring. Further, the fact that the new Board of Control had a newly elected conservative majority meant that the day of reckoning for the faculty had only been delayed.

Resolution 3-12, introduced by the floor committee on seminary issues, charged Tietjen with allowing and fostering false doctrine, failing to mediate doctrinal disagreements, irresponsible administration, wrongfully assuming Board of Control responsibilities, intimidating Board of Control members, demeaning certain faculty members and synodical president Preus, refusing to cooperate with the synodical president, insubordination to the BHE, and failure to supervise adequately the spiritual welfare, personal life, and conduct of the student body. On the basis of these charges, the resolution asked for Tietjen's resignation. If his resignation was not tendered by the end of the convention, 3-12 proposed that the synodical president be given the power to dismiss Tietjen and initiate the procedure for calling a new seminary president.[97]

Since the seminary resolutions had been so time-consuming, the committee on seminary issues decided not to attempt passage of this highly controversial 3-12, even though it had already been printed and distributed in the agenda. Instead, Resolution 3-12A was substituted at the time of convention consideration. It proposed

> that the matter of Dr. John H. Tietjen as president and professor of Concordia Seminary, St. Louis, shall be dealt with in such manner as is permitted under applicable substantive and procedural provisions of the Handbook of the Synod.[98]

As appeasing as this resolution may be, the "Whereas" section called attention to the "matters contained in the above named overtures," which are the same accusations of the original 3-12. In other words, the accusations were clearly made and the only reason that action was not taken on them by the convention was that these "matters . . . cannot be adequately dealt with on the floor of the convention, because of the press of other business and the time available."[99]

Resolution 2-40 requested the suspension of altar and pulpit fellowship with the ALC. However, by the time this resolution came to the attention of the convention, the delegates felt they had debated enough; this motion was laid aside by the adoption of another that read

> until such a time as we do not have an atmosphere of fear pervading the discussion, no decision (shall) be made on this matter.[100]

Postponing the ALC fellowship decision indicated not only a weariness on the part of the delegates but the contentiousness of the issue, even in 1973. Neither moderates nor conservatives were willing to fight yet another battle at this convention.

E. Aftermath of New Orleans

The faculty majority was extremely prompt in responding to the New Orleans resolutions. On July 24, 1973, they published "A Declaration of Protest and Confession" protesting the accusations leveled against them by the floor committees, the way coercive power was being used in matters of conscience and doctrine, the way they were being judged by procedures other than those prescribed in the constitution, and the way the confessions and scriptures were being ignored while synodically adopted statements were being elevated unduly. Their major concern was summarized in the concluding portion of their protest, "An Appeal":

> Our church confronts a crisis. The gospel is at stake. *Our church is in danger of losing its truly Lutheran character and of becoming a sect.* In issuing this "Declaration of Protest and Confession" we join with those delegates to the New Orleans Convention who stood together to protest convention actions and to confess the Bible's Gospel. We call upon our brothers and sister to join in a common movement of protest and confession within the Synod.
> We need to stand together in our concern to be truly Lutheran.
> We need to stand together in our concern to be the church.[101]

The wording reflects an obvious struggle between those who regarded the LC-MS as a sect of limited doctrinal tolerance and those who regarded the denomination as a broadly based church. However, these were not the words of a faculty merely concerned with what sociological niche their denomination would occupy. These men had a real fear that the liberty of the Gospel was endangered by what they regarded as the oppressive authoritarian measures of the conservatives led by Jacob Preus. Ecclesiastical politics were hereby impassioned for the faculty of Concordia Seminary and their sympathizers with the belief that the very essence of the Gospel message was at stake.

On August 17-18, 1973 the newly elected seminary Board of Control met and suspended Tietjen on the grounds listed in Resolution 3-12. However, legal issues were involved so the board delayed implementation of the suspension until legal advice could be obtained. The suspension was later "vacated" because the constitutional experts of the Synod, the members of the Commission on Constitutional Matters, advised the Board to direct the complainants to meet with the accused. That way "no person can say he wasn't treated with Christian love."[102]

While the complainants pursued their charges against Tietjen, the Board of Control made use of its newfound conservative majority power in their meeting of November 19, 1973. Buoyed by a statement of the faculty minority asking the authors of "A Declaration" to submit and return to the Synod,[103] the Board of Control asked the faculty majority to answer some of the accusations raised by the New Orleans convention. They also asked Tietjen to explain his actions and policies in light of his position as president of a synodical seminary. As well, Paul Goetting, a moderate professor, was refused a contract renewal. It was decided that seven professors aged sixty-five and over would be honorably retired in February of 1974; it was no coincidence that all but one were of the moderate persuasion.[104] In short, the Board flexed its new muscles in a way that informed the faculty majority that they would have to submit to the will of the synodical administration or leave their positions.[105]

Though it is certainly true that contributing factors in the controversy included the clash between two determined and capable leaders and the struggles of a denomination as it felt its way into the mainstream of American religion,[106] the explosiveness of Missouri's controversy was fired by the religious issues. The 1973 New Orleans convention focused decades of debate regarding denominational authority, biblical interpretation, and fellowship issues in the context of seminary problems at St. Louis. At the Milwaukee convention, congregational authority was subordinated to the power of a synodical resolution; at the New Orleans convention, Preus enacted that newly articulated power by stacking the floor committee appointments and by ensuring the passage of Resolution 2-12. Resolution 3-01, adopting Preus's "Statement," set out plainly the Synod's position on biblical interpretation though 45 percent of the convention delegates did not want to adopt that "Statement." The ALC fellowship issue received little attention, though the party lines were clearly drawn. In short, religious issues such as biblical interpretation were coalescing with structural issues such as division of authority within the Synod to create the questions that would ultimately lead to schism: What type of "church" should the LC-MS be? Would it be characterized by doctrinal tolerance, and if so, what should constitute the limits of that tolerance? Or would it be a church in which doctrinal uniformity was required? Early indications of the degree of doctrinal tolerance the church body would allow were apparent in the resolutions dealing with Tietjen and the faculty; those indications gave the dissenters reason to organize.

"If You Can't Stand the Heat . . .": Events Between 1973 and 1975

Once the battle lines had been drawn, two fundamental steps remained in the schismatic process for the Missouri Synod. The first was the organization of the moderate movement into a coherent group that demonstrated a willingness to take drastic action if necessary. The second step involved the synodical effort, initiated by Preus, to expel those who refused to obey synodical resolutions. Neither of these steps occurred without serious religious debate about scriptural interpretation and what it meant to be a Lutheran.

A. ELIM Organizes

Comparing themselves to the sixteenth-century reformers,[107] eight hundred clergy and laity met August 28-29, 1973 at Des Plaines (Chicago), Illinois, in a Conference of Evangelical Lutherans chaired by John Tietjen and F. Dean Lueking, pastor at Grace Lutheran, River Forest, Illinois. They met "to protest errant actions of the majority at the New Orleans convention of the LC-MS," to "form an organized confessing movement" within the Missouri Synod,[108] and to help those people whose ministries were in jeopardy as a result of convention action.[109] Ten members of a fifteen-member board were elected. Elwyn Ewald, a former missionary from New Guinea, was hired to raise funds and serve as editor of the group's newspaper, *Missouri in Perspective*. The group was incorporated as Evangelical Lutherans In Mission (ELIM) in October of 1973.[110]

At this same meeting a declaration of dissent, "In the Name of Jesus Christ and for the Sake of the Gospel," was adopted. This document protested the most disputed resolutions of the New Orleans convention[111], arguing that the synodical constitution had been violated by using majority vote to impose doctrine on the membership. According to ELIM's interpretation of the constitution, doctrine was to be extracted from Scripture and the Confessions only. Because "popes and councils do err, such binding resolutions must be resisted."[112] By so stating, ELIM was linking doctrinal tolerance and ecclesiastical freedom with the truth and liberty of the Gospel.

"Where Does This Lead Us?," a second document, declared that the group was not interested in schism or in forming a "church within the church."

With all previous confessing movements, we will "speak truth to power," without fear of consequences or personal inconvenience. We will "wait and see" in what direction our Lord will guide our common activity. We call upon our church body to reverse its recent actions. We are not schismatics and will not be responsible for schism. We shall continue our movement of confession and protest within our Synod.[113]

When the goals and objectives of ELIM were introduced to the synodical membership, missions and education were the chief emphases. A statement regarding "the maintenance and strengthening of the bond of faith with other Lutherans" was also included.[114]

These emphases might seem out of place if the synodical conflicts are characterized as concerned strictly with the interpretation of Scripture; they make perfectly good sense in the context of a dispute concerning what the church is and should be. While the synodical administration thought of the church in terms of a tight membership among whom no variation or error in doctrine was to be publicly tolerated, ELIMites thought of the church in much more inclusive terms. As ELIM president Sam Roth put it when discussing the objectives of ELIM: "The ultra-conservative voices are calling for a split. We oppose that idea. We believe that some diversity in the Synod will make us stronger, not weaker."[115]

The synodical administration reacted just two weeks later. Opposite the news reports of the ELIM meeting in *The Lutheran Witness* was an article by Preus condemning the conference. Outlining the proper channels for dissent, which did not include organizing bodies such as ELIM, Preus asserted that the Synod had already decided that it did not want the faith of the faculty that those attending the ELIM conference were advocating. In answer to the criticism that majority vote cannot determine doctrine, Preus quoted Article VIIIc of the constitution, which made provision for the Synod to witness to the truth on the basis of Scripture. He argued further, "How else can a synodical convention confess its faith? Does it not do so by voting?"[116]

In December the Commission on Theology and Church Relations published its official notice, "Opinion on Dissenting Groups." Reaffirming earlier convention rulings, the CTCR reasoned that dissenting organizations subvert the constitution of the Synod. Since union was the original and major concern at the time of the Synod's founding, the quest for oneness was paramount. In the absence of a clear-cut Word of God, issues are to be decided by majority principles and such decisions applied in Christian love and restraint. "When the majority has been determined it must be respected."[117]

This same issue of the *Witness* also announced that the CTCR had approved "Guiding Principles for the Use of 'A Statement.' "[118] The opening line of "Principles" acknowledged that there may be objections to the adoption of "A Statement" and stated that the CTCR wants to "listen carefully" to all such objections. Since registering dissent was the first step in correcting a synodical position, "Principles" outlined the procedure for expressing dissent.[119] The role of the CTCR was to determine the nature of the dissent, weigh all criticisms, and determine if the dissent disagreed with the Scriptures or Confessions. If the dissent was valid, "The process . . . may well lead to a modification or clarification of the statement of belief"; but if the dissent was in error, "it may also result in the application of the evangelical and fraternal disciplinary procedures specified in our synodical Constitution and Bylaws."[120]

With more specific reference to "A Statement," "Principles" declared that it

> is now to be regarded as an official synodical document which is to be used throughout the Synod rather than as the statement of an individual for a somewhat limited use. . . . "A Statement" is not to be used mechanically or legalistically to discipline members of the Synod, but it is to be honored, upheld, and used fraternally and evangelically throughout the Synod in an effort to assist the Synod in remaining faithful to its confessional position.

The CTCR was treading a fine line here between saying that "there shall be no effort to have 'A Statement' formally and individually subscribed by the members of the Synod" and "assent to the Synod's doctrinal statements is assumed in all cases."[121]

No matter how diplomatic the CTCR may have wanted to be, this position could not hope to satisfy the moderate dissenters who found "A Statement" theologically inadequate, had voiced their dissent, did not think the measures levied against them in their dissent were "the evangelical and fraternal disciplinary procedures specified in our synodical Constitution and Bylaws,"[122] and thought the "Statement much too constricting as it precluded the diversity they perceived as being a necessary and strengthening aspect of their vision of a church."[123]

B. Seminex Established

After the attempted suspension of Tietjen in August 1973, the faculty majority at Concordia realized they would have to take their case to the people. Between October 21 and 29, Operation Outreach was organized by the faculty majority and students to explain their position to the synodical membership regarding the New Orleans resolutions.[124]

In early December, the student body adopted a document entitled "With One Voice," which was sent to the synodical membership on December 12. Declaring their intent to support the faculty majority, the students demanded that the decisions of the Board of Control meeting of November 19 be rescinded. As a tentative ultimatum, they hinted that they might leave the Synod. "We believe that the church ought to know that we are individually struggling with our Christian commitments to the Lutheran Church Missouri Synod."[125] This was a dramatic signal that matters were getting worse at the showcase seminary.

At a meeting in early January 1974, the Board of Control demonstrated its intent to enforce the New Orleans resolutions by cutting nineteen courses from the seminary curriculum because course descriptions suggested methods of study contrary to those endorsed in New Orleans. In a January 20 meeting of the Board, Tietjen refused to cooperate any more in the Board's investigation because of the collusion of the Board, Preus, and the complainants in pressing charges against him.[126] At 9:00 P.M. that night, Victor Bryant, public relations director for the synod, announced that Tietjen had been suspended because of his alleged "malfeasance in performing the duties of the office of president." In describing the evidence presented by the complainants, *The Lutheran Witness* said that a twenty-page document of charges "deals primarily with the charge that Dr. Tietjen holds, defends, allows and fosters false doctrine contrary to the Synod's constitution." Martin Scharlemann was declared acting president of the seminary the next day.[127]

Also on January 21, leaders of Students Concerned for Reconciliation under the Gospel (SCRUG) and the Expanded Commission on Seminary Concerns (ECSC) ratified "A Student Resolution," which called for a moratorium on all classes if the professors were not formally charged or the investigations stopped immediately.

At this same student meeting, Tietjen released a press statement that claimed that agents of Preus had approached him to make a deal in which he would accept a call to a parish.[128] Tietjen called the deal "immoral" because it used human beings as pawns in a larger political maneuver.[129] He repeated his charge of collusion among the conservatively controlled Board of Control, Preus, and his accusers. As proof of that charge, he released his booklet "Evidence Presented by John Tietjen."[130]

After this impressive set of accusations was presented and an announcement made that the popular Arthur Repp, a critic of Preus, was also to be forcibly retired, the students adopted the moratorium resolution by a vote of 274 to 92; until something changed, students would not be attending classes. The resolution was delivered to the Board of Control and synodical headquarters.[131]

On January 22, the faculty majority also decided to act. They delivered a letter to Preus, declaring their loyalty to Tietjen and his cause; if Tietjen was suspended, so were they. The faculty gave Preus two options: side with the Board of Control and press charges, or clear the professors, including Tietjen, of false doctrine charges. The faculty also issued a personal attack against the new acting president, Martin Scharlemann.[132]

When a meeting was arranged between the students and Scharlemann on January 23, Scharlemann informed the students that the seminary would continue to operate, since 120 students were still attending classes. However, all classes were suspended until January 25 to allow the dust to settle. The next morning, Scharlemann informed the faculty and students that students could still graduate and that the Board of Control would take action on Resolution 3-09 quickly. He also asked that faculty and students return to classes the following Monday, January 28.[133]

In a letter addressed to the faculty dated January 24, Preus stated what he considered the critical issues. Emphasizing that the faculty had not been suspended, he asked, "Are you still the faculty of Concordia?" If the faculty's answer was negative, there were no problems; if they answered affirmatively, Preus ordered them to return to classes immediately. Implicit was the accusation that the faculty were breaching their contracts by not teaching classes.[134]

The faculty reply was dated January 26. Though suspended, they still considered themselves faculty. Asserting that they had not violated synodical doctrine, they argued that Preus was caught in a dilemma: either Resolution 3-09 of New Orleans was right and they should not be teaching as synodical faculty, or 3-09 was to be ignored and they should be allowed to continue as they were.[135]

The faculty offensive backfired. On January 28, Preus issued his reply, "A Message to the Church," which was to be read in synodical congregations on February 10. Given the faculty position as stated in their letter of January 26, Preus agreed that they were wrong in continuing to teach after the adoption of Resolution 3-09; but since they had agreed to teach after New Orleans, Preus argued their discontinuation of teaching duties after Tietjen's suspension was a deplorable political ploy.[136]

Preus made a critical tactical error in this letter by including "Appendix Six" to support his contention that the liberal faculty had bullied students of the more conservative persuasion.[137] This served to unite the student body; conservative and moderate students alike reacted with missives to Preus and

Scharlemann decrying the un-Christian behavior of students who, in the first place, had not confronted their professors and then did not even have the courage to sign their name to "Appendix Six."[138] A second outreach was planned for July 25-31.

Support for the faculty and staff, both moral and financial, poured in from many sources. The student body at Concordia Senior College of Fort Wayne sympathized with their fellow Concordians of St. Louis.[139] The faculty at Concordia Teachers College, River Forest, affirmed their stand with the faculty majority.[140] The Board of Directors of the Atlantic District adopted a position statement that said that since 1969 the Synod had lived under an administration that "replaced confessional conservatism with dogmatic rigidity and evangelical pastoral leadership with an authoritarian style."[141] The English District asked its members for money to support the seminary professors who found themselves without income.[142] President Samuel Roth of ELIM spoke to faculty and students on campus promising financial and moral support.[143] In short, the Concordia faculty and students knew they were not alone as they continued to meet with the administration in an effort to resolve the issues.

On February 6, the students participating in the moratorium discussed the possibility of continuing their education away from the seminary campus. At a rally at the Episcopalian Christ Church Cathedral on February 7, Dr. Bertram outlined a Seminary-in-exile proposal, informing those gathered that $50,000 had already been pledged from the Atlantic District. On February 8, the Council of Presidents met unsuccessfully to resolve the crisis. A forum of all involved parties was scheduled by the synodical Board of Directors for February 15 and 16. On February 11, James Adams of the *St. Louis Post-Dispatch* reported that all preliminary arrangements had been made for a Concordia Seminary-in-exile.[144] With their plans in place, the faculty released a statement on February 12 that it would return to classes only if the following demands were met by the Board of Control by February 19: only Scripture and Article II would form the confessional basis for their teaching (not Preus's "Statement"); Tietjen would immediately be reinstated as seminary president; and Goetting and the "retired" professors would be rehired. If these demands were not met, the faculty threatened to move to another location where they would continue their call of preparing young men for the ministry.[145]

Since the Board of Control was not scheduled to meet until February 17, the faculty ultimatum gave the Board only two days to meet all the conditions. Because the Committee on Constitutional Matters (CCM) had ordered the

Board of Control to interview each of the forty-six striking faculty members regarding Resolution 3-09, there was no possible way the Board could satisfy the demands of the CCM in the time allotted. Hence, the Board issued a statement on February 17 declaring that faculty who failed to report to classes by noon February 18 would be considered in breach of their legal contract and would forfeit their position at the seminary. None of the faculty reported, many of them protesting that they did not get notice of the Board's directive until it was too late anyway.[146]

On February 19, the faculty majority and students staged a mock funeral complete with a wooden cross for each suspended faculty member. After readings from Jeremiah and Lamentations, prayers and the doxology, the group proceeded with a peal of bells down the road to St. Louis University. In cooperation with Eden Seminary (United Church of Christ) and the St. Louis Divinity School (Roman Catholic), faculty and students began classes at Concordia Seminary-in-Exile on February 20, 1973. Their academic structure was officially called the Joint Project for Theological Education with degrees granted from the Lutheran School of Theology in Chicago. Ninety percent of the faculty (forty-six men) and 85 percent of the students of Concordia Seminary comprised the new institution.[147]

The purpose and format of the new institution were summarized by Dean John Damm on February 7 at Christ Church Cathedral:

> Concordia Seminary-in-Exile ("Seminex") is the temporary name for a joint effort of the vast majority of the student body, faculty, and executive staff aimed at completing programs of theological education. Seminex means that the same students and faculty are getting back to the same synodically approved curriculum working out of the same Lutheran confessional commitment.
>
> Seminex is not a new seminary, not a new institution; it is Concordia Seminary but in exile. Seminex represents not a departure from Synod but a commitment to the Synod which has been rapidly departing from the best in its tradition. It is the only way we can see to complete theological education and simultaneously to call the Synod back to its own evangelical fountainhead.[148]

This document also expressed the hope that the dispute would be resolved in time for the students to graduate from Concordia Seminary, as Seminex was meant to be only a temporary institution that would draw the attention of the Synod to the gravity of the problem. That hope was never fulfilled.[149]

C. The Dispute over Missions

Problems in the mission field involved the same issue of church definition except that instead of the debate swirling around scriptural interpretation as contained in Preus's "Statement," the focus of the controversy was the "Mission Affirmations" adopted at the 1965 convention.

It is important to remember that the "Affirmations" was a moderate document stressing ministry to the whole person. Its view of the Synod was that of a confessional movement within Christianity, not of an institution with members who are expected to follow a certain set of doctrines. Under the Board for Missions (BFM), which had moderate leadership until 1971, the objectives of the mission staff, following what they perceived to be the directives of the "Affirmations," had involved establishing a mission program in a region and developing that program in cooperation with the indigenous peoples. Cooperation with other denominations, both Lutheran and non-Lutheran, was common in establishing these outposts.[150]

All these emphases were obvious efforts by the LC-MS mission staff to enter the American denominational mainstream where ecumenical cooperation and religious pluralism were assumed; these assumptions became objects of heated religious debate when combined with the controverted issue of scriptural interpretation and doctrinal tolerance.

After the conservatives had stationed their man in the presidency of the Synod in 1969, they sought control of the BFM. With the election of more conservative members to the BFM in Milwaukee in 1971, the arch-conservative Waldo Werning assumed the chairmanship and control of the Board.[151] The first action of this BFM was the effective firing of Martin Kretzmann, author of the "Affirmations," as secretary for Planning, Study and Research late in 1972. In response to a directive of the 1971 convention, the conservative BFM carried out a study of the "Affirmations" and found the document deficient, particularly in its lack of emphasis on the Word of God and its overemphasis on ecumenical endeavors in the mission field. Stressing that the confessional question is important in missionary work, the board majority singled out tri-Lutheran campus ministries and ecumenical communion services as examples of rampant ecumenism gone awry.[152]

The minority report to the 1973 convention in New Orleans signaled the depth of the dispute, not just within the Board but between the conservative majority on the BFM and the mission staff that sided with the BFM minority. Affirming their obedience to the Synod and its resolutions, this minority report declared that tri-Lutheran efforts were not necessarily wrong. They argued that the mission was God's mission and that cooperation with other Christians was justified as fulfilling various aspects of the mission call.[153]

After the New Orleans convention, mission policy took a whole new direction. At the January 10-12, 1974 meeting of the BFM, James Mayer, Area Secretary for Southeast Asia and a staunch defender of the "Affirmations," was fired from his post. Protests poured in from the mission staff, both in North America and abroad.[154] The chasm between the two factions deepened. To deal with all these complaints and problems, the BFM established the Mission Study Commission in March of 1974.[155]

On April 10, William Kohn, Executive Secretary for Missions, resigned, complaining of the "spirit of isolationism and centralization" and the "arbitrary use of power to obtain greater centralization." His resignation was eagerly accepted by the BFM majority, who complimented Kohn for his integrity when the obvious intent of his resignation was to protest the BFM's firing of Mayer. Kohn's resignation was followed almost immediately by the resignations of four more mission executives who, together with Kohn, announced that they intended to establish a separate mission society that would follow the directives of the "Affirmations."[156]

Much more disconcerting to the BFM was the threat from the New Guinea, Indian, and Philippine churches that they would reconsider their synodical ties if the BFM did not do something about the complaints of isolationism and centralization that they shared with Kohn and the resigned executive members. To discuss their problems, representatives of these national churches met July 15-19 in Hong Kong in what was called the Consultation of Asian Churches. They discussed their relationship to the Missouri Synod and stated their position for the Synod's consideration. The minutes of their meeting with a cover letter describing their concerns about the current BFM were distributed to the synodical membership for discussion.[157]

The resolutions of the minutes of the Consultation centered around two main issues. The first issue was summarized by President Waesa of the New Guinea church:

> They [the BFM members] are pressing down and disregarding a national church with its own dignity, integrity, and independence. There is a demonstrated lack of sincerity because they are making merely a lip-service claim to being a brother.[158]

The second major issue for the young Asian churches involved how the Missouri Synod was steering away from ecumenical contact with other Lutherans in the mission field and from the spirit of the "Affirmations" in general. As they put it, "the mission is Christ's and not that of the Lutheran Church-Missouri Synod." One of the strongest resolutions of the Consultation said that if there was not a return to mutual trust and a reaffirmation of the "Affirmations," not only in word but also in action, the Asian churches would demand the resignations of the members of the BFM.[159]

From the establishment of the Mission Study Commission in March of 1974 to the release of its report in May of 1975, thirteen of the Synod's eighteen staff members resigned. The Commission's report blamed everyone involved in the controversy. It called for the implementation of existing board-staff-field operational guidelines, which had been a complaint of the resigned staff members. The concerns raised by the Asian churches should be addressed; this could be done at least in part by including representation from "a divergence of cultural and geographic backgrounds" on the Board for Missions.[160] The most critical recommendation of the Commission involved establishing a new office, directly responsible to the synodical president, which would supervise overseas sister church relationships. At the 1975 convention, Resolution 2-02 was adopted, which commended this report and directed that its recommendations be adopted.[161]

The problems in the mission field were just as extensive, though not as well publicized, as those at the St. Louis seminary. The disputes were certainly connected with the effort of the synodical mission staff to enter the American religious mainstream, but in fact the controversies revolved around the issue of church and how exclusive it should be. On the one hand, people like Mayer and Kohn thought the mission staff, as part of a confessing movement within the context of a larger church that extended across and included other denominations, could cooperate with other church bodies. The important task was the taking of the gospel to those who needed it; the "Mission Affirmations" served as a guide for that service. The name of the mission society they formed upon leaving the Missouri Synod reflected that concept; it was called "Partners in Mission."[162] On the other hand, the conservative majority of the mission board subscribed to a concept of church wherein denominational doctrine was equated with the pristine Christian truth, which truth was not to be contaminated by extensive cooperation with others, even in the mission field where the benefits of such cooperation were obvious. The "Affirmations" was seen as leaning too far in the direction of cooperation for the sake of expediency.[163] For that reason, a purge of those who interpreted the document in this radical manner was necessary and accomplished, at least at the higher levels of the mission executive.[164]

D. Attempts at Reconciliation

Shortly after the walkout in February of 1974, the synodical Board of Directors called a forum where members of the seminary's Board of Control, the faculty majority, and the student body met in a tense atmosphere to discuss the crisis. At the beginning of the second day of the two-day forum, acting seminary president Scharlemann announced that the faculty would receive no more paychecks unless they returned to class; the discussions broke down soon after this announcement.[165]

A second failed effort was dubbed the "Committee of Twenty" since it consisted of twenty representatives from the seminary Board of Control, the faculty majority, the students, and major synodical boards. It consisted of two sets of meetings in October 1974, the first one ending on an optimistic note as the two sides engaged in earnest debate. By the time of the second meeting on October 22, 1974, Tietjen had been officially dismissed by the Board of Control on charges of false doctrine.[166] This conciliation effort ended with Robert Bertram of the faculty majority pleading for "a church which is big enough so that there is some diversity under the umbrella of the Scripture and the Confessions" and Ralph Bohlmann of the faculty minority and increasingly a spokesman for the synodical administration lamenting the severe disturbance "because of what the church has heard . . . on Scripture, its authority and inspiration."[167]

Synodical president Preus initiated a third major effort at reconciliation, called the Advisory Committee on Doctrine and Conciliation (ACDC). It consisted of representatives from the seminary, the faculty majority, the CTCR, the COP, and pastors and teachers. Its purpose was to define issues and propose suggestions for resolution but not to act as an arbitrator in the seminary dispute, simply because no group had the authority to negotiate or compromise.[168] Though its participants had agreed to a news blackout, there was an exchange of public letters in *The Lutheran Witness*. The effort dragged on for more than a year. Finally, in December of 1975, Preus received a final report from the Committee wherein four major issues of controversy were identified: 1) inspiration and inerrancy of Scripture; 2) relationship of Gospel and Scripture; 3) use of the historical-critical method; and 4) third use of the law.[169]

Neither side was happy with the ACDC report[170] but both sides agreed about the contents of their disagreement. The conservatives maintained that the only basis for God-pleasing concord is "mutual agreement in doctrine and all its articles" because this is the goal clearly required by Scripture. They regarded the moderates as willing to settle for a consensus based only on the Gospel, "in its narrowest sense."[171] The moderates said almost the same thing, only without the negative implications: "In short the conservative group saw as its goal to make clear what they believed to be disunity in Synod. The moderate group saw as its goal to make clear what they believed to be our unity."[172]

Oliver Harms, past president of the Synod, proposed the last major effort at reconciliation, a convention to rediscover a basic doctrinal consensus and to reevaluate and reassess the theological differences.[173] Three hundred of the Synod's best minds met April 14-18, 1975 to discuss the convention theme, "The Nature and Function of Scripture."[174] All the evaluations of this convention were cautiously optimistic in that consensus was found and the differences did not seem overwhelming.[175]

While the theme of the theological convention was the interpretation of Scripture, the critical discussions that prevented any sort of meaningful, lasting reconciliation concerned the amount of diversity to be tolerated within the church. Ralph Bohlmann, who in May 1975 was named president of Concordia Seminary, was not at all conciliatory in his address "The Church under the Scriptures." He maintained that the external unity of the church is to be based on agreement in the purely taught Gospel.[176] The tool of historical criticism, in claiming that there are inconsistencies in the Bible that cannot be fully understood, has contributed to the false ecumenical assertion that doctrinal positions can exist side by side within the same fellowship, he argued. In a succinct statement that characterized so much of the conservative reconciliation efforts, Bohlmann said:

> For the church under the Scriptures, considerations of truth must take precedence over considerations of love, should these be in conflict, for Christian love is always dependent upon the truth of the Gospel. *When a choice must be made between external unity and the truth of the Gospel, unity must yield to truth.*[177]

E. ELIM Confesses Its Inclusiveness

The issues confronting ELIM's second assembly were described by Thomas Spitz, executive associate of ELIM. Spitz spoke of the theological freedom needed in a renewal of the church.

> What we really have to be concerned about is whether the Church of Jesus Christ can long survive among us on the theology which is used to support that political machine. And we dare not forget that the political power is justified by an appeal to the authority of theological positions.

Acknowledging that it is a Missouri Synod tradition to make doctrinal statements, Spitz said that the difference between those adopted in New Orleans and those adopted before 1973 lay in their application. Previously the resolutions had been used to express the position of a particular group of people assembled, but since New Orleans they had become a means of discipline, used to separate the true from the false believers.[178]

In an evening sermon, the spiritual leader of the movement, John Tietjen, repeated some of these sentiments in terms of freedom from the law of the Missouri synod. His pointed question, "Does that mean leaving the Missouri Synod behind?," was answered indirectly but clearly.

> If there are structures and functions in the old system that can still help us with our mission of bringing God's gift of life to the world, let's use them. If the institution is going to stand in our way, ignore it or bypass it. If the powers that be throw us out, what does it matter?[179]

After Ewald's speech, the assembly adopted "Here We Stand," which explained ELIM's existence as a "confessing movement" that would "boldly confront any traditions, rules, authorities or fears."[180] Together with "In Statio Confessionis" or "A Confession of Faith and Declaration of Protest,"[181] ELIM declared its relationship with the Missouri Synod as that of a confessing movement in a state of protest that hoped to have those reasons for protest removed. Documents such as Preus's "Statement" and the Board for Higher Education's "Limitation of Academic Freedom" were declared offensive because they imposed beliefs on the individual over and above those demanded by Article II of the synodical constitution.[182]

Most important to an understanding of ELIM's raison d'être was its confessional statement "We are Persuaded," which was commended for study at this assembly.[183] The inclusiveness of the church and its mission in the world was emphasized.

> The truth of our distinctive witness is not so fragile that it needs to be protected by isolation from the rest of the church; neither is our understanding so superior that it does not need the correction and enrichment of the larger Christian community. Concern for doctrine and concern for unity must not be set against one another. Our belief in the unity of the church is doctrinally grounded and our struggle to manifest that unity is doctrinally imperative. We therefore repudiate the charge that we are indifferent to doctrine, or libertarian, or wanting fellowship at any price.[184]

This document viewed the controversies within the Synod as more than political or procedural, stemming from theological differences. Regarding the use of the Scriptures, the document declared that it is

> not only permissible but mandatory that the Scriptures be understood in their historical context, using the best tools available in our time. The purpose of the "historical-critical method" as it is called, is not to criticize the scriptures but to keep *our own partial understanding of the Scriptures* under constant and critical examination.[185]

The document also hinted at separation from the Synod.

> We cannot and will not compromise the Gospel in order to preserve the human institution that is the Lutheran Church-Missouri Synod.[186]

In the more concrete matter of how the goals of ELIM were to be accomplished, the assembly looked ahead to the synodical convention at Anaheim in 1975. ELIM's board of directors was directed to publish an educational package for the convention announcing ELIM's minimum demands. These included rescinding Milwaukee Resolution 2-21 and New Orleans 2-12.[187] Seminex was to be recognized as a legitimate synodical school. Fellowship with the American Lutheran Church (ALC) was to be embraced without qualification and fellowship with the more liberal Lutheran Church in America (LCA) actively pursued.[188]

F. Debating the Fate of Seminex Graduates

The existence of Seminex graduates was a real problem for the synodical administration. Seminex was obviously not a synodically approved institution yet its 1974 graduates had been trained at the St. Louis seminary for more than three of their four years under a faculty who, until only months previously, had not been officially condemned for anything more than breach of contract. Further complicating matters was the fact that there was a perennial shortage of preachers in the Synod; missing a whole graduating class could make the situation critical.

Most calls for graduates were usually filled in the spring. The increasingly powerful and conservative Commission on Constitutional Matters (CCM) ruled in April 1974 that no congregation issue a call to a Seminex graduate unless it wanted to forfeit its membership in the Synod. The reasoning was that Seminex candidates had not completed all the required courses and did not have synodical (Concordia) faculty endorsement. Anticipating the argument that this threatened the autonomy of the congregation, whose right to call its own clergy had been enshrined in the synodical constitution, the CCM reasoned that a congregation could call uncertified candidates but only if synodical procedures were followed that ensured that the candidate would be as acceptable in one congregation as in another.[189]

The Council of Presidents (COP), composed as it was of moderate and conservative district presidents, was much more ambivalent on the graduate issue and resolved on May 3 that, for that graduating year only, all Seminex graduates would be considered for the ministry. The synodical faculty remaining at the Concordia campus would review a list recommended by the Seminex faculty and then issue a theological diploma for those graduates. If any of the list from the Seminex faculty were challenged by the Concordia faculty, then the individual would be interviewed by a five-man committee consisting of three district presidents, a professor from Concordia, and a professor from Seminex. The interview was to center on the confessional basis of the Synod as outlined in Article II of the constitution. After the interview, "the interview committee shall determine the justice of the challenge and so advise the [Concordia] faculty."[190]

The resolution was vague. It did not specify whether the recommendation of the interview committee had to be accepted by the Concordia faculty or whether the Concordia faculty was still free to refuse to issue the requisite theological diploma. The Concordia faculty interpreted the resolution to mean they had the right of refusal. When the COP disagreed with this interpretation, the Concordia faculty announced on May 9 that it wanted to interview all candidates. The Seminex students refused, issuing a statement on May 21 that they would receive calls from any Missourian congregations that were willing to recognize the Seminex certification as sufficient for ministry.[191] The issue was passing from the purview of the seminaries to that of the congregations.

The crisis deepened when Preus advised the congregations through *The Lutheran Witness* that it would be better to do without a preacher than to take one from Seminex. When the conservative CCM ruled in June that the Concordia faculty did in fact have the final determination regarding which Seminex graduates were eligible for a call, any hope of cooperation was lost.[192]

By July 7, only six candidates had been endorsed by the Concordia faculty and another thirty-nine had already accepted calls without official endorsement.[193] Eight district presidents, by ordaining these unsanctioned candidates, had disobeyed synodical bylaws as found in the *Handbook*.[194] Their public argument was that the autonomy of the congregation in calling its own minister must be maintained at all costs.[195] As servants of the congregations, the district presidents argued, they were only fulfilling their elected roles in ordaining the Seminex graduates.[196] The synodical administration did not share this view.

At a September 16 meeting of the COP, Preus presented a paper that described the district presidents not as servants of the congregations but as extensions or arms of the synodical president with a responsibility to implement synodical resolutions. Listing the eight district presidents who had authorized Seminex ordinations, Preus said that a

> very grave hour in the Synod's history has been brought on by this action of the district presidents. Not only has the corporate integrity of the COP been virtually destroyed . . . but the very life of the church body is threatened by the deliberate violation of constitutional authority.[197]

Preus was supported by other district presidents, who said that the congregations recognized the synodical president as having the authority to supervise doctrine and that the rulings of the CCM were binding.

With an increasingly powerful and organized ELIM backing them, the eight district presidents continued to support the ordination of Seminex graduates. The lines of demarcation between the two groups became even more pronounced with the CCM's "Opinion regarding the Removal of District Presidents from Office." This ruling stated that a district president could be removed from office by being expelled from membership in the Synod for offensive conduct. Failure to carry out the bylaws of the Synod was deemed offensive because the first object of the Synod "is the conservation and promotion of the unity of the true faith and *a united defense against schism and sectarianism*." Such direct removal of a district president from office could be taken by action of the synodical or district convention or, in cases of emergency, by the president of the Synod.[198]

Despite the adoption of a resolution by the majority of the COP in early May of 1975 that assured the Synod that its presidents would abide by synodical resolutions, the eight dissenting district presidents continued to support the ordination of Seminex graduates. In early June, they affixed their signatures to "A Call to Face the Issues." This document affirmed the right of congregations to call their own pastors and to disregard synodical resolutions if they deemed them against the will of God. According to this document, the Seminex graduates possessed a valid call.[199]

Further developments on this issue had to wait until after the rulings of the 1975 Anaheim convention, but the lines of schism were drawn clearly. If the dissenting presidents did not obey synodical directives regarding the ordination of Seminex graduates, they would be removed from the Synod. Individuals and congregations would leave with them.

G. The Lutheran Church in Mission

For some unhappy Missourians, ELIM and the district presidents were not moving quickly enough. One of these was C. Thomas Spitz, executive associate of ELIM. In a letter to interested congregations Spitz announced the Lutheran Contingency Conference, to be held February 7-8, 1975 at Des Plaines, Illinois. The purpose of the conference was to establish a corporate entity that would be "available on a stand-by/ immediately-usable basis, should life and mission within the LC-MS remain at its present level of decline or fall even further."[200] Spitz suggested the conditions under which the corporation might be activated: they included the continued harassment of pastors, teachers, and congregations; the failure to amend the injustices of the past two years; and further withdrawal from Lutheran unity.

The minutes of the February 7 meeting chaired by Spitz indicate that there were many concerns about incorporation. After lengthy discussions, it was finally decided that incorporation had its advantages.[201] A Continuation Committee was struck to initiate the incorporation and a resolution adopted indicating that the incorporation was not intended in any way "to be prejudicial to the existence" of ELIM.[202]

At the conclusion of the next meeting of the Continuation Committee, a public statement announced the name of the new organization as the Lutheran Church in Mission (LCM). The primary message of the release was the inclusive aspect of the new organization.

> The Lutheran Church in Mission does not claim any corner on truth or wisdom but it does raise the signal that peace, joy and unified purpose can characterize Christians working together. It is dedicated also to the promotion of Christian fellowship in the Gospel as exhibited in the historic Lutheran Confessions.

The statement also emphasized that the organization was of a stand-by nature,

> . . . until it becomes clear whether the kind of witness, mission, and ministry it envisions will be encouraged in the Lutheran Church-Missouri Synod, of which its organizers are presently members.[203]

Any congregation or individual could become a member of LCM merely by notifying its chairman, Spitz, of its intent.

The remaining meetings of the LCM before the Anaheim convention were relatively uneventful, dealing with the development of a constitution and bylaws. Of some significance was the printing and distribution of fifteen thousand copies of a pamphlet entitled "Catechism on LCM." The "Catechism" outlined the reasons LCM existed and listed its main purposes.

> Lutheran Church in Mission is a not-for-profit corporation which will have the capability of functioning as an interim church body when and if its members find that to be necessary. . . . LCM will serve as a facilitating agency with two purposes: first, to hold together individuals and congregations forced to sever their ties with the LC-MS: second, to play a role in the realignment and greater unity of American Lutheranism.[204]

On April 21, 1975, the LCM was officially incorporated in the state of Illinois.[205] Synodical authorities were thereby warned that if the Anaheim convention did not act on the concerns of the moderates, a corporate structure was in place to begin the schism.

H. Further Actions Against Tietjen

As noted, Tietjen was suspended from the seminary's presidency on January 20, 1974 for allowing false doctrine. On October 12, 1974, Tietjen was officially fired from the presidency by the Board of Control on the basis of ten charges, the most important of which was the holding, defending, allowing, and fostering of false doctrine contrary to Article II.[206] In an October 15 statement Tietjen said he was not surprised, since the whole investigation

> was a charade designed to achieve predetermined objectives announced by the president of the Synod to remove me from office and from the pastoral ministry of the Synod. The Board of Control has completed the charade.[207]

The synodical administration was not finished with Tietjen. In its February 22-23, 1975 meeting, the CCM ruled that if the charges of false doctrine against Tietjen were indeed true, Tietjen should be expelled from the Synod. They ordered a new investigation by H. Scherer, president of the Missouri District, but in early June Scherer disqualified himself on the basis of his involvement in the election and dismissal of Tietjen. He handed the case over to O. Gerken, first vice president of the Missouri District, a well-known conservative and yet also something of a maverick.[208]

After meeting with Tietjen on June 24, Gerken found him innocent of the charges of false doctrine even though he admitted that he did not agree with Tietjen's exact articulation of the issues in every instance. Gerken stressed that he did not investigate whether Tietjen was guilty of allowing false doctrine at the seminary but only whether Tietjen himself held false doctrine. Because Gerken found that Tietjen did not hold false doctrine in the major doctrines of the Lutheran confessions or with respect to the specific doctrines of inerrancy, creation, the historicity of the Jonah, or virgin birth accounts, he ruled that Tietjen should not be excluded from the Missouri ministerium or fellowship.[209] There was no comment from Preus regarding the Gerken verdict, though the conservative editors of *Affirm* argued that Gerken missed the point of synodical supervision in his verdict.[210]

The problems in the mission field and at Concordia were related and similar. They were related insofar as those faculty opposing the central authority of the synodical administration were supporters of the "Mission Affirmations." They were similar in that both faculty and mission department challenged the central authorities on questions that ultimately asked, "What kind of church will the Missouri Synod be in the modern world?" The efforts at reconciliation and the reasons given for the breakdowns in those efforts substantiate this thesis. The emergence of a group that encouraged continuing the confessional movement outside the Synod is the first indication of a schism germinating. The issue that seminary, lay, and even mission people could debate was the ordination of Seminex graduates.

More important is the fact that the ordination debate focused the old issues of fellowship, denominational authority (structural issues), and biblical interpretation (a religious issue) on a single, concrete question that could not be ignored because it involved too many people. That convergence of structural and religious issues was necessary before the schism could begin.

"Get Out of the Kitchen!": From Anaheim to the Schism

The importance of the 1975 convention was recognized by both sides in the dispute well before the meeting was convened.[211] ELIM seems to have had a pessimistic view of the balance of voting power at the Anaheim convention. As early as September 1974, *Missouri in Perspective* admitted that victory by ELIM majority was simply not possible at Anaheim. In May of 1975, ELIM presented a platform of positions for the convention that they hoped even a conservative majority would find attractive.[212]

A. The Anaheim Convention, 1975

The *Workbook* for the 1975 convention set the tone for the convention with resolutions on both sides of the ordination and mission controversies. Regarding ELIM, some resolutions were specific enough to suggest that if a congregation could not drop its ELIM membership, it should leave the Synod.[213] Of an even more contentious nature were those resolutions requesting the dissolution of the English District. Though the motion to dissolve the English District had been put before the convention before,

English District administrators and ELIM sympathizers were genuinely concerned that the conservative majority might be powerful enough to dissolve the nongeographical, moderate district at Anaheim.[214]

In an effort to avoid the debacle of New Orleans and to ensure the consideration of more resolutions, some procedures were changed. New standing rules were adopted[215] and a professional parliamentarian was hired. The floor committees were directed to meet months before the convention, giving delegates time to consider the resolutions. Each floor committee was to hold public hearings to help them formulate resolutions. Small group Bible studies were to be convened every morning of the convention in the hopes that having conservatives and moderates mingle in a relaxed setting would dissolve some tension on the convention floor.[216]

Preus's "President's Report," given at the beginning of the convention, contained ominous forewarnings of the Anaheim issues and how they would be resolved.

> It is evident that for the past two decades we have had two opposing theologies, particularly with reference to the doctrine of Holy Scripture. No church body can long support two theologies which are in conflict.[217]

The church vision that Preus articulated is one whose orderly organizational structure is of paramount importance.

> Since the Synod exists for the "protection of pastors, teachers and congregations in the performance of their duties and the maintenance of their rights" (Art. III), it is imperative that the church have officers at every level beginning with the presidents of our districts, who are carrying out their work in keeping with the Constitution and Bylaws of the Synod. God is a god of order, and the apostle has commanded that all things be done decently and in order. If we are to maintain a blessed and useful walking together, we must all carry out our duties in keeping with the regulations which the church has established for the performance of those duties.[218]

Most important to Preus's church vision was that there was no room for those who did not conform to the established doctrines. Dissent was to be voiced through the channels provided by the Synod; if the dissenters could not conform to that procedure or if after pursuing their channels of dissent they found that they could not follow the synodical line, Preus advised them to find another church.

I would beseech those who have been involved in divisive movements that they come to terms with their church and try to live at peace with their brethren. If there are those who are doctrinally at such odds with the church that they cannot live at peace with their church or teach in conformity with our doctrinal position, then for their own good, as well as that of the Synod, it would seem that wisdom would dictate that they try to find a church home in which they could live with greater happiness.[219]

Under the synodical administration of Preus, the message was clear: diversity is fine if eventually it conforms to synodical standards.[220]

We want to be fair in our treatment of all of our officials, yet at the same time we must be firm. No church can run on organizational anarchy.[221]

The conservative attitude, where diversity is a necessary transitional stage before the pure goodness of uniformity is attained, permeated the resolutions adopted at this convention. The first major resolution introduced, 5-02A, was entitled "To deal with district presidents who have ordained or who have authorized ordination of persons who are not properly endorsed." According to this resolution, if the district presidents refused to implement synodical resolutions as adopted by convention, and if, after conferring pastorally with them, the synodical president was not able to sway them from such refusals, the president's duty was to vacate the offices of the disobedient district presidents and inform the districts sixty days before a regional convention.[222] Each of the dissenting eight district presidents was given a chance to speak when this resolution was first introduced; Preus then took the floor, stating that he would have this resolution withdrawn if the district presidents would "walk with the Synod and abide by its Constitution." After the district presidents refused this opportunity, the resolution was adopted.[223]

Rev. Emil G. Jaech, president of the Northwest District and one of the eight presidents affected, was given permission to speak after this resolution was adopted. His comments exemplify the moderate stance. Jaech dwelt not on the motives of the convention in passing the resolution but on freedom of conscience under the Gospel. This freedom extends particularly to the congregations.

Even the small congregation in the Synod is possessed of an authority higher than that of the most impressive church assembly, for all authority is derived from the Word of God. Where the Gospel is proclaimed and the sacraments administered, there is the Word of God.[224]

In this concept of church, "walking together" does not demand conformity as dictated by synodical resolutions. Diversity is possible because authority rests not with the synodical meeting but with the individual congregation as it studies the Word of God.

The synodical impatience with the situation was amply displayed again in the adoption of Resolution 6-02, which advised Seminex to close or be considered like any other extradenominational school. According to 6-02 and 6-04, students of Seminex would receive final approval for ministry in the Synod only after a colloquy procedure and/or a year's stay at Concordia.[225]

Preus called for and received the passage of Resolution 3-03A, "To Respond to Concerns re Former Faculty Members," wherein all faculty members would be interviewed by a committee of five to determine those teaching false doctrine.[226] According to Resolution 5-06, congregations that ordained Seminex graduates would be reminded that they had made a solemn covenant with their brethren to follow synodical rules.[227]

The harshest pronouncements were reserved for the devotees of ELIM. Resolution 3-06 stated that ELIM was no longer a confessional movement but a schismatic one because it had its own mission agency, newsletter, and educational facility for teachers. ELIM members were called upon to discontinue their ELIM roles or leave the Synod. The leader of LCM, Thomas Spitz, stated that such a resolution may force him to leave the Synod. Even with such a symbolic threat, the resolution was adopted and ELIM officially condemned as a schismatic movement.[228]

The effort to dissolve the ELIM-sympathetic English District into the geographical districts was stalled only after some skillful negotiating by English District officials. They convinced the delegates that this question would receive proper treatment under the new Preus-instigated commission on synodical structure initiated earlier in the convention.[229]

As if these resolutions condemning ELIM, Seminex, and the eight district presidents did not indicate the type of church wanted by the synodical convention, more general resolutions did. Resolution 3-04 affirmed the Synod's right "to adopt doctrinal statements and establish procedure."[230] The CTCR document "Guiding Principles for the Use of a Statement with Specific Reference to the Expression of Dissent" was commended to the synodical membership for reference and guidance under Resolution 3-05.[231] Though Resolution 5-09 did not deal specifically with doctrinal statements, its flavor was even stronger as it stated that adopted opinions of the CCM were to be considered binding.[232] Since the CCM had become involved in more than merely constitutional matters, this resolution indicated how tightly the parameters of the synodical boundaries were being drawn.[233]

B. Formation of the AELC

ELIM members reacted to the clear message of Anaheim at their own assembly in Chicago on August 13-15, 1975. In the words of ELIM's president, Sam Roth, the "crunch point" had arrived; since it would be only a short time before Anaheim's resolutions were implemented, ELIM's proclamation of the Gospel would soon be impossible from within the Synod.[234] Keynote addresses by ELIM board member Rev. Roger Schleef and C. Thomas Spitz, chairman of LCM, supported Roth's assessment though both men were much more emphatic in the call for new organizational forms to facilitate ELIM's ministry.[235] The eight district presidents, represented by Paul Jacobs of the California-Nevada District, issued a joint declaration that protested the loss of congregational autonomy, the misuse of power, and the violation of the "Doctrine of Call" by the Synod. They also offered their leadership for alternative organizational forms if the synodical administration implemented the Anaheim decisions.[236]

This third ELIM assembly adopted "Resolution 75-1 and 2 Alternative Forms in Mission and Fellowship," which explained ELIM's new situation in the Synod.

> The Missouri Synod convention in Anaheim changed the situation by officially declaring ELIM schismatic and by calling participation in its programs divisive of fellowship and contrary to the common bond between Missouri Synod members. In short, ELIM now offers no safe haven from which to protest because the Missouri Synod views it as a separate church. The eviction notice has been given. Implementation will follow.

The same resolution acknowledged that there were still disagreements within ELIM regarding its purpose. Therefore ELIM would serve at least two purposes:

> 1. For those who feel that in spite of the eviction notice served on ELIM they can most effectively carry out their mission and ministry within the institutional context of the Missouri Synod, we look to the organization of ELIM to support, encourage and assist them in their mission and ministry not only to the world but also to the Missouri Synod.

2. For some the institutional structure of the Missouri Synod no longer adequately serves as an effective instrument for mission and ministry. We recognize the Lutheran Church in Mission is a promising alternative for some. For others ELIM must facilitate a process by which they can begin to form a new association.

a. Form clusters of congregations, groups and individuals within a given geographic area throughout the United States and Canada, who can most effectively carry out their mutual mission and ministry within that given area. . . .

b. Out of this must come a meeting of the clusters to consider how to relate together, and to determine how to do together what no one cluster can do alone (e.g. coordination, leadership training, pension and welfare, etc.)

We call upon the ELIM Board of Directors to facilitate bringing representatives of these clusters together no later than the end of February 1976, the purpose of which meeting will be to define their direction and when and where an association of clusters will be activated.[237]

The two resolutions that demonstrate best the broader concept of church being employed by ELIM are 75-5, "Lutheran Unity and Cooperation with Other Christians," and 75-13, "Christian Unity." The first calls for efforts that "celebrate Lutheran unity . . . and . . . complete pulpit and altar fellowship with all Lutherans" as well as those efforts that "work for greater cooperation with all other Christians." The second declared an eagerness to talk with other interested Christian communities, to "engage in worship and mission activities which will promote, deepen and expand a God-pleasing unity," and to "refrain from setting up false barriers to pulpit and altar fellowship so that we may share Gospel and Sacrament with all who accept our Lord's invitation to participate in His lifegiving presence among us."[238]

After the ELIM assembly, the Synod assumed a temporary negotiating posture as many moderates continued to organize their departure from the Synod. In September of 1975, Preus wrote the congregational leaders pleading for "a more balanced approach."[239] An interview committee was appointed in October to give the Seminex faculty an opportunity to clear their names.[240] On the moderate side, LCM president Spitz wrote individuals and congregations, inviting them to apply for membership with LCM, even though LCM was not yet a functioning church body. Spitz also informed moderates of the clustering possibility suggested by ELIM and that LCM would "yield to a broader concept and coalition" when it became organized.[241] At a special meeting of the English District in September, district president Hecht was directed to continue ordaining Seminex graduates.[242] Even *The Lutheran Witness*, the official synodical publication, admitted in its report on

89

this special district convention that the English District was considering leaving the Synod.[243]

By November, the Synod's negotiating posture had dissolved and the moderates had publicized their schismatic plans. Preus began procedures to remove the eight dissenting district presidents.[244] At the request of Pastors Buelow and Harnapp, Preus began his own investigation of the Tietjen case.[245] The English District, emerging as the most concentrated and active moderate organization, issued a position statement that said they were "prepared to ask [their] congregations to revert to [their] status as an independent Synod or to seek other institutional affiliation."[246] In December 1975, the eight district presidents repeated publicly their intention to continue to ordain Seminex graduates.[247]

By February of 1976, an adequate number of congregations had been contacted to warrant a meeting of those interested in starting a new church body. It appeared that the moderates were organizing around three main groups: the LCM, the ELIM clusters, and the English District. At an ELIM "cluster" meeting on February 26-28, representatives of the three groups met. English District president Hecht said that the congregations in his district were considering the formation of an English synod but that the decision was theirs alone.[248] Spitz reported great interest in his organization but "loyalty to the local districts blunted the response to a call for membership." Elwyn Ewald stated that the ELIM cluster effort was not going as well as hoped.[249]

Alternatives were discussed for the better part of the three days. Finally, after breaking off into small groups, a consensus was reached that a coalition of some type was needed. A resolution was adopted, proposing the formation of "The Coordinating Council for the Moderate Movement" (CC), whose task was to study the alternatives open to those unhappy with the LC-MS situation.[250] Funding and staffing needs would be met by ELIM resources. The first meeting of the CC was to be convened no later than March 30, 1976 by ELIM cluster meeting chairman William Kohn. Until alternatives materialized, congregations were asked to keep their present affiliations or join the LCM or English District.[251]

On the same weekend, the LCM coordinated their plans with the new CC by deciding it would activate as a separate church body if no other coalition alternative appeared by September 30. In other words, LCM was going to wait to see if the CC was able to organize a viable coalition before striking out on its own; if the CC seemed to be making a successful bid, the LCM would lend its resources to a combined effort.[252]

Though the CC met within ten days of its formation (March 8-9), no real action was taken until after the events of early April. On April 2, Preus fired four district presidents on the basis of Anaheim Resolution 5-02A. Those fired were H. Frincke of the Eastern, H. Hecht of the English, R. P. F. Ressmeyer of the Atlantic, and R. Riedel of the New England districts.[253] There is a geographical localization of moderate sentiment evident in these firings that one could argue was reflective of a geographical split within the denomination; however, Preus said the reason the other four district presidents had not been fired was that they had not ordained Seminex graduates. In other words, denominational uniformity as it mixed with religious concerns was still the controverted issue.[254]

As a result of these firings, the April 14 meeting of the CC became very important. First, this meeting recommended that none of the eight deposed presidents appeal and that, if the four dismissed presidents were not recognized at the next COP meeting, the other four would walk out in support. Second, the CC agreed to establish a new corporation that would facilitate the association of interested moderate congregations. The districts immediately affected by the firings were directed to prepare alternative associations outside the Synod; regional meetings were suggested for those of the other districts so congregations wanting to leave the Synod could be identified. Finally, it was agreed that the "trip wire" for full activation of regional associations would be any legal action taken by the synodical administration regarding the four fired district presidents.[255]

After a series of regional meetings in April and May, Elwyn Ewald, the only full-time CC staff member, reported that all the meetings authorized the incorporation of an agency outside the Synod. Since it seemed that most of the congregations involved were waiting for the four districts affected by the firings to make the first move, Ewald suggested that the existence of an alternative might challenge the congregations into making a decision. For that reason, discussion of a constitution for a proposed Association of Evangelical Lutheran Churches (AELC) began at the third meeting of the Coordinating Council on May 26, 1976.[256]

Concrete support for the new organization was received from the English District at its district meeting June 17-20 at River Forest, Illinois. Excerpts from President Hecht's address to the assembly support the thesis that it was the idea of the church that was the major point of contention between the moderates and the synodical authority.

Our convention *theme* is our clarion call to be the church, with commitment to the life that responds to the challenge of this day. We have chosen the singularly strong words of our early church father, St. Augustine: IN NECESSARY THINGS, UNITY; IN DOUBTFUL THINGS, FREEDOM; BUT IN EVERYTHING, LOVE. What a wonderful summary of what the church is about. It tells us how we are constituted. It surely establishes our relationship with each other in Jesus. A fellowship that is inclusive of all believers who share this faith and common mission.

A discussion followed of what the church meant for the moderates. Quoting Article VII of the Augsburg Confession (1530), Hecht gave his inclusive definition of the church.

The church is the congregation of saints in which the Gospel is rightly taught and the sacraments administered. And to the true unity of the church it is enough to agree concerning the doctrine of the Gospel and the administration of the sacraments. Nor is it necessary that human traditions, that is rites of ceremonies, instituted by men should be everywhere alike.

This inclusive nature of the church was being destroyed by the adoption of documents such as Preus's "Statement."

It is of this church that we are concerned that its mission and its ministry increases, not allowing itself to be diminished. We cannot narrow down the Confessions of our Lutheran Church nor allow additional statements which have divisive effect. Such additions have tended to tear us apart from our Lutheran brothers and sisters and set us apart. . . . As people of God who have unity as God's gift, we need to assert that, proclaim it and live it in the church.[257]

With that inclusivistic convention theme and these words of their president ringing in their ears, the majority of the English District agreed to an amicable separation from the Missouri Synod by a vote of 296 to 75. Under the leadership of Harold Hecht, who formally resigned the English District presidency at this convention, a separate English synod was formed that sought application in the developing AELC.[258]

By the time of the fourth meeting of the CC on June 29-30, it was decided that at least four and possibly five regional "synods" could be formed. The mood of this meeting was optimistic as concrete objectives were set out and comparisons made to another great Lutheran event.

Basic *time lines* were discussed: *regional synods* have *already legally incorporated*; *initiation meetings* are to be held during the *next month* or so, with *constituting meetings* to take place at the *time* of the *Reformation*. Shortly thereafter, the *first delegate meeting* of the Association of Evangelical Lutheran Churches (AELC) would take place.[259]

That first delegate meeting was scheduled for December 4-6 in Chicago. At a meeting of the Board of Directors of the AELC held on June 30, it was resolved to include the CC on the AELC's Board of Directors. Bill Kohn, ELIM chairman and member of the CC, was elected AELC interim chairman.[260]

Since the AELC was only a small organizing body at this point, moderates looked to the annual assembly of ELIM in August for moral and material support; they received just that from the opening speeches to the resolutions passed. In his presidential report, Roth said that the AELC was currently the most appropriate expression of a confessing movement, encompassing as it did all other Lutherans.

The ultimate goal is not a separate church body but unity among all Lutherans. . . . The emerging synods are only a step toward something else, namely bringing all Lutherans into a much closer fellowship as a witness to that unity which is absolutely essential to the Gospel message.[261]

The resolutions of the 1976 ELIM assembly reflected these sentiments. Resolution 76-2 recognized the AELC as "one of the fruits of the Confession of ELIM."[262] Because ELIM's role as a confessing movement within the Missouri Synod seemed to be coming to an end, many ELIMites found the AELC's concrete objectives easy to support. For that reason, Resolution 76-3 spoke of ELIM's program being "altered . . . to reflect changing needs and resources." In other words, ELIM would fade so that the AELC could grow.[263] Resolution 76-7 repeated Roth's hope that this new organization would eventually lead to greater Lutheran unity and even to "an ultimate manifestation of Christian unity."[264] The inclusive church idea was assumed in all these and other resolutions and stood in direct contradistinction to the exclusivistic model of the Missouri Synod, which found expression in the resolutions of New Orleans and Anaheim.

From this ELIM assembly to December 1976 was a time in which synodical authorities released statements warning those who left the Synod of the consequences of their actions. In late August, the conservative and increasingly powerful Commission on Constitutional Matters published a judgment with obvious implications for ELIM congregations: it was judged improper for a synodical congregation to be a member of two church bodies at once.[265] Two months later, the synodical board of directors asked the synodical president to appoint a task force that would establish the necessary procedures for implementing this CCM ruling.[266]

Yet the crystallization of the schismatic movement continued. Another of the district presidents not fired by Preus resigned.[267] By the end of November 1976, ELIM's official newspaper reported that 141 congregations from 6 synods (5 regional groupings plus the English Synod, still nongeographical) had signed up for the AELC.[268] Also by the end of November, inaugural meetings of the six synods of the AELC had provisionally approved constitutions, bylaws, officers, and policies with all synods, stressing the temporary nature of their new bodies.[269] The new AELC denomination was ready for launching.

According to the AELC's own news release, 150 congregations with a total of 75,000 members were represented by 172 delegates at the founding convention in Chicago, December 3-4. The release stated that the moderates were cutting their formal ties with the Lutheran Church-Missouri Synod because they believed the Synod had become "too conservative, separatistic, oppressive and unjust."[270] The interim and soon-to-be-elected president, William Kohn, gave the keynote address, "Our Church in Mission in Today's World." At times quoting the "Mission Affirmations," Kohn dwelt not on the institutional barriers being erected with the formation of this new church body but the mission opportunities that they as a group were being freed to accomplish. A necessary part of that freedom involved learning and accomplishing the mission task in unity with others, particularly those subscribing to the Lutheran Confessions.[271]

The delegates supported Kohn's sentiments by adopting resolutions that offered full fellowship not only to the Missouri Synod but also to the Lutheran Church in America, the American Lutheran Church, and other Lutheran bodies. Membership in the Lutheran Council in the USA and the Lutheran World Federation (LWF) was also to be pursued. Even the question of membership in the National Council of Churches of Christ in the USA and the World Council of Churches was to be studied by the AELC Board of Directors.[272] This type of broad ecumenical contact had never been seriously contemplated by the Missouri synod.[273]

C. Distinctive Features of the AELC

Not surprisingly, the constitution of the new denomination stressed the "association" aspect of the body's organizational structure; a quick comparison of the AELC with the LC-MS constitution illustrates this. The "Objects and Purposes" section of both constitutions (Article III) lists the obvious, such as training of ministers, the mission enterprise, and the provision of pensions for clergy. However, the Missouri Synod constitution lists one object as "the endeavor to bring about the *largest possible uniformity* in church practice, church customs, and, in general, in congregational affairs" (emphasis mine). The AELC's corresponding statement implies, if anything, an acceptance of diversity: "To promote and participate full in *any and all expressions* of confessional Lutheran unity in the U.S.A. and throughout the world" (emphasis mine).

A comparison of the "Conditions for Membership" and "Relation to Members" in each constitution illustrates the same difference.[274] As well, very few powers were centralized in the new body's Board of Directors or the body's convention rulings. Instead, Article VIII stressed the governing authority of the individual congregation.

> [T]he AELC is not an ecclesiastical government exercising legislative or coercive powers, and, with respect to the individual congregation's right to self-government, it is but an advisory body. Any authority not expressly granted to the national organization is reserved for the synods and the congregations.[275]

An example of how this decentralizing principle affected the functioning of the AELC is obvious in the founding convention, where the ordination of women received free debate by the delegates. Resolution 76-5 "To Assist the Synods Concerning Ordination of Women," stated that "the scriptures neither forbid nor require that women serve in the ministry of Word and Sacrament." Though the Pacific Synod was commended for approving the ordination of women, pressure was not applied to the other congregations and synods to follow suit. Rather, the Board of Directors was directed to

> coordinate the process by the which the synods deal with the issue of women serving in the ministry of Word and Sacrament and to arrange for the preparation of educational materials to assist the congregations in understanding and resolving the issue.[276]

Since the accusation had been made that this new denomination had no doctrinal content,[277] it must be noted here that the new AELC constitution included the Missouri Synod's Article II, which subscribed the denomination to the Scriptures and the Lutheran Confessions. As with the Missouri Synod, this article was considered unalterable.[278]

What was qualitatively different about the new denomination relative to the Missouri Synod was that it did not think of itself as an exclusive institution, a "brotherhood" from which others could be barred.[279] Nor did it think of itself as a body that could not enter into fellowship with others who did not share exactly the same doctrine. The organizational structure of the new AELC actually lacked powers to enforce exclusivistic actions because such actions offended the basic premise of the new denomination, that it is a confessing movement in mission with each congregation possessing the authority to make its own decisions.[280]

> The truth of our distinctive witness is not so fragile that it needs to be protected by isolation from the rest of the Church; neither is our understanding so superior that it does not need the correction and concern for unity of the larger Christian community. Concern for doctrine and concern for unity must not be set against one another. Our belief in the unity of the Church is doctrinally grounded and our struggle to manifest that unity is doctrinally imperative. We are committed to the Gospel of God's grace in Christ alone. That Gospel is our very life, and the only ground and hope for true unity.
>
> Resisting every temptation to seek security in schism or a sense of rightness in isolation, we commit ourselves to join with others in working for the renewal of the Lutheran confessional witness within the whole of Christ's Church.[281]

In his analysis of this schism, Takayama identified three "non-theological sources of conflict" that are obvious in the history presented here: the struggle of an ethnically based denomination to remain "true to its theological roots" even as it was increasingly "Americanized"; the intraorganizational authoritarianism of the synodical president and the conservative machinery; and the vulnerability of Concordia Seminary, so dependent on the Synod for its existence. Takayama's analysis relegates doctrinal purity to secondary importance by calling it merely the "overt issue."[282] While his analysis is helpful in identifying the nontheological factors, his disparaging of the religious element generally leaves one wondering what it was that provided the drive behind the schismatic process if not the religious disputes involved.

Not only did the issues provide the passion that fueled the debate but only when those religious issues coincided with the structural problem of what authority would prevail in the denomination was it possible for the schism to occur. This convergence of religious and structural issues around the ordination question drove the schism to its logical end. The new body that emerged from this debate carefully developed a structural organization that would reflect the doctrine of church it wished to practice. Organizational structure and religious issues again converged, this time in the birth of a new denomination.

FOUR

Schism in the Episcopal Church

"A Branch Shall Grow"

Ever since its arrival on the eastern seaboard early in the eighteenth century, American Anglicanism has wrestled with the problem of its identity.[1] Lacking the security that comes with state establishment and without determinative doctrinal statements, Anglicanism has survived by drawing on its tradition of apostolic succession.[2] In the beginning, even such survival was a struggle for the transplanted Church of England.

After the Revolution, American Anglicans lacked a resident bishop, a governing body, or any other recognizable form of leadership. Parishes were scattered, disorganized, and financially broken, having lost many of their best-trained to Canada and the West Indies in the Loyalist migrations. In the early 1780s, Revs. William White and William Smith organized the clergy and laymen of the Middle States while Samuel Seabury sought consecration as a bishop in England. Though these initial efforts at establishing leadership and church government were not always coordinated, regional conventions did meet in 1785 and 1786. Finally in 1789, the first General Convention of the Protestant Episcopal Church in the United States of America was convened. The new church was Episcopal in that it claimed to follow the line of apostolic succession as maintained in the Church of England; it was also Protestant in affirming the principles and theology of the reformers in their battles with the Roman Catholic church. At this General Convention, an American Book of Common Prayer and constitution were adopted. The American Prayer Book was virtually the English Prayer Book with the requisite revisions for the American context.[3]

The constitution reflected not only the disestablishment of the American church but also the involvement of the laity in every level of ecclesiastical decision making. According to the constitution, whose basic outline has changed little since the eighteenth century, the Protestant Episcopal Church in the United States of America (PECUSA)[4] is a federal union of independent diocesan units usually divided along state lines. Each diocese consists of an association of independent parishes. The dioceses meet annually in a convention presided over by a bishop and comprised of clergy and elected lay representatives of parishes and missions. Every three years, the dioceses meet at a General Convention in bicameral legislative assemblies called the House of Bishops and the House of Deputies. The two houses deliberate and vote separately but all proposals require the approval of both houses to become the rule of the church. Any legislation that would alter the constitution requires passage by both houses in two successive General Conventions; all other legislation requires the passage of both houses at any one General Convention.[5] Between General Conventions, business of the church is administered by an Executive Council, which is to implement all convention mandates and recommend future action for the delegates.[6]

The House of Bishops includes every consecrated bishop including retired bishops; they usually number around 150 at a General Convention, though approximately 230 are entitled to attend. As well as meeting at the General Convention, the bishops also meet at least once and usually several times during the year. A Presiding Bishop or chief officer of the denomination is elected by the House of Bishops "at the General Convention next before the expiration of the term of office of the Presiding Bishop"; his election must be confirmed by a majority of the House of Deputies. The House of Deputies consists of eight elected representatives from 113 dioceses for a total of 904 delegates. Of the eight elected from each diocese, four are laypeople and four clergy.[7] Normally a straight majority vote in the House of Deputies will pass a resolution, but at any time any deputy may call a "vote by orders"; this means that on that particular debated question each diocese has one vote for its clerical deputies and one for its laity. In these instances, a proposal must be passed by a majority in both the clerical and the lay orders to become law. If a vote is divided within a diocesan order, whether in the clerical or lay orders, that vote is not counted; in effect the divided vote acts as a negative vote.[8]

As many commentators have suggested, the close fellowship of the Anglican communion results from its heritage of faith (the episcopate) and its church order and worship (the Book of Common Prayer), not from any uniformity of belief.[9] No oath of obedience was attached to any confessional statement; only the oath of ordination asked the candidate if he believed "the Holy

Scriptures of the Old and New Testaments to be the Word of God, and to contain all things necessary to salvation."[10] Even when a group of "low-churchmen" left to form the Reformed Episcopal Church in 1873, the response of the Protestant Episcopal Church was to adopt a ritual canon in 1874 "that enabled conflicting views and traditions to live together in a measure of tolerance." Anglican theologians such as W. Norman Pittenger refer to this doctrinal tolerance or inclusiveness as Anglican "comprehensiveness," since all theological traditions are accorded equal standing.[11]

The Book of Common Prayer has been the one document that bonds diverse groups within the Episcopal Church. High and low, catholic and evangelical, charismatic and broad Episcopalians all rely on the Prayer Book to provide them with a common worship and order manual as well as a doctrinal heritage that most agree to in principle though they will almost surely agree to disagree in specifics of interpretive issues.[12]

In a denomination where doctrine plays such a minimal role in forging group identity, is it possible that a religious controversy was instrumental in producing a schism? Answering this question necessitates showing how the challenges to the Episcopal tradition had a religious content that was articulated and amplified by the dissenters.

"Other Seeds Fell on Good Ground . . .": Polarizing Issues of the 1960s and 1970s

While most observers agree that the Episcopalian schism of 1978 was precipitated directly by the decision of the 1976 General Convention to ordain women to the priesthood, starting with that issue would miss the polarization that had previously developed in the PECUSA.[13] By noting briefly some of the issues that received attention in the two decades before 1978, we can observe that polarization developing.

Though never noted for its evangelical zeal,[14] the Episcopal Church experienced a sharp drop in its membership figures after 1969.[15] Part of this may be due to the national decline in church attendance around this time, but the Episcopal Church especially was affected. Lacking any specific theological vista, perceived as the church of the rich and white, the PECUSA was increasingly characterized as "the Republican party at prayer."[16] Williamson observes that at least part of the problem was that no consensus existed within the church regarding the necessity of converting the unconverted.[17] Only a few small Episcopal churches with a charismatic or conservatively evangelical bent grew; the rest of the church attended less, gave less, and generally lost influence in the religious sphere.[18]

The church leadership attempted to solve the problem, but in some respects their efforts only made things worse. Declining membership combined with a surplus of clergy[19] prompted the establishing of a Special Committee on Episcopal Theological Education in the mid-1960s. The study this committee produced indicated that not only were ill-suited candidates being accepted into the ministry but that those who were being trained were not given the necessary educational preparation for ministers to serve the modern age. Closer supervision of the seminaries by the church as well as cooperation with universities and other seminaries was recommended.[20] This study only widened the gulf between clergy and laity since the clergy were reproved for lax educational standards and a substantial portion of the laity were vindicated in their conviction that the clergy were neglecting theological study and the spiritual welfare of the membership in favor of an aggressive social work program.[21]

The social action program instigated by Presiding Bishop John Hines, commonly called the General Convention Special Program (GCSP), was another source of controversy in the late 1960s and early 1970s.[22] The most publicized issue involved the allotting of $200,000 to the militant Black Economic Development Committee, which advocated violence to attain its goals.[23] However, other aspects of Hines's social action program also came under scrutiny. Funds were given to militant farm workers; to the American Indian Movement, which was connected with the hostage incident at Wounded Knee, South Dakota, in 1973; and to Third World liberation movements. The polarization precipitated by such actions was especially obvious in 1970 when the Foundation for Christian Theology (FCT), a conservative Texas-based group, demanded Bishop Hines's resignation.[24] As evidence of the church's increasing secularization, the FCT cited the warnings of the Internal Revenue Service to Episcopalian leaders that the church was in danger of losing its tax-exempt status if it continued to fund political strikes.[25]

Paralleling this concern of an overzealous social action program and an underdeveloped concern with spiritual matters were charges that what little theology there was coming out of the pulpits was not orthodox. Many conservatives felt that the Episcopal Church was relying less on the Bible as

102

its authority and more on tradition and reason. They found evidence for their charges even in the writings of more conservative Anglican theologians like John Macquarrie, who spoke of six "formative factors" for the Christian of which Scripture was only one.[26] However, it was the theological speculations of men like Bishop James Pike and Rev. John Spong, who questioned basic dogmas of orthodox Christianity like the Incarnation, that really offended conservative laity and clergy. Despite the fact that the House of Bishops denounced Pike's theologizing as "offensive" and "irresponsible," many felt that the Episcopal Church had exercised its disciplinary function poorly in failing to bring Pike to trial on charges of heresy.[27]

Conservatives perceiving a slide into a secular humanism that had little to do with Christian theology found further evidence in recent decisions of the General Convention regarding Christian morality. Prior to 1973, divorcees wanting to remarry had to wait one year before taking another spouse; after the General Convention of that year a priest was allowed to marry a couple with his bishop's consent even if a full year had not elapsed.[28] Homosexuals were considered full church members by convention resolution in 1976, though not without some debate as to whether homosexuality was an aberration of God's will or an extension of it.[29] The 1976 General Convention also adopted a moderate stand on abortion, which was regarded by many to violate the Christian concern for human life.[30] These are just three examples of moral issues that many Episcopalians thought indicated a backsliding by the church into a form of secular humanism that had little, if any, contact with Christian morality and theology.[31]

The conservative extremes of this polarization can be found in the very small splinter groups that left the PECUSA in the 1960s. James Parker Dees of North Carolina organized the Anglican Orthodox Church of North America in the mid-sixties because he and others like him thought the views of many Episcopal clergymen to be heretical in doctrinal matters such as the Trinity, the virgin birth, and Christ's resurrection. They also objected to the PECUSA's membership in the National Council of Churches.[32] In May 1968, the American Episcopal Church was organized by a group of Episcopalians who, in opposition to the speculations of Bishop Pike, joined their presiding bishop James H. George Jr. in declaring, "The faith of the apostles has been watered down."[33] Of the conservative groups remaining in the church until 1970 and not directly involved in the schism under study here, the Foundation for Christian Theology was one of the most vocal in raising concerns of individual salvation while the Episcopal Charismatic Fellowship reflected a pentecostal movement among the clergy that crystallized in 1973.[34]

This polarization within the Episcopal Church made it ripe for a major schism. That polarization was undoubtedly based in part on a reaction against the turbulence of the 1960s and the methods of the national leadership that many conservatives considered too authoritarian.[35] Still, this polarization would probably not have gone beyond dissent had contentious issues not arisen that threatened the very identity of the church; such issues of contention were found in the proposals to revise the Book of Common Prayer and ordain women to the priesthood.

". . . And They Sprang Up . . .": Resolution of the Two Main Issues

A. The Book of Common Prayer

Sydney Ahlstrom describes most succinctly the centrality of the Book of Prayer:

> Stately in language, scriptural in quality and in much of its substance, it endeared itself to generation after generation, becoming in time the quintessential expression of Anglicanism.[36]

When Seabury was consecrated as bishop by the Scottish episcopate in 1784, he promised to incorporate elements of the Scottish communion liturgy into the American Book of Common Prayer. In the compromise arrangement with the other two American but English-ordained bishops that resulted in the establishment of the PECUSA, Seabury agreed to omit the Athanasian Creed in return for the incorporation of these elements. Hence, from the beginning, the American Book of Common Prayer was a revised version of the First English Prayer Book of 1549.[37]

That was not the last revision. This 1789 Standard Edition of the Prayer Book (also called the 1793 edition because that was the year it was actually published) was significantly revised in 1892 and again in 1928.[38] It was this 1928 version that was at the center of the controversial proposed revision of the 1960s and 1970s.

The most recent drive for Prayer Book revisions finds its origins in the 1949 General Convention, when a new series of revised worship services, which became known as the Prayer Book Studies, was commissioned.[39] In 1950, the first of these was published. Each study centered on a specific service or act. Seeking a more comprehensive format in contemporary language that would reflect modern concerns, the 1964 General Convention asked the Standing Liturgical Commission (SLC)[40] to prepare a revision of the 1928 Prayer Book. Acting cautiously on what it perceived to be a sensitive item, the SLC proposed a "Plan of Revision," which the 1967 General Convention approved.[41] The 1967 General Convention also authorized for trial use a new Liturgy of the Lord's Supper.[42] This liturgy was included in the "Services for Trial Use" (commonly called the "Green Book" because of its cover). It was published in 1970 and authorized for use by the General Convention of that same year.[43]

Opposition to the "Green Book" grew rapidly in the spring of 1971. At that time, the Society for the Preservation of the Book of Common Prayer (SPBCP) was established by six professors, one priest, and one editor.[44] They rented a post office box in Nashville and mailed a statement of purpose to the Episcopalian membership. In their letter to perspective members, they emphasized the moderate nature of their organization:

> Our design is not to prevent any change whatsoever in the 1928 rite but to defeat the trial liturgies now before us in the "Green Book," because we consider them to be poorly written, ill-conceived, and in some particulars, contrary to the Faith. . . . Our primary aim is to represent those churchmen who feel that the proposed revisions, if adopted, would be disastrous for the life of the church, and to make that representation as forcefully as we can to the bishops severally and also to both houses at the 1973 General Convention.[45]

Preventing a poor revision of the 1928 Prayer Book was the only goal of the Society as SPBCP president Walter Sullivan emphasized repeatedly. "We intend to stick to our single effort, and forward this one cause as best we can at Louisville [site of the 1973 General Convention] and beyond."[46]

At all times, the SPBCP stressed the importance of working within the system; in fact, they argued that the system favored their position since some dioceses had already illegally eliminated the use of the 1928 Book of Common Prayer. They also argued that their position represented the best interests of the denomination; if the trial rites as put forward by the few in the "Green Book" were permitted to "displace or compete with the Book of Common Prayer, the church cannot survive the shock [of] such schism as is almost certain to follow."[47]

The SPBCP obviously struck a responsive chord with some; by 1973 they claimed a membership in excess of seventeen thousand. Even if these figures are be somewhat exaggerated, the fact that the SPBCP was able to employ five full-time and two part-time staff in their Nashville office indicates the strength of their movement.[48]

However, the work of Prayer Book revision continued. In 1973, the SLC presented to the General Convention a "Report on Trial Use."[49] As a result of this report, the General Convention authorized the continuation of trial-use liturgies as presented in the SLC's "Services for Trial Use and Authorized Services, 1973" (also called the "Zebra Book").[50] In view of the increasing opposition to the revisions, the 1973 General Convention also directed the SLC to solicit responses from the general membership regarding the changes. Based on those responses, the SLC was to prepare another draft of the Prayer Book revision for the 1976 convention.[51] The convention also set a timetable for the completion of these revisions: all the consulting and research was to be completed by September 1975 with the proposed draft to be published by April 1976. This would enable the entire membership and in particular the convention delegates to study the draft before September of 1976 when the next convention was scheduled for Minneapolis. The 1973 Convention delegates also specified that two full days of debate were to be set aside in 1976 to consider the proposed draft. Since a prayer book change involved a constitutional change that required the approval of two successive conventions, the 1973 convention also directed that only the 1976 version, agreed on in the General Convention, would be considered by the decisive 1979 General Convention.[52] In essence, then, the course of the revisions had been charted; they would either be approved with this time line or the whole procedure would have to start over again.

The SLC dutifully went about their business distributing questionnaires, holding public hearings, and encouraging discussion through the public press. Discussion centered around how much of the 1928 Prayer Book was to be preserved, in what form, and what irrelevant rites could be removed. However, little of significant theological import seemed to be at controversy. In October 1974, the House of Bishops met in Mexico to protest the effective removal of the confirmation rite from the revised draft, but this protest was lodged more on the basis that deemphasizing the rite would distance the bishop from the members of his diocese rather than on theological argument.[53] In late 1974, the SPBCP met in Nashville to state once again that they were not against revision per se but wanted to preserve the beauty of the 1928 version, which the previous drafts had not done.[54]

By December 1974, the SLC had finished their research and consultations; in January 1975, they were behind closed doors drafting the proposed revision. Realizing that their job was one of public relations as well as scholarship, they wisely appointed an Education and Communication Committee in January 1975 to promote a better understanding of the proposed revisions.[55]

In September of 1975, the SLC finished its delicate duty of drafting the revised book; in February 1976, *The Draft Proposed Book of Common Prayer and Other Rites and Ceremonies of the Church* was published.[56] The SLC said that this particular revision was undertaken so that the church could speak to the modern age in a language it could understand, the missionary posture of the denomination could be reflected, better ecumenical dialogue with other denominations could begin, and more opportunities could be provided for the Episcopal membership in the worship format of the church.[57] For these reasons, the old English of the 1928 version had been dropped, as had most of the sexist language.[58] Bishop Powell of the SLC noted that the *Proposed Book* emphasized the Eucharist as the church's principal act of worship.[59] Weil of the SLC said that the proposed revision reflected the input of the Episcopalian membership in that the "liturgical norms were not clerically dominated."[60]

The SLC certainly catered to the laity when they enlarged the catechism "to give an outline for instruction . . . which is not meant to be a complete statement of belief and practice; rather it is a point of departure for the teacher."[61] It was also obvious that the House of Bishops had managed to persuade the SLC that confirmation was significant enough to keep as a reaffirmation of one's baptismal vows.[62] To pacify the traditionalists who were concerned that the Thirty-Nine Articles would no longer be available, a Historical Document section containing this document as well as the Chalcedonian definition of the person of Christ, the Athanasian Creed, the Preface to the First Book of Common Prayer, and the Chicago-Lambeth Quadrilateral was included.[63]

There was an unmistakable effort to play down the Prayer Book controversy in *The Episcopalian*. For instance, the April 1976 edition proclaimed on page 1 that the *Proposed Book* was so well received that the only negative reaction came from SPBCP president Walter Sullivan, who said the new book has the "same, colorless, mushy language, the same effort to weaken the faith." The

107

article also clearly implied that the SPBCP was a small organization and that Sullivan was venting his frustration as an individual.[64] In the September 1976 *Episcopalian*, the editors were even more explicit in their belittling of the Prayer Book controversy when they stated that the threat of schism derives not from the revision of the Prayer Book but rather from the controversy regarding the ordination of women.[65]

However deemphasized by *The Episcopalian*, the opposition to the *Proposed Book* does seem to have had some support. In preparation for the General Convention in Minneapolis in 1976, the SPBCP voiced their opposition to the *Proposed Book* by taking out full-page advertisements in many periodicals, including the high-profile *Episcopalian*.[66] An editorial in the June 20, 1976 edition of *The Living Church* (p. 9) claimed that the *Proposed Book* had too many variations and that what worshiping unity the Episcopal Church did have would be lost with this revision. Dorothy Faber, editor of *The Christian Challenge*, an independent conservative newspaper commenting on affairs in the Episcopal Church since 1962, voiced her disapproval of the whole revision project by claiming that the final cost to the denomination would be approximately $36,000,000.[67] Again there was a minimum of real theological debate as the disputants were more concerned with the endangered Episcopal uniformity and tradition than with any theological deficiencies in the *Proposed Book*.

Despite the protests, the revision process continued. There were at least three alternatives the General Convention could consider. Total rejection and total acceptance were both highly unlikely options as neither side wanted to alienate the other in a highly volatile environment. Revising the document seemed the best hope, though with the controversy heating up, the entire two days of debating time allotted the *Proposed Book* would be required for revisions satisfactory to a majority. Such a revised draft could receive preliminary acceptance in 1976 and be considered again for final approval at the 1979 General Convention.[68]

Discussion at the Minneapolis convention was passionate. Most of the substantive theological differences were actually resolved in the hearings before the convention[69] or dealt with in quick order once the proceedings officially started.[70] However, the emotionally charged and practical issue of giving up the 1928 Prayer Book altogether attracted attention from all in attendance.[71]

Presiding Bishop Allin, ever the mediator, proposed a compromise that would have allowed dioceses to retain the 1928 Book of Common Prayer unconditionally but neither the SPBCP nor the SLC liked this idea since it was thought this would result in a nonuniform pattern of worship throughout the church.[72] The turning point of the debate came when the SLC suggested that the continued indefinite use of the 1928 Prayer Book should be studied and reported on at the 1979 General Convention; with this compromise, opponents of the *Proposed Book* lost most of their moderate support and the General Convention adopted the *Proposed Book* by lopsided majorities. The House of Bishops passed the adopting resolution almost unanimously while 95 percent of the clerical order and 80 percent of the lay order in the House of Deputies also voted in the affirmative. It was also decided that in the interim before the 1979 General Convention, the dioceses could chose whether to use the *Proposed Book* or the 1928 Book.[73] When accepted without change in 1979, the revised *Proposed Book* of the 1976 General Convention became the new Standard Book of Common Prayer of the Episcopal Church.

While the Prayer Book debate alone was not contentious enough to provoke a schismatic movement, the debate did define more clearly the conflicting constituencies within the Episcopal Church. On the one hand, the minority group of conservatives objected to the eroding of their Episcopal tradition in general and regarded the new Prayer Book as a direct threat to what it meant to be an Episcopalian. On the other hand, the denominational leadership with majority support from the membership sought to keep Episcopalianism relevant even if it meant altering what had become the sacred form of that tradition, the 1928 Prayer Book. As vigorous as the debate may have been at times, no schismatic movement resulted solely as a result of the Prayer Book issue because it lacked the religious ingredients to drive the debate beyond the bounds of human preference for a particular style of worship. However, those religious ingredients were present in the ordination of women debate.

B. The Ordination of Women

The place of women in the church had been a source of some agitation for the Episcopalians before it finally erupted into the controversy of the 1970s. In 1946, the first woman was seated in the House of Deputies, but this was clearly regarded as an exception because the same General Convention declined to reinterpret "laymen" to allow the seating of women on a regular basis. Efforts to reinterpret the same term in 1949 and even as late as 1961 were also unsuccessful.[74] Not until 1967 was a constitutional amendment passed that enabled women to serve in the House of Deputies; ratification of that amendment three years later enabled women to sit in the House for the first time in 1970.[75] The 1970 General Convention also debated whether women should be ordained to the diaconate and the priesthood.[76] Ordination to the priesthood was defeated, but the 1970 Convention did authorize the ordination of women to the diaconate as equals with men.[77]

With foreign dioceses giving women's ordination to the ministry serious consideration,[78] some foreign bishops actually ordaining women in 1971 and 1973,[79] and international organizations such as the Anglican Consultative Council in 1971 and the Lambeth Conference in 1968 approving such ordination,[80] the pressure was on the American Episcopalians to consider seriously women's ordination to the ministry. In 1972, the House of Bishops took an unofficial vote, which favored women's ordination.[81] Since there was no question that the matter would receive attention and probably be voted on at the General Convention in Louisville in 1973, public debates were convened,[82] advertisements were placed in church periodicals,[83] and organizations were established that either favored or denounced women's ordination.

C. 1973 General Convention at Louisville, Kentucky

Those for and against women's ordination to the ministry campaigned energetically at the 1973 General Convention.[84] Proponents of women's ordination argued that men and women are equal in God's sight, that representing Christ is part of "being in Christ," that the gifts and talents of half of God's people could not be ignored, that classic statements opposing women's ordination were based on sexist assumptions, that it was more important to move closer to God than to worry about what Rome would think of the decision, and that the worldwide Anglican communion was moving in the direction of women's ordination. Opponents argued that the role of women was not the same as that of men in the church, though this did not mean it was less of a role, only a different one. The idea of an apostolic succession based on the fact that Christ did not call any female apostles and that there is a sacramental nature to the priesthood, especially in relation to the celebration of the Eucharist, rounded off the theological arguments of ordination opponents. On the practical side, they claimed that ecumenical relations with denominations such as the Roman Catholic and Orthodox churches would suffer if such a measure were passed without first convening an international ecumenical council.[85] Obviously, the question not only struck at the heart of the Episcopal tradition as articulated in the apostolic succession of bishops but also had religious implications. Conservatives in particular considered it threatening to what it was that made them Episcopalian.

It was significant for the delegates to the convention that in addition to the hot items on the agenda,[86] they were also going to pick a new leader. When the liberal Presiding Bishop John Hines announced his retirement, observers thought that the developing factions within the church would try to consolidate their position with one of their own as the episcopal head.[87] It appeared that the conservatives had gained the advantage when Bishop John M. Allin of Missouri was elected to the top spot on the second ballot.[88] However, his actions at this convention and immediately following it indicated the conciliatory position the affable bishop wished to adopt. Consequently his election was applauded by diverse groups within the denomination even before his term of office began in January 1974.[89]

At the convention, both factions claimed victories. Liberals rejoiced that those remarrying within a year of divorce would no longer be automatically excommunicated and that the local priest was given greater authority regarding remarriage.[90] The convention also directed that a revised Book of Common Prayer was to be drawn up for the 1976 Minneapolis convention.[91] However, the conservative forces squeaked out a major victory when, on the resolution calling for a canonical amendment that would have allowed women to be ordained to the priesthood, they called for a vote by orders in the House of Deputies. As proponents of women's ordination claimed later, the majority of the House of Deputies actually voted for women's ordination but because of the procedure whereby a split vote within a diocese is not counted in the final tally (thereby acting as a negative vote in counting the majority), the measure failed. Fifty-six bishops signed a statement favoring women's ordination after this vote but, given the result of the House of Deputies, the House of Bishops spent little time discussing the issue.[92]

Not surprisingly, the question of a "divided vote," or vote by orders as it is more correctly called, received attention after this.[93] A resolution was presented to abolish this "vote by orders," but that very resolution was subjected to a divided vote and it also lost.[94] Those favoring women's ordination claimed that a resolution can be defeated by as few as 25 percent of those voting even if it is approved by the majority.[95] In effect, the Episcopal

111

Church was being forced to face the question of the nature of its organizational as well as its religious structure. Should the denomination remain true to its diocesan base of ecclesiastical order that justified the existence of voting by orders? Or was a representative democratic vote more appropriate for the modern organizational structure of the church?[96]

Despite the fact that Allin had voted against women's ordination at the House of Bishop's meeting in 1972 and claimed that the whole issue was secondary to that of a general church renewal, his stance at the 1973 General Convention was much more conciliatory. He asked the bishops to approve the appointment of an ad hoc committee to provide two study papers; the first concerning the definition of the priesthood and the second developing a definitive statement of contemporary Christian sexuality.[97] In December of 1973, he again publicly opposed women's ordination but pleaded for understanding between the opposing forces.

> We must not proceed to ordain women because there are no theological grounds against it; we must make this change when we agree there are strong theological reasons for it.[98]

Little substantive action was taken between October 1973 and June 1974. Discussions continued among women deacons, their bishops, and their standing committees. There were calls from some prominent churchmen to ordain women.[99] For a time it seemed that Allin's call to conciliation was having its effect.

D. The "Philadelphia Eleven" Are Ordained

By July 1974, however, proponents of women's ordination were preparing to act. On July 10, twenty Episcopalians met in Philadelphia; retired Bishops R. L. Dewitt, E. R. Welles, D. Corrigan, and C. F. Hall agreed to be the ordaining bishops in an ordination ceremony for a number of women deacons.[100] Bishop Hall approved the ordination of Deacon Alison Cheek on July 19; however, the diocesan standing committee on ordinations declined permission by a 5-4 vote with three absent.[101] On July 20, Bishop Ogilby of Pennsylvania wrote to the members of his diocese that though he supported the proposed ordinations and considered them theologically valid, he was denying his required consent as governing bishop of the jurisdiction where the ordinations were to take place. That same day, the three ordaining bishops and eleven ordinands sent letters of intention to the press and the other bishops. The bishops claimed that they were acting out of "Christian obedience"; the women claimed they knew their proposed ordination to be "irregular" but they also believed "it to be valid and right."[102] Presiding Bishop John Allin begged the deacons and bishops to reconsider. On July 26, Bishop Ogilby wrote to the diocese, warning that if the proposed ordinations were carried out, the fourteen would be "conducting themselves in violation of the Constitution and Canons of the Church" and would be subject to ecclesiastical discipline.[103]

Nevertheless, on July 29, the Feast of St. Martha and Mary, eleven women were ordained under the rubrics of the 1928 Prayer Book at Philadelphia's Church of the Advocate by retired Bishops DeWitt, Corrigan, and Welles and by active Bishop J. A. Ramose of the Missionary Diocese of Costa Rica.[104] In a service described as a "circus-type atmosphere" because of the number of media attending, Charles V. Willie, vice president of the House of Deputies, claimed in his sermon that it was the Episcopal Church and not the ordaining bishops who were wrong.[105] During the service Rev. Charles Osborn, executive director of the American Church Union (ACU),[106] Rev. DeWitt Mallary, chairman of the Committee for Apostolic Ministry,[107] and Rev. George Rutler, rector of the Church of the Good Shepherd in Rosemont, Pennsylvania, read statements of protest. Rutler accused the ordaining bishops of breaking "laws of the church" and, even worse, "the law of creation: God's gift to the universe of man and of woman, each holy and each different, each with certain gifts which cannot be exchanged."[108] According to the conservative *Living Church*, these protests were greeted with "jeers and boos from the 'worshippers.' "[109] In replying to the protests, Bishop Corrigan spoke of the conflict between "revelation in the Scriptures and the doctrine of the Church, on the one hand, and the discipline, rules and regulations, and common practices of the Protestant Episcopal Church, on the other hand." He claimed that in ordaining those women they were only choosing the truth of the Scriptures and doctrine over claims of truth by the denomination.[110]

After consulting with the presidents of the Provinces of the Episcopal Church, Presiding Bishop Allin called a special meeting of the House of Bishops in Chicago on August 14-15. They heard reports from Bishops Arthur Vogel and Donald Parsons from the Committee on Theology. Both sympathized with the sincere crisis of conscience for those involved in the ordinations. Parsons gave the main concerns of the Committee.

The action of these four bishops raises serious questions about 1) the nature of the church 2) the nature of ministry 3) the authority of the bishops and 4) the meaning of ordination. . . .

The points of concern may be briefly summarized as follows:

1) The Church which God created is by its very nature a community.

2) Jesus Christ gave the ministry to serve the Church and to help express its essential nature.

3) The bishop is the sign of the unity of both the local and the universal Church. This function does not belong to him as an individual but by reason of his membership in the episcopal college.

4) Ordination is therefore an action in and for the community, not simply to confer a gift but also to admit the ordinand into the ministerial community within the Church.

Vogel developed the concept of "validity," saying that it connotes "ecclesiastical recognition" and that in this respect the Philadelphia ordinations were lacking.[111]

The influence of these reports on the final text of the resolution adopted by the bishops on August 15 is obvious. After noting their sympathy for the position of the ordaining bishops, the House of Bishops said:

We believe that they are wrong; we decry their acting in violation of the collegiality of the House of Bishops as well as the legislative process of the whole Church.

Further we express our conviction that the necessary conditions for valid ordination to the priesthood in the Episcopal Church were not fulfilled on the occasion in question; since we are convinced that a bishop's authority to ordain can be effectively exercised only in and for a community which has authorized him to act for them, and as a member of the episcopal college; and since there was a failure to act in fulfillment of constitutional and canonical requirements for ordination.[112]

The bishops also asked that the 1976 General Convention in Minneapolis reconsider the ordination question and that all parties wait until after that convention before taking any more action.[113] Immediately following adoption of this resolution, Bishop B. R. Hull of Virginia asked if the "Philadelphia eleven" were in fact ordained for the priesthood; Allin replied in the negative. Some bishops disagreed with this judgment and attempted to have the resolution reconsidered. When that failed, these bishops, some having supported the resolution, voiced their opposition to its adoption.[114]

The decision by the House of Bishops seemed to draw fire from all sides. There was some question as to whether the House of Bishops could legislate such disciplinary action without acting in concert with the House of Deputies.[115] Willie, who officiated at the Philadelphia ordinations, resigned as vice president of the House of Deputies because of the "male arrogance" of the bishops.[116] The Primate of the Antiochian Orthodox Church in America protested that "the ordination of women is theologically impossible"; he also chastised Allin for his focus on the issues of church discipline and constitution when he felt Allin should have invoked theological doctrine to condemn those participating in the ordinations.[117]

In fairness to Allin, it must be noted that he agreed that theological issues were at the root of the ordination controversy. In opposition to other commentators, Allin argued that the issue was not a sexist or ecumenical one but a theological one in which he desired "theological reasons" for ordaining women, not just secular rhetorical reasoning that asked "Why not?" However, he also acknowledged that the bishops, not renowned for their interest in theological debate, played down this aspect of the controversy. When asked if the real issue was theological, Allin replied, "Yes, but it's damn hard to get bishops to discuss theology."[118]

Still, Allin managed to present himself as the pastoral conciliator when he wrote all involved in the Philadelphia ordinations pleading with them again to wait before taking further action.[119] At the meeting of the House of Bishops in Oaxtepec, Mexico, in mid-October 1974, Allin claimed that he, like the average Episcopalian, was confused regarding what stance to take on the issue of women's ordination. He urged a churchwide discussion of the subject. The House of Bishops was less confused, as they affirmed the principle of women's ordination by a 3-1 vote at this same meeting. Supporting Allin, they urged caution, repeating Allin's warning to delay further action until after the Minneapolis General Convention.[120]

Trying to avoid charges that the bishop was merely a representative of the community in the act of ordination, the bishops also adopted a theological report that grappled with the root issue of the controversy as they saw it:

> A bishop can legitimately function and be himself only within community for community although his ministry derives from Christ in ordination, not from the community.
> The difficulty we confront here concerns our understanding of the nature of the Church. . . . It was the very structure of our church as a church which was attacked in the Philadelphia service. . . . Certainly a rite of ordination used by

our Church was employed in Philadelphia. A visible incorporation into the prayer of the Church thus *appears* to have taken place. Such incorporation did not take place, we believe, because the act was done in defiance of the Church whose rite was used rather than by the authorized commission of that Church. When the communal structure and process of the Episcopal Church are respected, then ordination *for* that Church is possible.[121]

The qualified support given by the bishops to the principle of women's ordination did not satisfy two of the eleven ordained in Philadelphia, Alison Cheek and Carter Heyward. On October 27, 1974, they celebrated the Eucharist at the nondenominational Riverside Church in New York.[122] There was surprisingly little reaction from official circles; however, when Cheek announced plans to celebrate the Eucharist again in November in the Episcopal Church of St. Stephen and the Incarnation in Washington, D.C., Bishop Creighton of the diocese of Virginia asked that she refrain from doing so and instructed the rector, Rev. William Wendt, to prevent it. When Wendt did not do so, Creighton refused to discipline Wendt because he said it would not accomplish anything; however, other diocesan clergy brought charges against Wendt soon thereafter.[123] As if that was not enough to force the issue, Cheek and Heyward celebrated the Eucharist again in December at Christ Church Episcopal Church in Oberlin, Ohio, where Rev. L. Peter Beebe was the rector. By the end of the year, both Wendt and Beebe were charged in ecclesiastical courts with "violations of the constitution and canons of the Protestant Episcopal Church in the United States of America, the rubrics of the Book of Common Prayer and acts violating [their] ordinations."[124] The trials of both clergymen revolved around questions of obedience to their bishops, though related issues such as the degree of authority any one congregation can exercise were also discussed.[125] Both Wendt and Beebe were found guilty and were admonished by their bishops, the lightest sentence they could be given.[126]

E. 1976 General Convention in Minneapolis

Meanwhile the debate intensified on other fronts as the denomination prepared for the decisive 1976 General Convention in Minneapolis. The subject of women's ordination became more of an issue in ecumenical dialogues.[127] New boards were established to investigate new charges against more priests and bishops.[128] In April 1975, the House of Bishops appointed a ten-member Board of Inquiry to handle the charges against the three ordaining bishops because "the core of the controversy is doctrinal."[129] Other bishops favoring ordination increased the passion of debate by threatening to resign if ordination was not approved or by stating that they would not ordain any more priests, male or female, until after Minneapolis, when they would reassess the situation.[130] In June of 1975, the Executive Council pleaded with the membership to delay further action until after the 1976 General Convention, though at least one bishop dissented from the decision because it abrogated the right of dioceses to decide their own affairs.[131] At their scheduled autumn meeting in 1975, the House of Bishops "censured" the three ordaining bishops for not obeying the jurisdictional bishops but, as Allin had requested, did not bring them to trial.[132] In anticipation of a ruling favoring women's ordination in 1976, the House of Bishops asked Allin to appoint an ad hoc committee to deal with the practical problem of ordaining women, especially those already having an "invalid" ordination.[133] At a meeting of the diocese of Missouri in February 1976, Allin withdrew his opposition to women's ordination.[134] Even more important, opposition groups formally established organizations to campaign against women's ordination for the convention.[135]

Finally, the decisive Minneapolis convention was convened. Due to the contentiousness of the ordination issue, it was decided that no applause or demonstrations would be allowed during the five days allotted to the debate, which was described even by conservative magazines as "moderate" in tone.[136] During the debate, Allin suggested a compromise that would have permitted diocesan discretion in ordaining women, but to no avail.[137] On September 15, by a decisive majority vote of 95-61, the House of Bishops approved the canonical change that applied the ordination canons equally to both sexes.[138] Thirty-eight bishops, led by Rev. Stanley Atkins, presented a statement that they could not accept the action of the House because it decided "unilaterally and in the face of the expressed disapproval of our Roman, Old Catholic and Orthodox brethren, a question which ought to be decided by an ecumenical consensus."[139] The following day, the House of Deputies, again on a vote by orders, narrowly approved the same canonical change and thereby authorized that the first ordination of women could take place on or after January 1, 1977.[140] Reports indicate there were quiet tears of joy and disappointment at the announcement of this deciding vote.[141] Much more than tears would develop as a result of this decision, as the months to come would demonstrate.

117

As in the other schisms already studied, a denominational split became imminent when an issue of some religious import became linked with a problem affecting the authoritative structures of the denomination. In this case the issue of the ordination of women, a matter of religious import to those on both sides of the question, was linked to the question of the origin of episcopal authority, which was a vital aspect of the very definition of the Protestant Episcopal Church. All that remained for the completion of this schismatic process was the organization of the dissenters into a cohesive unit that could challenge the right of the denominational leadership to lead the denomination in the tradition by which it was named.

". . . And Bare Fruit an Hundredfold": The Schism Crystallizes and Splinters

A. Fellowship of Concerned Churchmen

The controversies over the Prayer Book revision and women's ordination created a bond between conservative factions in the PECUSA that eventually led to the formation of the Anglican Church in North America. That bonding first received formal definition in the creation of the Fellowship of Concerned Churchmen (FCC).

> The FCC was formed in the summer of 1973 as an umbrella organization of Episcopal and Canadian Anglican organizations and publications which were deeply concerned by the apparently increasing slide of the Episcopal Church and the Anglican Church of Canada into heresy and apostasy. . . . [It] was forged in order to present a united front of opposition to the priesting of women, to the replacing of the Book of Common Prayer and to the tolerance of the Episcopal Church on moral issues such as divorce, abortion and homosexuality.[142]

Among its founding members were Canons Albert J. DuBois and Francis W. Read of the American Church Union, Walter Sullivan, John Aden, and Harold Weatherby of the Society for the Preservation of the Book of Common Prayer; Dorothy Faber, editor of *The Christian Challenge*; and Perry Laukhuff, editor of *The Certain Trumpet*.[143] Under Laukhuff's chairmanship from 1974 to 1978, the FCC included over fifteen organizations and publications.[144]

118

Though the 1973 General Convention declined to ordain women to the priesthood, the fact that a majority in both houses voted affirmatively for ordination prompted the FCC on October 2, 1973 to issue "Here We Stand," also known as the "Louisville Declaration." In it, they rejected any act "that would weaken or compromise the tradition" which they defined in terms of seven principles: the authority of the Holy Scriptures; the Catholic creeds; baptism and confirmation; the Holy Eucharist; the Holy Orders of Bishops, Priests, and Deacons; the integrity of the episcopate; and The Book of Common Prayer "as a doctrinal standard and a bond of fellowship, allowing moderate revision . . . provided the substance of the Faith be kept entire."[145] The most contentious principle was the fifth, where the Holy Orders were "restricted to men as the universal practice of the Holy, Catholic Church, and as intended by The Book of Common Prayer." The Declaration stated further that circumvention of any of the above Principles was

. . . a breach of communion and a formal act of schism intolerable to the faithful body of the church. . . . To perpetuate these Principles, we pledge ourselves to take every step necessary toward the continuation of the Episcopal Church in its historic form.[146]

Despite the harshness and exclusiveness expressed in the declaration, FCC spokesman DuBois denied any intention of leaving the PECUSA, promising a "fight for the issues . . . as a loyal opposition."[147]

As already noted, representatives of the ACU and the CAM protested publicly at the ordinations of the eleven women in Philadelphia on July 29, 1974. Conservatives were increasingly agitated in the last six months of 1974 when the bishops levied the lightest possible penalty on the ordaining bishops and actually approved the principle of women's ordination at their October Mexico meeting. In response to the bold celebration of the Eucharist by Cheek and Heyward in late 1974, the FCC issued "A Call to Anglican Integrity" on January 11, 1975. They spoke of the Episcopal Church being "buffeted by innovation, strange doctrines and disorder. . . . The Church is in disarray. Its membership and outreach are clearly diminishing." They pleaded with church leaders "to draw back from a course which, if continued, can only divide the Episcopal Church" and called upon others to exercise leadership in preventing this. As a remedy to this disastrous course, "A Call" prescribed increased evangelizing, "a return to reverence and beauty in worship . . . to order and discipline in the Church . . . to a renewal of the spiritual inner life."[148]

Just as it appeared that the FCC was gaining momentum, signs of dissent appeared within its ranks as members wrestled with the problem of whether they should remain in the denomination. After failing to convene an ecumenical council of the whole Catholic church,[149] the ACU's executive committee initiated a witness program entitled Episcopalians United (EU) in September 1975. EU's slogan, "No Surrender—No Desertion," encapsulated its goals of resisting the surrender of essential principles as found in the Scriptures, the Book of Common Prayer, and the tradition of the apostolic church while still promising "no desertion from the Episcopal Church in the battle for survival on the basis of its nature as declared in its Constitution, Canon Law and the Book of Common Prayer."[150] Just five months later, ACU's executive director, Charles Osborne, felt obliged to resign after receiving great criticism for his position that the ACU would not leave the Episcopal Church under any circumstances.[151] As if to indicate the point of origin for that criticism, the FCC issued in February 1976 "An Open Letter to the Bishops of the Episcopal Church," indicating that schismatic movements would be initiated if "the most immediate threat to the Church's life," the ordination of women, was approved by the denomination.[152]

By July 17, the FCC was more specific about its intentions should the ordination of women be approved at the 1976 General Convention.

> It is our conviction that any action altering the Apostolic ministry of bishops, priests and deacons, as these Orders were received by the Church and have been preserved to the present time, would be beyond the power of a General Convention and would result in the creation of a new body outside the Holy Catholic and Orthodox Church.
>
> We go into General Convention praying and fighting for the continued unity of the Church. If, however, this Convention should be led into a break with Apostolic Faith and Order, we would convene a meeting as soon as possible of those who share our concerns, allowing time for divine guidance and for the careful planning required to deal with the new situation of apostasy in the Church.[153]

Immediately following the decisions of the 1976 Minneapolis General Convention, the FCC issued "Hold Fast," lamenting that the Episcopal Church "by deciding to ordain women, officially departed from the ancient Apostolic faith and became simply another Protestant denomination." The document also asserted that by departing from the Book of Common Prayer, the denomination had "turned to new formulas which no longer express the fullness of the faith." "Hold Fast" advised "the faithful" to discontinue financial contributions to the "apostate national Church" and refuse the sacraments from its priests. A convention was promised for early 1977.[154]

At an FCC meeting in Nashville in early November 1976, the following resolution acted on that promise:

> The Fellowship of Concerned Churchmen has resolved to hold a Church Congress on September 14-15, and 16, 1977 in St. Louis, Missouri, for the purpose of presenting the spiritual principles and ecclesial structure of the continuing Episcopal Church. The Fellowship urges all faithful Episcopalians in the United States, Anglicans in Canada, and churchmen in other provinces of the Anglican Communion to attend that congress and to unite themselves with this Continuing Church.[155]

The same meeting also "commissioned the drafting of a statement of moral and devotional principles upon which a continuing church will be based, and appointed a steering committee to develop detailed plans for organization and financing."[156]

Again, just as the "continuing Church movement" seemed to be gaining momentum, signs of dissent reappeared within its ranks. Aside from the parishes that had already left the Episcopal Church to stand as independent congregations,[157] the March 1977 *Episcopalian* listed five organizational options for the dissenters. The two most prominent were the FCC and The Evangelical and Catholic Mission (ECM). While the FCC proceeded with plans for a new church structure, the ECM, "as a fellowship of orthodox churchmen who intend to work *within the structure* of the Episcopal Church," spoke of its goals to "pray, preach, and teach the full Catholic and Apostolic Faith."[158] A joint statement issued by the FCC and ECM on June 22 illustrated their similar views on the ordination of women, morality, and abortion, as well as their differences in strategy.[159]

B. The "Affirmation of St. Louis"

Before the St. Louis Church Congress convened, yet another issue formed a bond between conservatives. The group Integrity had championed the rights of homosexuals within the Episcopal Church for many years.[160] The granting of full church membership to avowed homosexuals at the 1976 General Convention was a mixed victory for the gay community, as the discussion preceding adoption of the resolution and the preamble to the resolution had

121

not condoned the homosexual act or life-style.[161] Bishop Paul Moore of New York made a more positive statement on January 10, 1977 when he ordained Ellen M. Barrett, a lesbian, to the priesthood.[162] Presiding Bishop Allin issued a statement shortly after the ordination saying that Bishop Moore had so acted out of concern for Barrett and that policy for the whole denomination had not been determined by Barrett's ordination. However, this "exception" explanation did not satisfy those who were particularly annoyed that the action preceded a study on homosexuality being prepared by church officials.[163] When Moore explained that Barrett's ordination was not a political act and "besides, homosexuality is not a sin,"[164] conservative reactions were loud and numerous.[165]

By the time of the St. Louis Church Congress in September 1977, a group of churches had withdrawn from the PECUSA and formed the nongeographical Diocese of the Holy Trinity, whose priests promised "fealty and obedience" to Bishop Albert Chambers.[166] Organizers announced Trinity as the "start of a continuing Episcopal Church";[167] they also said that

> . . . the Church Congress is for all who reject the acts of the General Convention. We repeat that kindly but firmly. No one should plan to attend who believes the General Convention is on the right track; that argument is over and done with.[168]

Perry Laukhuff, president of FCC and chairman of the St. Louis Church Congress, described its purpose: "to witness to and express the faith of the participants and to offer a platform and a provisional plan for a future church organization."[169] Discussions at the congress were concerned with what was wrong with the PECUSA[170] and the logistics for congregations leaving the denomination.[171] At the conclusion of the congress, the diocese of San Francisco became a partner with the new diocese of the Holy Trinity by claiming membership in the provisional church.

The closing session of the congress adopted the "Affirmation of St. Louis," which outlined a provisional ecclesial structure called the Anglican Church in North America (ACNA).[172] The "Affirmation" authors claimed that this "continuing Anglican Church" was necessitated by the "unlawful attempts (of the PECUSA) to alter Faith, Order and Morality (especially in their . . . General Convention of 1976)."[173] "Continuing Anglicans" did not see themselves alone in this quest for the Catholic Faith, Apostolic Order, Orthodox Worship and Evangelical Witness of the Traditional Anglican Church. We are upheld and strengthened in this determination by the knowledge that many provinces and dioceses of the Anglican Communion have continued steadfast in the same Faith, Order, Worship and Witness, and that they continue to confine ordination to the priesthood and the episcopate to males. We rejoice in these facts and we affirm our solidarity with these provinces and dioceses.[174]

The "Fundamental Principles" section of this document began with a declared "intention to hold fast the One, Holy, Catholic and Apostolic Faith of God . . . which has been believed everywhere, always and by all, for that is truly and properly Catholic." "Essential principles" of belief included the Holy Scriptures, the creeds, tradition, and the sacraments. Not surprisingly, the sacrament of the Holy Orders had its own section, where the Orders were described as "consisting exclusively of men in accordance with Christ's Will and institution (as evidenced by the Scriptures), and the universal practice of the Catholic Church." A section was also devoted to the "Incompetence of Church Bodies to Alter Truth," where none of the Ecumenical Creeds, Scriptures, or "essential prerequisites of any Sacrament" were regarded as susceptible to change. Most important to the "Affirmations" was "The Nature of the Church," where a church was described as having had its "true religion . . . revealed to man by God."[175]

We cannot decide what is truth, but rather (in obedience) ought to receive, accept, cherish, defend and teach what God has given us. The church is created by God, and is beyond the ultimate control of man.

The church is the Body of Christ at work in the world. She is the society of the baptized called out from the world: In it, but not of it. As Christ's faithful Bride, she is different from the world and must not be influenced by it.[176]

The concept of church embraced by the St. Louis "Affirmations" contrasts sharply with the one envisioned and articulated by the PECUSA House of Bishops less than one month after the St. Louis Congress. At the Port St. Lucie, Florida, meeting, Presiding Bishop Allin surprised his colleagues by offering to resign his post if the fact that he could not accept women as priests impaired his function as leader of the denomination.[177] Allin's statement of conscience prompted the House of Bishops to approve their own "Statement on Conscience," which said those who could not accept women as priests should not be discriminated against for acting according to their consciences.[178] What is of particular interest is the concept of church

123

articulated, which was envisaged as a much more dynamic, inclusive institution than that offered by the "Affirmation of St. Louis."

> We hold fast to the Anglican tradition which seeks to distinguish between what is required or not required of believers. Anglican comprehensiveness is not weak so-called "tolerance." . . . Rather it is this distinction between what must be believed by a Christian and what cannot be clearly demonstrated from basic Christian sources, together with the awareness that the Spirit leads the Church into further penetration of the Truth (John 14:26, 16:13). Since Jesus Christ is the Truth, there can be no adding to the Truth, but there is a promise of deepened understanding of that Truth as the Spirit guides the Church. It is tempting to cry to others as to ourselves, "The Church—love it or leave it." Yet to say it hastily assumes that we already know fully what it is, much less what the Church will be like when brought at last to "nothing less than the full stature of Christ" (Ephesians 4:13). Leaving this Communion or forcing others to leave interferes with the process of searching together for that fuller penetration of the Truth.[179]

Hence this debate compelled even the liberal bishops, whose distaste for theological debate has already been noted, to describe their Anglican tradition in terms of a religious truth.

C. Emergence of the Anglican Catholic Church et al.

By early January 1978, five dioceses were eager to have their bishops consecrated.[180] On January 18 at Augustana Lutheran Church in Denver, four priests were consecrated as bishops of the Holy, Catholic, and Apostolic Church[181] in the rite given by the 1928 Prayer Book. The consecrator was Albert A. Chambers, retired bishop of Springfield, who was assisted by Bishop Francisco J. Pagtakhan of the Philippine Independent Church. Episcopal tradition stipulates that there be three bishops conducting the consecration[182] so there was some question about the validity of the first consecration of Rev. C. Dale Doren.[183] Once Doren's consecration had taken place, he, together with Chambers and Pagtakhan, consecrated Bishops Robert S. Morse, Petter F. Watterson, and James O. Mote.[184] Hours after the consecrations, the Most Rev. Donald Coggan, Archbishop of Canterbury, announced that he "would not recognize either the consecrations or any organization formed by the new bishops." ECC officials had a ready answer: "Canterbury does not define Catholicism but only Anglicanism."[185]

Having acquired bishops and established dioceses, the ACNA held a constitutional assembly October 16, 18-21, 1978 in Dallas. Seven dioceses at the convention represented by 140 delegates changed the name of the provisional church to the Anglican Catholic Church (ACC).[186] In his keynote address, Perry Laukhuff pleaded for unity and asked that the delegates remember "to remain Catholic in an Anglican way."[187] Despite such noble pleas, the assembly was torn by controversy. At one point, two of the four bishops, together with the delegates from their dioceses, walked out of the convention protesting the seating of the delegates from the newly formed Southwestern diocese. It appears the two bishops were protesting the fact that they had not been involved in the formation of the new diocese. Only after twenty-four hours of bargaining and the assurance that the new diocese would not have a vote at the assembly did the bishops and their delegates return.[188]

When the intended business of the convention was finally acted on, a constitutional proposal was drawn up designating the 1928 Prayer Book as the official service book and the "Affirmation of St. Louis" as a positional statement.[189] As a result of this assembly, it was decided that four dioceses needed to ratify the proposed constitution to bring the ACC into existence. On May 4, 1979, the Diocese of the Southwest elected Robert C. Harvey as bishop and became the fourth diocese to ratify the constitutional proposal.[190] On May 26, five ACC bishops met at Grand Rapids and announced the legal existence of the Anglican Catholic Church. A subsequent meeting of the five named Bishop Doren as Prime Bishop of the College of Bishops.[191]

Of the seven dioceses that met in Dallas, two refused to ratify the constitution and so did not join the emerging ACC.[192] Though Christ the King and the Southeastern dioceses adopted the "Affirmations of St. Louis," they thought the ACC's concept of church only "pseudo-Catholic";[193] both wanted a tradition much more in the Anglo-Catholic style. This was only the beginning of the splintering of the "continuing Anglican Church."[194] Of the groups who left the PECUSA, the ACC was the largest and remained so for some time thereafter.[195]

Among the post-1976 groups, most use the 1928 Prayer Book and all ordain only males to the diaconate, priesthood, and episcopate. Most do not belong to the National Council of Churches or the World Council of Churches, as they do not want to be connected with the liberalism of those groups.[196] There is a common concept of the church among those of the "continuing Anglican Church" that is perceived as a vessel that has already received God's truth and whose mission is to preserve that truth.[197] That

125

concept is embodied in the "Affirmations of St. Louis" adopted as a formative position statement by the Anglican Catholic Church and those who first left the Episcopal Church after the Minneapolis General Convention of 1976.

In a denomination where ecclesiastical "comprehensiveness" is considered a virtue, the schism of 1978 was an unusual and unsettling event. Undoubtedly it had its origins in tensions that developed long before 1978. At least some of that tension developed as a result of the turbulence of the 1960s, but an even greater polarization occurred in the Prayer Book controversy. However, that polarization did not become potentially schismatic until an issue, the emotionally volatile ordination of women, dominated the denominational gatherings. When that passionate issue of significant religious import was linked with the establishment of alternative authority structures, ecclesiastical schism was the result.

FIVE

Conclusion:
The Fuel of Schism

Gustaaf Johannes Renier described the historian as one whose task is "to see one particular portion of life right side up and in true perspective."[1] He roundly condemned those who try to use history for any purpose other than making the story of the past generally available.[2] Even with this severe judgment of the "supererogating historian,"[3] Renier asserted that a limited complementary relationship exists between the historian and the sociologist. For Renier, as a historian, the sociologist needs history and its data to support generalizations regarding human groupings; however, the historian can also learn from the sociologist. "By reading the views of sociologists, he may find it easier to search for relevant events."[4]

Two Existing Sociological Models

The two extant sociological models articulated by Takayama and Wilson of the phenomenon of schism, already mentioned, deserve attention here in the effort to understand the schismatic histories. Of the two, Wilson's model is much more detailed in its schematic outline; therefore his will provide the foundation for this discussion. Basing his model on Neil Smelser's,[5] Wilson identifies five determinant stages, "each of which is dependent on the occurrence of the preceding stage."[6]

> a) structural conduciveness which are those constructs of the group that permit given types of collective behavior[7]
> b) structural strain or the ambiguities, deprivations, conflicts and discrepancies which give rise to the behavior[8]
> c) mobilizing agent where the behavior of the leaders is usually regarded to be of primary importance[9]

d) precipitating factor or a specific event/situation that prompts the group to take action[10] and

e) social control including all those counter-determinants which prevent or interrupt the accumulation of determinants outlined above. Some of these forces of social control would minimize structural conduciveness and strain while others would only aggravate them.[11]

Wilson notes that the cornerstone of the whole scheme is structural strain, which he defined as "a disjuncture between norms and values." Values are paramount in system control. Norms are the application of those values. In the need to "get a fit" between norms and values, strain occurs. The manifestations of this inappropriate fit are uneasiness, frustration, and an increasing inhibition to the social rules one is expected to follow. A schismatic group will have its origins in a dispute over norms and allegations that the main group has departed from those implicated in the values of the original movement.[12]

Because Wilson sees religious movements as particularly ideological, he maintains that there is a "fund" of issues over which conflict "legitimately" could take place.

It is not sufficient, then, to point to the doctrinal disputes, or to the underlying social differences in cases of schism. We must look also at strains inherent in the movement which these other factors may only exacerbate.[13]

In his discussion of the sociology of schism, Takayama describes his key concern as the discovery of the "major conditions for the development of severe conflicts that may lead to denominational splits." He holds that

. . . the major conditions for divisions are a high degree of environmental permeability and ideological concern regarding the legitimacy of organizational authority and the behavior of the leadership, rather than the doctrinal purity per se.[14]

In developing his thesis, Takayama says that denominations are challenged from the outside by external conditions. The mode of response by the organization depends on the nature of the religious tradition, the type of religious leadership, the internal strains, the social characteristics of its members, and the secular interests involved.[15]

In addition to the external challenges or strains, Takayama maintains that there are internal strains that are ubiquitous and particularly critical: the discrepancies between the "ideal" and the "actual," and shifts in the authority structure.[16] The first involves the very nature of religious organizations in that they are the repositories of "ideals" of truth, value commitments, and aspirations. In affecting the lives of people, these ideals are subject to conventional norms and procedures.[17] Shifts in the authority structure are related to this ideal/actual discrepancy because as an organization becomes more efficient in pursuing the goals set out for it, the more readily it will be viewed as "overcentralized" by the constituency it is attempting to serve. For Takayama these internal sources of strain illustrate "the internal structural inconsistencies and their accompanying uncertainties which always exist and develop beneath the apparent stability and continuity of the denominational structure."[18]

According to Takayama, internal strains by themselves are not likely to cause splits in denominations. "Rather, external environmental changes act as catalysts to internally generated and unresolved strains, producing crises." Denominations are not susceptible only to the environmental changes that are a major source of uncertainty for all organizations, but they are particularly susceptible to cultural and moral aspects of that environmental change. As Takayama says, "Denominations have highly environmentally permeable boundaries." Any erosion of community cohesion, uprooting of traditional human bonds, or shifting of cultural values and symbols will have a profound influence on institutional religion.[19]

Takayama complements Wilson in many ways; he is particularly helpful in adding some details to the first two stages of Wilson's scheme. Takayama helps explain why the structural organization of religious groups may be conducive to severe conflict. "Environmentally permeable boundaries" leave religious groups open to the influence of external catalysts, which are an important factor in the production of Wilson's structural strain. More important for the historian of schism, Takayama's factors, which determine the mode of response by the organization, are helpful in identifying aspects of Wilson's "structural conduciveness."[20] There are also great similarities between Takayama's "internal strain" and Wilson's "structural strain," which are especially obvious in the synonymous meanings of Takayama's ideal/actual and Wilson's value/norm terminology. Both authors agree that the discrepancy between the "ideal and the actual" (Takayama) or the "values and the norms" (Wilson) is the cause of structural strains that eventually may become great enough to produce conflict and even schism.

Applying Wilson and Takayama

These complementary sociological perspectives regarding the patterns of schism are helpful in analyzing the histories of the schisms related here. All three of the denominational conflicts involved disputes regarding how the values or ideals were to be translated into norms or actuals in the modern context. The conservative forces in each dispute wanted to preserve the pristine meaning of the founding ecclesiastical documents; little concern was evident for the liberal sentiment that the documents were increasingly irrelevant to the contemporary age. This "static" interpretation of the denominational faith was accompanied by an intolerant attitude toward all those who did not share the identical version of the founding truth. Their liberal or moderate counterparts in the dispute were much more tolerant of other interpretations, even of the static conservative type, because the liberals viewed the interpretation of the founding documents as a dynamic enterprise. For them, no divine truth could ever be enshrined in human words; even the best formulations had to be interpreted in the light of growing scientific knowledge, modern theological advances, and the contemporary context.[21] These disputes over what constituted the ideals and the actuals were a vital aspect of what Takayama and Wilson call "structural" or "internal" strain.

By their nature and by virtue of their existence in a pluralistic, modern society, American denominations are environmentally permeable, subject as they are to every outside influence that any other individual or group experiences. When denominations that have been sheltered through regional or ethnic isolation grope their way toward a more open, national existence, they find themselves subject to external influences and structural strain soon develops. This is certainly the case with the LC-MS and PCUS denominations, which increasingly were exposed to the broader American way of life in the twentieth century and to an aggressive secularism in the 1960s. As these two denominations were exposed to unfamiliar influences, they were forced to grapple with the problems associated with modern methods of biblical interpretation, the extent of ecumenical relations, and the degree of historic confessional subscription. Whereas these concerns were not especially relevant to the LC-MS when it was a predominantly ethnic church or to the PCUS so long as it was a southern regional church, once these denominations considered and then became increasingly identified with American mainstream denominationalism, they were forced to deal with the application of their historic confessional ideals in the modern situation. That attempted application produced internal or structural strains as different interpretations of these actuals or norms were championed by various groups. Though it is not appropriate to make the same case for the regional or cultural isolation of the Episcopalians, this denomination also felt the pinch of falling membership and declining revenues. As a result, Episcopalians were earnestly attempting to make a statement of their relevance to the American public with the Prayer Book revision (begun in 1949) and later the ordination of women. Some conservatives thought such innovations to be destructive of the very essence of Episcopalianism, especially since the core beliefs of the tradition were so often defined in terms of the Prayer Book and the apostolic succession. No Episcopalian would want to argue with the premise that the denomination had to make an effort to remain relevant. However, some conservatives thought the effort would be truer to the ideals of the Episcopalian tradition if such relevance was sought along more evangelical or Catholic lines.

Takayama also identifies "shifts in the authority structure" as a ubiquitous and critical aspect of the structural strain. This characteristic is most obvious in the PCUS history, where a restructuring was underway that threatened conservative voting strength. In a more subtle way, the locus of denominational power was also shifting from the presbyteries to the General Assembly. For instance, the equalization policy increased the power of the Assembly to the detriment of the congregations and presbyteries offering the gift. This type of authority shift also occurred in the Episcopalian schism as dioceses and bishops looked increasingly to the General Convention for leadership. Evidence for this is found in the attempts to eliminate the vote by orders convention procedure that demanded unanimity within the diocese before a diocesan vote could be counted and that ensured the strong voices of the dioceses at the General Convention. When voting by orders was eliminated, the diocesan foundations of ecclesiastical government were eroded and the General Convention effectively became a collection of delegates from a national denomination that prescribed actions for its members.

While the LC-MS did not experience any legislative shift in authority, under Preus there was a definite shift to a centralized authority concentrated in the person of the synodical president.[22] By controlling appointments to the seminary Board of Control, the Board for Missions, and the powerful convention floor committees, Preus ensured that his office controlled the important decision-making bodies and even the convention itself. Further, his publication of "A Statement of Confessional and Scriptural Principles" was

131

more than an indication of the conservative attempt to reinterpret Lutheran ideals for a modern situation. It effectively made the synodical president not only the "pastor of pastors" but also the chief synodical theologian. This also involved a shift in the authority structure because until that time, the Commission on Theology and Church Relations had been the theological voice of the synod; under Preus's supervision, the CTCR became a mere echo of presidential authority.

Other aspects of the structural strain in each denomination have already been mentioned. Glock and Ringer (*To Comfort and to Challenge*) cite the disparity between clergy and laity as a major source of strain in the Episcopal denomination; that disparity is obvious at the conventions where the House of Bishops and House of Deputies so often voted contrary to each other. Concordia Seminary was obviously a moderate leader in the LC-MS in matters of biblical interpretation, but the failure to relay that knowledge to the grass roots of the denomination resulted in a gulf between denominational scholars and the laity; consequently, conservative allegations of heresy had a ready audience in the Missouri laity when the crisis developed. A chasm was also developing between denominational leadership, or the "radical ecumenists" as conservatives called them, and certain factions of the PCUS, who thought their church could continue to function as if it was the isolated South of yesteryear. These are all aspects of structural or internal strain that Wilson and Takayama discussed in their models of schism; they are all an important part of the beginning of the schismatic process.

However, using the sociological models of either Takayama or Wilson to follow the story line of the examples will not result in the completion of any of the schismatic histories. Wilson and Takayama have helped us understand the factors involved in denominational conflict and what heightens that conflict; thereby they have given us clues in the "search for relevant events" in the early stages of a schism. But once it has been established that the denominations are structurally conducive to schism and that a certain structural strain has developed, neither sociologist helps us understand what keeps the conflict going until it finally concludes in schism.

Takayama and Wilson leave several other questions unanswered. Does the discrepancy between the ideal/value and the actual/norm continue to operate in each of the schisms past the stage of structural strain? Since both authors virtually ignore the religious issues of the conflict once the structural strain is established, what is it that carries the conflict past the stage of internal conflict or structural strain to the finality of the schism? Or to put it another way, why do some conflicts result in schism and others do not? Without doubt the personalities involved sustained the conflict and acted as mobilizing agents in the schism. As well, a crisis situation developed in each historical example that precipitated the schism. But what is it that made these denominational conflicts schismatic while other conflicts are resolved less dramatically? Is it the amount or type of internal/structural strain and environmental dissensus/precipitating factors that makes the difference? Is it the personalities involved that make one conflict schismatic while in another situation reconciliation results? Or is it merely the coincidence of particular internal and external strains that is critical to the continuing process of schism?

Obviously there are no conclusive answers. However, the examples indicate that Wilson and Takayama have not given sufficient emphasis to the power of the religious concerns that drives the polarizing conflict through to its schismatic end. In all the schisms studied, the religious considerations affected the schismatic event beyond merely producing some internal problems identified in Wilson's and Takayama's models as "structural" or "internal" strain. Lewis Coser provides some insights regarding the potency of religious differences in situations of social conflict.

Coser's Propositions and Their Applications

Relying heavily on the theories of Georg Simmel in his analysis of *The Functions of Social Conflict*, Coser argues that conflict is a "form of socialization" that is functional as well as dysfunctional. He identifies two types of conflict: realistic, which arises when people clash in pursuit of claims that have a specific content; and unrealistic, those conflicts in which hostility and aggression are the sole content of the conflict.[23]

Coser proposes that conflicts tend to be more intense and radical when the parties involved are in a very close relationship with one another. This is due to the fact that when conflicts do arise, the whole of each party's identity is threatened by the conflict.[24] Most relevant is Coser's example of the heretic. While the renegade or the apostate attacks the past of the originating group or the values of the originating group itself, the heretic poses a more serious threat by upholding the values of the group and claiming that he or she is conforming more strictly to those standards. Intense hostility is a distinct possibility in such situations: "In conflicts within a close group, one side hates the other more intensely the more it is felt to be a threat to the unity and the identity of the group."[25]

Coser relates this point to the study of sects and churches.

> Groups engaged in continued struggle with the outside tend to be intolerant within. . . . Such groups tend to assume a sect-like character: they select membership in terms of special characteristics and so tend to be limited in size, and they lay claim to the total personality involvement of their members. Their social cohesion depends upon total sharing of all aspects of group life and is reinforced by the assertion of group unity against the dissenter. The only way they can solve the problem of dissent is through the dissenter's voluntary or forced withdrawal.[26]

Sects tend to be structurally rigid so that any conflict that has simmered for a period of time can very well explode when fueled by other conflicts of even more volatile force.[27] On the other hand, groups assuming a more churchlike character do not presume total involvement of the individual; they are also larger and more structurally elastic, "allowing an area of tolerated conflict within."[28] Churchlike structures usually solve a conflictual situation with legislation that offers a compromise to the disputing parties, thereby alleviating any pressure that could develop if the conflicts were not resolved or at least confronted.[29]

Coser's propositions regarding intimacy and sect-type denominations are very helpful in explaining why the conflicts within the PCUS and LC-MS developed into schisms. Both denominations leaned toward the sect-side of the ecclesiastical spectrum because of their isolating tendencies that were based on peculiarities of ethnicity and geography. Hence both tended to have a certain intimacy about them that other, more broadly based, denominations lacked. Their heavy emphasis on a strict confessional subscription helped maintain a barrier between themselves and other denominations, even those of the same broad confessional background. Each denomination's social isolation bred not only an intimacy but a dependence among its members that extended beyond the purely religious needs. When the unity of such closely knit denominations was threatened by dissenters within, whether moderate or conservative, the intensity of conflict escalated rapidly because denominational unity and security were so dangerously threatened by intimates in the faith.

The same linkage between sectlike characteristics and rapidly escalating social conflict cannot be made for the Episcopal Church. Though sectlike characteristics may be influential, they are not the only determinants in producing schism. The other factors involved may be even more determinative. Coser's discussion of functional and detrimental conflicts is very helpful in uncovering those other factors.

> Internal social conflicts which concern goals, values, or interests that *do not contradict the basic assumptions* upon which the relation is founded tend to be positively functional for the social structure. Such conflicts tend to make possible the readjustment of norms and power relations within groups in accordance with the felt needs of its individual members or sub-groups.[30]

On the other hand, conflicts that involve group "goals, values or interests" or that do "contradict the basic assumptions upon which the relation is founded" may be detrimental to the functioning of the group.[31]

> Internal conflicts in which the contending parties *no longer share the basic values* upon which the legitimacy of the social system rests threaten to disrupt the structure.[32]

The schismatic histories studied all exemplify Coser's principle of functional and disfunctional conflicts. All three denominations had experienced tensions and polarizations prior to the schismatic actions. All had issues, both religious and sociological, that endangered their unity. The Episcopal Church had witnessed heated disputes over the propriety of many of its social programs and had experienced a widening gulf between its clergy and laity. The PCUS had debated ferociously its ecumenical ties, the extent of its social involvement, and theological positions on many matters as it moved into mainstream American denominationalism. The LC-MS had witnessed factions fighting over the missions of the church, its ecumenical ties, and various questions of social import as the distinctly ethnic background of its membership faded into the American melting pot.

Yet none of these denominations experienced schisms of any major proportion until "the basic assumptions upon which the relation is founded" were questioned. In the PCUS, the 1969 decisions to write a new confession and to explore ties with another denomination whose ties to the PCUS confessional standards could be questioned were pivotal in stirring the voices of schism. In the LC-MS, Preus's new "Statement" was regarded by moderates as an effort to supplant the established Lutheran Confessions with another standard. In the Episcopal Church, the effort to revise the Prayer Book and ordain women attacked the very foundations of the church, namely the apostolic succession and the values found in the 1928 Book of Common Prayer. The polarizations in each denomination intensified and the rhetoric of schism began shortly after church members questioned these "basic assumptions." Wilson's scheme, enhanced with Takayama's insights, is still helpful, as mobilizing agents and precipitating factors are involved in all the schisms studied. However, it is the questioning of and disagreement over the basic assumptions of each denomination as those assumptions are found in the denominational standards that propelled the polarization from structural strain to schism. Without due consideration to these religious concerns, there is an insurmountable gap in the understanding of the schismatic process.

Coser also discusses how ideological concerns and the appeal to those ideological concerns can have a continuing power in a conflict even once the conflict is well underway.

> Conflicts in which the participants feel that they are merely the representatives of collectivities and groups, fighting not for the self but only for the ideals of the group they represent, are likely to be more radical and merciless than those that are fought for personal reasons.[33]

In elaborating this point, Coser demonstrates that, in viewing oneself as the representative of the group, one may also come to view oneself as the embodiment of the group's purposes and power. Making sacrifices for the organization increases one's loyalty to it, and in relinquishing one's personal interests one also projects upon the group one's own personality. Threats to the group are regarded as threatening to one's own personality; hence bitterness and intensity of conflict are escalated even though strictly speaking the conflict has been objectified by this appeal to a higher ideal.[34]

There is also a polarizing function that occurs between the adversaries when self-interested motivation on either side is rejected and each is committed to some higher cause.

> The effect of objectification here may be exactly the reverse of unifying: it draws a sharp line of distinction between the antagonists with the result that each is more likely to seek to defeat the other through intensive struggle. . . . What is integrated primarily is each party within itself.[35]

Again, there is ample evidence for this proposition in the denominational schisms studied. Even after the mobilizing agents have been identified and the precipitating factor or crisis has occurred, the battling factions appealed to a higher principle. Usually that higher principle was a confession or other ecclesiastical standard, but often it was something a bit more nebulous, like the "Spirit of Christ" or "true Presbyterianism" or the "tradition of our fathers." Even when the debated issue was something as blatantly materialistic as the fate of property rights, Presbyterian conservatives appealed to a higher authority like the right of the congregation vis-à-vis the presbytery. Without this appeal, the mobilizing agents would be regarded as self-serving schismatics; with this appeal to religious concerns, the processes of schism were fueled through their final stages.

Not only are the mobilizing forces legitimized with this appeal to a higher ideal but the precipitating factors or specific events that result in the schismatic action are easily identifiable. For instance, in the Episcopal Church the ordination of women struck at the very heart of the principle of apostolic succession; in the PCUS, the deletion of the "escape clause" meant that conservative congregations could be forced into an ecumenical union with which they disagreed or a confession to which they could not subscribe. The precipitating factor in the Lutheran schism is a little less obvious, probably because the groups that eventually left the denomination wanted to remain but were effectively thrown out by the conservative authorities. Still, one can reasonably argue that the 1973 convention in New Orleans was the crisis event that forced moderates to realize that their existence within the denomination was of a limited duration.

Most important is the fact that the precipitating factor was an event that left the schismatic party with no option other than to pursue its vision of what it meant to be true to the pristine standards outside the denomination. Not only would remaining inside the denomination make it much too difficult to pursue the vision, but remaining in fellowship with the majority could compromise the vision. This pattern is especially obvious in the Presbyterian and Episcopalian schisms but is also true in the LC-MS if one identifies the schismatic party as the conservative party that held the majority power.[36] In other words, the conservative groups in each dispute were concerned not only that the presence of the liberal party within their ranks would make it more difficult to remain truly Presbyterian, Lutheran, or Episcopalian, but also that the very presence of the liberals or moderates was a compromise to the type of church they were seeking to obtain.

Concluding Comments

Over three decades ago, scholars felt compelled to show that "more than doctrine divides the churches."[37] In an ecumenical spirit that deemphasized the significance of religious differences of belief, polity, and ritual, commentators spoke of schisms caused by sociological factors such as race, geography, and ethnicity as well as more idiosyncratic features such as personality clashes and struggles of ecclesiastical politics.[38] Increasingly, the religious aspects of ecclesiastical disputes lost importance.

This tendency is reflected in the sociological models of schism available. Though these models are helpful in identifying many of the events in the schismatic processes, they lack any serious consideration of the religious concerns of the groups involved. The religious issues are more than a "fund" out of which conflict could "legitimately" arise as in Wilson; nor are they merely part of the "internal strain" to which Takayama ascribes only secondary importance in the conflict that leads to schism. Rather, the religious issues are central to the dispute; as well, these issues have the power and the passion to escalate the conflict, even to the point of schism. Since polarizations and tensions existed in the denominations long before the schismatic event began, one can surmise that the religious issues could not be simply any religious issue nor could the religious issue of one denomination have fueled the schismatic process of another. Without the issues that impinged on the core religious content of the traditions involved, there is no reason to believe that the disputes would have escalated into schisms. When the religious issues became concerned with what it meant to be a Presbyterian, Lutheran, or Episcopalian, the schismatic process had its ideological fuel.

One should not infer from these conclusions that sociological factors were of no consequence; an interdependence between the sociological events and religious matters was obvious in all three schisms. That interdependence became even more apparent in light of Coser's observations that ideological concerns as a higher principle have a tremendous power in legitimizing a social conflict.

This study has demonstrated that the participants' concerns must be taken seriously and that the religious elements in any development must be accorded serious consideration. As Richard Weaver said, "ideas have consequences."[39] In the 1970s, ideas acted together with existing sociological tensions to produce ecclesiastical schism and the formation of three new denominations.

Notes

CHAPTER ONE

1. K. Peter Takayama, "Strains, Conflicts and Schisms in Protestant Denominations," in *American Denominational Organization*, ed. Ross P. Scherer (Pasadena, California: William Carey Library, 1980), p. 299.
2. William Rusch, *Ecumenism—A Movement Toward Church Unity* (Philadelphia: Fortress Press, 1985), pp. 95ff.
3. For instance, the merger of the Lutheran Church in America (LCA), American Lutheran Church (ALC), and the Association of Evangelical Lutheran Churches (AELC) in the U.S.A. to form the ELCA in 1987 and the formation of the Evangelical Lutheran Church in Canada in 1984.
4. Takayama, "Strains and Schisms," p. 299.
5. The schism occurring in the Lutheran Church-Missouri Synod has been the topic of two books and one dissertation, but none has told the whole schismatic story and all the authors were interested parties in the event. See Frederick W. Danker, *No Room in the Brotherhood: The Preus-Otten Purge of Missouri* (St. Louis, Missouri: Clayton Publishing Company, 1971); Kurt E. Marquart, *Anatomy of an Explosion: Missouri in Lutheran Perspective* (Fort Wayne, Indiana: Concordia Theological Seminary Press, 1977); Larry Neeb, "The Historical and Theological Dimensions of a Confessing Movement within the Lutheran Church-Missouri Synod" (Doctorate of Ministry dissertation, Seminex, 1975). The same can be said of John Edwards Richards, *The Historical Birth of the Presbyterian Church in America* (Liberty Hill, South Carolina: The Liberty Press, 1987).
6. Takayama, "Strains and Schisms," pp. 298-329; John Wilson, "The Sociology of Schism," in *A Sociological Yearbook of Religion in Britain*, ed. Michael Hill (London: SCM Press, 1971), 4: 1-19.
7. Takayama, "Strains and Schisms," p. 299, 311, 313.
8. Wilson, "Sociology of Schism," pp. 5-6.
9. For three of the more obvious examples of this tendency to disparage religious considerations, see E. T. Clark, "Non-Theological Factors in Religious Diversity," *Ecumenical Review* (July 1951): 347; Christopher Dawson, "What About Heretics? An Analysis of the Causes of Schism," *Commonweal* 36 (18 September 1942): 513-16; and C. H. Dodd, G. R. Cragg, and Jacques Ellul,

Social and Cultural Factors in Church Divisions (New York: World Council of Churches, 1952).

10. My use of the word "tradition" here is heavily dependent on Edward Shils's discussion in *Tradition* (Chicago: The University of Chicago Press, 1981), especially pp. 213-309. A couple of points seem of particular interest. First, tradition is maintained because people want to continue it; they are unable to live without it (p. 213). Second, most traditions of belief are vague, so that the tradition is easily reinterpreted for the changing circumstances in which they occur (p. 264).

11. Rodney Stark and William Sims Bainbridge, *The Future of Religion Secularization, Revival and Cult Formation* (Berkeley: University of California Press, 1985), p. 107.

12. Paul Tillich, *Dynamics of Faith* (New York: Harper & Row, Publishers, Inc., 1957). In borrowing this phrase, I do not use the full import of Tillich's definition of faith. Rather, I emphasize the all-consuming nature of the "religious" matter that elicits such drastic action by the schismatic groups.

13. There is no attempt to find an ideal type, as the differences between the histories are just as important and are duly noted. As Crane Brinton said of his study of revolutions and states, this work will "attempt to establish, as the scientist might, certain first approximations of uniformities." *The Anatomy of Revolution*, rev. ed. (New York: Vintage Books, 1938), p. 7.

CHAPTER TWO

1. T. Watson Street, *The Story of Southern Presbyterians* (Richmond, Va.: John Knox Press, 1960), pp. 10-11. Lefferts A. Loetscher, *A Brief History of the Presbyterians*, 4th ed. (Philadelphia: The Westminster Press, 1983), p. 64. Also *The Presbyterian Outlook* (hereafter abbreviated *PO*), 25 January 1971, p. 2.

2. This principle of freedom within limits continues to be the basic position of American Presbyterianism with regard to doctrine, though how much freedom and how much limit has often become an issue. Street, *Southern Presbyterians*, p. 11.

3. Sydney E. Ahlstrom, *A Religious History of the American People*, 2 vols. (Garden City, New York: Image Books, 1975), 1: 559-66.

4. Loetscher, *Brief History*, pp. 97ff.

5. Street, *Southern Presbyterians*, p. 64. See also Arthur C. Piepkorn, *Profiles in Belief: The Religious Bodies of the United States and Canada* (San Francisco: Harper & Row, Publishers, Inc., 1978), 2: 314, where Thornwell is quoted: "The provinces of church and State are perfectly distinct and the one has no right to usurp the jurisdiction of the other." Southern Presbyterians never professed a nonchalance regarding the problems of the world but maintained that its problems could not be solved without starting with the individual and his or her salvation. This was the church's chief concern; the resolution of social

problems was left to the efforts of individual children of God who had been saved.

6. There was no doubt regarding the "Federal government" in question here, as the same resolution described it as that "central administration appointed and inaugurated according to the forms prescribed in the Constitution of the United States." Morton H. Smith, *How is the Gold Become Dim: The Decline of the Presbyterian Church, U.S. as Reflected in Its Assembly Actions* (n.p.: The Steering Committee for a Continuing Presbyterian Church, 1973), pp. 4-5.

7. Street, *Southern Presbyterians*, p. 56; Loetscher, *Brief History*, p. 102; Smith, *How is the Gold*, pp. 6-7; Piepkorn, *Profiles in Belief*, p. 314.

8. Richards, *Birth of Presbyterian Church*, p. 27.

9. Quoted ibid., p. 30.

10. Smith, *How is the Gold*, pp. 10-11.

11. Maurice W. Armstrong, Lefferts A. Loetscher, and Charles A. Anderson, *The Presbyterian Enterprise: Sources of American Presbyterian History* (Philadelphia: The Westminster Press, 1956), p. 213.

12. "The Church of Christ is a spiritual body, whose jurisdiction extends only to the religious faith and moral conduct of her members. She cannot legislate where Christ has not legislated, nor make terms of membership which he has not made. The question, therefore, which this association is called upon to decide, is this: Do the Scriptures teach that the holding of slaves, without regard to circumstances, is a sin, the renunciation of which should be made a condition of membership in the Church of Christ?" Ibid., quoting from *Minutes of General Assembly*, Old School, 1845, p. 16.

13. Richards, *Birth of Presbyterian Church*, p. 38. Jack P. Maddex argues an interesting thesis in "From Theocracy to Spirituality: The Southern Presbyterian Reversal in Church and State," *Journal of Presbyterian History* 54 (Winter 1976): 438-57. Maddex says that the PCUS was vocal in political issues until the slavery issue forced it to adopt this "spirituality" perspective rather than condone the demolition of this beloved southern institution. See also Thomas Cary Johnson, "The Presbyterian Church in the United States," *Journal of the Presbyterian Historical Society* 1 (1901): 74-79, for the same type of argument.

14. Richards, *Birth of Presbyterian Church*, pp. 40-41. See also Armstrong et al. *Presbyterian Enterprise*, p. 200.

15. See R. McFerran Crowe's articles in *The Presbyterian Journal* (hereafter *PJ*), 26 April and 2 May 1972, regarding the drastic effects of the northern union on Presbyterianism in the United States.

16. Smith, *How is the Gold*, p. 12. Also Crowe, *PJ*, 26 April 1972, p. 7; *The Presbyterian Guardian* (hereafter *PG*), June 1966, p. 77.

17. Street, *Southern Presbyterians*, pp. 84-85.

18. Smith, *How is the Gold*, p. 12. In successive attempts by the northern church at reunion (1887-88, 1894-95, 1904-06), the spirituality of the southern church was cited every time. Other reasons usually cited included the mission work

among blacks, the place of women, the principle of property rights, and assorted doctrinal issues.

19. In the northern church and previous to this in the south, only two-thirds of the presbyteries needed to approve such amendments. Ernest Trice Thompson, *Presbyterians in the South 1890-1972*, 3 vols. (Richmond, Va.: John Knox Press, 1973), 3: 216.

20. Piepkorn, *Profiles in Belief*, p. 318; Loetscher, *Brief History*, p. 124.

21. Thompson, *Presbyterians in the South*, pp. 216-17.

22. Pastoral letter from the General Assembly of 1898 to the PCUS membership, quoted ibid., p. 218.

23. As Samuel Hill says in *Southern Churches in Crisis* (New York: Holt, Rinehart and Winston, 1967), pp. 36ff., the homogeneous nature of the southern religious population means there is more similarity among Baptists, Methodists, and Presbyterians in the South than between their northern and southern counterparts. In a book on southern religion, Hill says there is no need for a section on Catholicism. Such an absence of pluralism and diversity among the popular denominations is due to a regionalism caused by the factors inherent in a frontier and rural situation where cultural insulation is the norm. For more on this topic of the PCUS as a southern regional entity that "buttressed a conservative social philosophy with an orthodox theology," see Hill, *Religion in the Southern States* (Macon, Georgia: Mercer University Press, 1983), pp. 409ff; and Charles R. Wilson, *Religion in the South* (Jackson: University Press of Mississippi, 1985), pp. 156ff.

24. Kenneth K. Bailey, *Southern White Protestantism in the Twentieth Century* (New York: Harper & Row Publishers, 1964), p. 24.

25. Thompson, *Presbyterians in the South*, p. 215.

26. Liberal commentators liked to highlight the fact that most of the schismatic leadership and congregations originated in Alabama and Mississippi. See Wilson, *Religion in the South*, p. 168; also *PO*, 25 October 1971, p. 10; 20 December 1971, p. 2; 3 September 1973, p. 9.

Especially relevant is the increased urbanization of the South after 1950; see Thompson, *Presbyterians in the South*, pp. 411, 486. Some historians link this demographic reality to increased tension within the denomination as the deep rural South remained theologically conservative and prosegregationist while the increasingly urbanized areas favored theological liberalism and racial integration; see also David M. Reimers, "The Race Problem and Presbyterian Union," *Church History* 31 (1962): 213.

There is no question that there was conflict within the denomination regarding integration and the support of the civil rights movement (see David Edwin Harrell Jr., *White Sects and Black Men in the Recent South* [Nashville: Vanderbilt University Press, 1971], pp. 66ff.), but this issue must be seen within the larger context of the spirituality of the church.

27. Takayama says that the significance of theological differences in the PCUS schism "lies in the fact that they provided ideological weapons to the conservative coalition to attack alleged violation of constitutional norms and

departure from historic Presbyterian doctrine of the PCUS," but the "critical factors in the split were social changes and shifts of cultural-moral aspects of the society." "Strains and Schisms," p. 317.

28. Bailey says that the southern rural homogeneity was disturbed around the turn of the century by immigration, industrialization, and new intellectual currents. *Southern White Protestantism*, p. 4. Others argue that an increasing emphasis on evangelism and scholarship in the PCUS forced some southern Presbyterians to deal with the views of their northern cousins and that exposure instilled some with liberal thoughts and methods. Loetscher, *Brief History*, p. 123, Street, *Southern Presbyterians*, p. 112. Still other authorities maintain that the real change took place much later during the Second World War, when the South and its religion were carried out of their cultural isolation into the mainstream of American social life and denominational Christianity. Hill, *Religion in the South*, pp. 418ff., Thompson, *Presbyterians in the South*, pp. 9ff.

29. A prime example was in 1906 when, in an effort to begin union talks with the Cumberland Presbyterians, an active group managed to get the General Assembly to change its strict stance regarding election by amending the Confession of Faith with a footnote that stated all infants were of the elect. *PO*, 8 March 1971, p. 5. A great protest followed this decision, led by Old School stalwarts who claimed that such a change endangered the integrity of the Confession. Within two years, the footnote was stricken from the confessional standards. Ibid; see also Thompson, *Presbyterians in the South*, pp. 219-22.

30. Thompson, *Presbyterians in the South*, p. 225.

31. For example, Rev. A. J. McKeludy, editor of *The Presbyterian Standard*, challenged southern Presbyterians to fight for racial justice, civic reform, and humane child labor laws. Ibid., p. 264. Others, like Rev. Walter Lee Lingle of Union Theological Seminary, taught favorably on Rauschenbusch's *Christianity and Crisis*. Ibid., p. 265.

32. Thompson, *Presbyterians in the South*, p. 338. See also Loetscher, *Brief History*, p. 123. Thompson made this assertion as a self-proclaimed PCUS liberal, but conservative historians agree with this assessment. See Smith, *How is the Gold*, pp. 20ff.

33. Smith, *How is the Gold*, p. 37. The act also said that if any minister had any reservation about the confession or catechism, "He shall at the time of his making said declaration declare his sentiments to the Presbytery or Synod," who could still admit him to the ministry if his scruple was judged by the Presbytery "to be only about matters not essential and necessary in doctrine, worship, or government." Conservatives also held that this same position was reaffirmed by the Synod in 1736. Ibid., pp. 37-38.

34. Ibid., p. 25.

35. Biblical criticism was dismissed in the 1880s and 1890s with logic like that of Henry C. Alexander, professor of New Testament at Union Seminary, who coined the phrase "if false in one point, then false in all." Loetscher, *Brief History*, p. 120. Even the attacks of science were turned aside, with defenders of the faith like G. C. Armstrong who said "God cannot err, science may err."

Thompson, *Presbyterians in the South*, p. 217. Thompson also tells that inerrant inspiration, rigid Calvinism, "jure divino Presbyterianism," and the nonsecular mission of the church continued to be taught at Union Seminary until 1930 (p. 208).

36. In *A Conservative Introduction to the Old Testament* Cartledge maintained that a conservative believer did not have to ascribe to scriptural inerrancy in all matters; Thompson, *Presbyterians in the South*, p. 496. Others of this same mind in the Presbyterian Church at the time included John Bright and James Robinson at Union Seminary.

37. By the 1960s, the *Southern Presbyterian Journal (SPJ)* had become *The Presbyterian Journal*. In addition to a defense of verbal inerrancy as the only legitimate means of interpreting the Scriptures, *SPJ* also called for a more spiritual church and opposed forced racial integration. Street, *Southern Presbyterians*, p. 118; *PJ*, 3 May 1967, pp. 11-12. See also Thompson, *Presbyterians in the South*, p. 488.

38. *PJ*, 19 January 1966, p. 17. Also 31 August 1966, p. 12; 10 January 1968, p. 13.

39. *PJ*, 8 June 1966, p. 23; 30 November 1966, p. 19.

40. Smith, *How is the Gold*, pp. 26ff.

41. An example of this conservative inability to prove an official doctrinal change regarding scriptural interpretation can be found in ibid., pp. 23-33.

42. Ibid., p. 40, quoting *Minutes of General Assembly*, 1898, p. 223.

43. These were not unlike the "fundamentals" of the fundamentalist controversy, as they included doctrines such as the "infallible truth and divine authority of the Scriptures," the virgin birth, the incarnation, the sacrificial death for the expiation of sins, and Christ's resurrection with the same physical body. Ibid., p. 41.

These essentials seem to be a belated reply by the PCUS to the widely publicized Auburn Affirmations (1924) written by members of the northern church. The authors of Auburn opposed the idea of "essential and necessary doctrines," which they argued would have the effect of amending the Westminster Confessions. In this regard, Auburn's authors quoted the Westminster Confession's modesty regarding claims of infallibility (XXI, iii): "all synods or councils since the apostles' time . . . may err, and many have erred; therefore they are not to be made the rule of faith or practice but to be used as a help in both." Armstrong et al., *Presbyterian Enterprise*, pp. 284-85.

44. Smith, *How is the Gold*, quoting Minutes, U.S. 1947, p. 45.

45. Armstrong et al., *Presbyterian Enterprise*, p. 268. The northern church had made the additions as part of an effort to effect a union with the Cumberland Presbyterian church, which denied the strong Calvinism of the Westminster Confession. Smith, *How is the Gold*, p. 52. Even PCUS liberals who favored the changes agreed that these chapters were added to de-emphasize Calvinism and elevate the views of Barth, Brunner, Bonhoeffer, and Tillich. Thompson, *Presbyterians in the South*, p. 12.

46. Smith, *How is the Gold*, pp. 52-53. "In the Gospel, God declares His love for the world and His desire that all men should be saved . . ." Ibid., p. 53.
47. This same report stated that the doctrine of election was not essential to reformed theology. Ibid., p. 57.
48. See Richards, *Birth of Presbyterian Church*, p. 237; *PJ*, 17 May 1961, p. 3; Thompson, *Presbyterians in the South*, pp. 12, 495.
49. Smith, *How is the Gold*, p. 56.
50. Conservatives argued this was a clear departure from the Book of Church Order. *PJ*, 27 May 1964, p. 3; 26 May 1965, p. 5; Smith, *How is the Gold*, p. 61.
51. This action was taken despite the fact that in 1961 the moderator of the General Assembly ruled out of order a proposal asking the PCUS to publish its disdain of capital punishment because it was "out of accord with the Constitution." Smith, *How is the Gold*, p. 63.
52. The assemblies cited had all affirmed that God created man directly and not through any other means such as evolution. Ibid., p. 58. Bailey discusses how this antievolution campaign was characteristic of southern regionalism. *Southern White Protestantism*, pp. 87ff.
53. See Smith, *How is the Gold*, pp. 73-76. Not surprisingly, the conservatives charged that the "few" given power were usually liberals.
54. Richards, *Birth of Presbyterian Church*, pp. 86, 242.
55. *PO*, 11 September 1972, pp. 5-7.
56. For an excellent article describing what PCUS conservatives expected Presbyterianism to be, see G. Aiken Taylor, "What is a Presbyterian?," *PJ*, 26 July 1967, pp. 7-9.
57. Piepkorn, *Profiles in Belief*, p. 316.
58. Thompson, *Presbyterians in the South*, p. 305.
59. Piepkorn, *Profiles in Belief*, p. 316; Thompson, *Presbyterians in the South*, p. 305; Smith, *How is the Gold*, p. 135.
60. Piepkorn, *Profiles in Belief*, p. 317.
61. Thompson, *Presbyterians in the South*, p. 419. Justification for the silence was that black power had been abused in the days of Reconstruction, that blacks were politically inept and dangerous, and that the South treated blacks better than did the North. In his eloquent summary, Thompson says that the southern Presbyterian church "in accord with its distinctive doctrine of the 'spirituality of the church' remained silent as disenfranchisement proceeded, and as segregation became first the practice and then the law of the various states. But its silence gave consent, and such cries as appeared gave religious sanction to the legal enactment" (p. 252).
62. Ibid., p. 540; Smith, *How is the Gold*, p. 151; Loetscher, *Brief History*, p. 121.
63. Thompson, *Presbyterians in the South*, p. 540. In 1956, *PJ* released a formal statement that "voluntary segregation in churches, schools and other social relations is for the highest interests of the races and is not un-Christian. . . . Racial integrity is something to be fostered, not to be broken down, and those

145

who would force a program countenancing and looking to the amalgamation of the races are doing great harm to the finding of the ultimate solution" (ibid.).

64. "It is debatable whether this conclusion [that the church should lead in the matter of integration] can really be based upon Scripture. As one looks at the stance of the Southern Presbyterians towards the slavery issue a century before, one finds that the Church refrained from getting into such social issues, and trying to decide such issues, because the Bible itself did not do so. The fact is that slavery had been legislated in the Bible, and therefore the Presbyterians in the South refrained from condemning slavery as sinful. *The same can be said of the matter of segregation.* The fact is that God Himself segregated Israel from the Canaanites. It is debatable as to whether the Church should get into the matter of trying to change that particular cultural pattern, and branding one form of culture sinful as opposed to another." Smith, *How is the Gold*, p. 153 (emphasis mine). The same attitude, with a slightly different emphasis, can be found in *PJ*, 9 August 1967, p. 18.

65. Smith, *How is the Gold*, p. 176; *PJ*, 1 July 1970, pp. 4-7; 11 June 1969, p. 5; 23 July 1969, p. 8; 3 December 1969, p. 4.

66. Smith, *How is the Gold*, pp. 160-61.

67. Project Equality was a program whereby businesses were boycotted and harassed if they did not hire minorities.

68. These included the use of face masks, hand-clapping, rock music, and psychedelic colors, all of which conservatives found objectionable and too secular.

69. An anonymous donor had provided $50,000 after the 1970 General Assembly had approved the practice in principle. *PJ*, 1 July 1971, pp. 4-7.

70. *PJ*, 1 February 1967, p. 3; 15 March 1967, p. 4.

71. *PJ*, 10 January 1968, p. 12. *The Presbyterian Survey* was the official periodical of the PCUS. The editors of *PJ* found particularly offensive a study book story that approved of the marriage of a Christian girl to a Hindu boy with a Unitarian minister and a Brahmin priest officiating. A neat summary of this movement toward more worldly concerns can be found in *PJ*, 13 October 1971, pp. 7-10.

72. Smith, *How is the Gold*, p. 162. Opposed to the paper's position, L. Nelson Bell, editor of *PJ*, argued that Christians as individuals "must" be concerned with social, political, and economic issues but that the church "does not exist as an ecclesiastical organization to wield secular power. Her message is spiritual and her power is spiritual" (21 December 1966, p. 13).

73. Thompson, *Presbyterians in the South*, p. 511; Smith, *How is the Gold*, pp. 162-63.

74. Smith, *How is the Gold*, pp. 109, 113-14.

75. Thompson, *Presbyterians in the South*, pp. 266, 268; Smith, *How is the Gold*, p. 130; Street, *Southern Presbyterians*, p. 114. Arguments against membership in the FCC and NCC usually centered on the secular and left-wing nature of the pronouncements made by these organizations, but there were also hints of

the old regional church still operating. For example, in the 18 January 1967 edition of *PJ*, the editor, G. Aiken Taylor, said, "We are Presbyterians. And the thing we resent most about the NCC is that it has replaced the constitution of the Church and the courts of the Church as the source of authority from which is derived most of what is going on in the church. We just don't like to look around and see everyone snake-dancing to the tune fiddled from New York especially when the tune is consistently off-beat" (p. 12).

76. Smith, *How is the Gold*, p. 131; Piepkorn, *Profiles in Belief*, p. 318. Conservatives were increasingly critical of the amount of money spent on the WCC, not only relatively small direct contributions but also through the increasingly socially active Board of National Ministries and the Board for World Missions.

77. Smith, *How is the Gold*, p. 119; Thompson, *Presbyterians in the South*, p. 301. Smith gives a good summary of those occasions when union with the northern church was stymied by the southern conservatives.

78. Smith, *How is the Gold*, p. 120; Loetscher, *Brief History*, p. 124; Street, *Southern Presbyterians*, p. 117.

79. Bailey, *Southern White Protestantism*, p. 126; Reimers, "The Race Problem," pp. 213-15. At this time, the PCUS was still calling for more fully black churches and could not boast one interracial congregation.

80. "One of these churches [northern] believes that 'brotherly love' demands the abrogation of segregation and the allowing of races to intermingle without any adherence to racial lines. The other branch [southern] believes that Christian love and helpfulness can be shown and be given while preserving racial integrity." *SPJ*, 24 September 1952, p. 3.

81. Smith, *How is the Gold*, pp. 114, 116.

82. *Presbyterian Guardian* (hereafter *PG*), September 1966, p. 103; *PJ*, 1 June 1966, pp. 12-13; 16 November 1966, p. 13; Smith, *How is the Gold*, p. 117.

83. *PJ*, 20 March 1968, p. 5; *PJ*, 3 April 1968, p. 4; *PJ*, 10 April 1968, p. 4.

84. *PJ*, 22 May 1968, p. 6. This seemed to confirm *PJ* editor Bell's concerns of 1 June 1966, p. 13: "The siren call to inclusivism, a willingness to subordinate matters of doctrine or polity for the sake of ecclesiastical union is seductive and dangerous."

85. Smith, *How is the Gold*, pp. 125-26; *PJ*, 25 October 1967, p. 6; 5 March 1969, p. 4.

86. Through the latter half of the 1960s, consultations were carried on with the RCA, a conservative denomination much like the PCUS but with a wider geographic and demographic base. At the General Assemblies of both denominations in 1968, union was approved and the proposal sent to the presbyteries for their consent. *PJ*, 19 June 1968, p. 4; 26 June 1968, pp. 6-7. In the PCUS the required three-quarters majority was easily obtained due to conservative support, but in the RCA the presbyteries defeated the proposal. *PJ*, 2 April 1969, p. 5; 26 June 1968, p. 7; 5 March 1969, p. 13; 19 December

1967, p. 5; 26 June 1968, p. 6; Piepkorn, *Profiles in Belief*, p. 318; Smith, *How is the Gold*, p. 126.

87. The title page of every issue described *PJ* as a "Presbyterian weekly magazine, devoted to the statement, defense and propagation of the Gospel, the faith which was once for all delivered to the saints." The *Journal* was published in Weaverville, North Carolina.

88. Thompson, *Presbyterians in the South*, p. 489.

89. *PO*, 12 February 1973, p. 5.

90. *PJ*, 27 September 1967, p. 11.

91. Dean Hoge, *Division in the Protestant House* (Philadelphia: The Westminster Press, 1976), p. 35.

92. *PJ*, 5 June 1968, p. 6. The text of Dendy's address to the closed meeting of the Fellowship of Concern can be found in *PJ*, 27 September 1967, p. 9; see also *PJ*, 31 January 1968, p. 6.

93. Liberals alleged that 1964 was simply the year that the Continuing Church Committee (CCC), a conservative lobby group organized in 1945, took on the new name of Concerned Presbyterians. This charge has some foundation in fact since it is a bit too much of a coincidence that the CCC disappeared so quickly after the CP organized. *PO*, 12 February 1973, p. 5.

94. Richards, *Birth of Presbyterian Church*, pp. xiv, 113-14.

95. *PJ*, 27 September 1967, p. 12; 31 January 1968, p. 6; 10 July 1968, p. 6. There are probably a number of reasons why the CP did not disband. The most obvious is that they felt the liberals had managed to grab control of the denominational leadership and that their views would not get a fair hearing without the profile offered by an organizational structure. It did not help that Dendy was a liberal who, in his appeal to CP, asked for the very thing the conservative organization opposed: "I appeal to you to recognize the fact that under the theology of our Church there is room enough for us who have differences of opinion, and that we ought to respect the right of people to differ." *PJ*, 27 September 1967, p. 12.

   PJ reported on 14 August 1968 that the leaders of the disbanded Fellowship of Concern began a new movement after the CP's announcement that it would continue. This movement pledged to work for "a radical reformation, renewal and unity of the visible Church beyond denominationalism, confessionalism and all else which hinders the oneness" (p. 5). However, the organization never seemed to receive a name and in any event, was not instrumental in further events, at least as an organization.

96. Richards, *Birth of Presbyterian Church*, pp. xiv, 188.

97. *PO*, 12 February 1973, pp. 5-6.

98. Smith was an avid pilot who, flying his own Cessna 150, established and taught a circuit of classes in Birmingham, Harrisburg, Kosciusko, Memphis, and Jackson. The operation was incorporated as the Reformed Theological Institute in 1965 and changed its name to Reformed Theological Seminary in 1966. *PJ*, 29 October 1969, p. 8.

99. Ibid., pp. 7, 9. Thompson, *Presbyterianism in the South*, p. 503.
100. Wallace Henley, "Southern Presbyterians: the Gap Widens," *Christianity Today* 13 (23 May 1969): 32-33. The chief ones are given in the text but two others worth mentioning include: a committee was established to study the unrest within the church and one of its first duties was to "visit" Reformed Theological Seminary; the recommendations of a theological study were adopted, which deemed evolution as no longer contradictory to Christian belief. *PJ*, 5 May 1969, p. 5.
101. This constitutional amendment required and received the approval of a majority of the presbyteries before the end of 1969. Only the second approval of the 1970 General Assembly was needed for the amendment to be effective. *PJ*, 26 November 1969, p. 5.
102. Conservatives were particularly annoyed at the way this amendment had been approved. Three presbyteries had cast their votes in the negative but since there had been some misunderstanding regarding what the resolution meant, they were able to change their votes immediately prior to the 1969 convention. As a result, the adoption of union presbyteries came as a something of a surprise to all, especially the conservatives. *PJ*, 14 May 1969, p. 5.
103. The Permanent Judicial Commission had studied the problem and delivered this conclusion to the 1967 General Assembly. Smith, *How is the Gold*, pp. 125-26.
104. The 1969 Assembly also ignored the Judicial Commission's warning in 1968 that providing for union presbyteries would mean that synods and presbyteries would have more power than the General Assembly. Ibid., p. 125.
105. *PJ*, 7 May 1969, p. 4; *PO*, 11 September 1972, pp. 11-13. The committee members were announced in *PJ*, 25 June 1969, p. 4, where it was noted that all were liberals. Henley observes that this is not surprising since the Assembly had commissioned the liberal moderator to assign the committee members. "Southern Presbyterians," p. 32.
106. *PJ*, 14 May 1969, p. 7. The Joint Committee for Union between the UPUSA and PCUS was also known as the Committee of 24 because it was composed of twelve representatives from each denomination.
107. For the best history of how the Confession came into being, see Edward A. Dowey Jr., *A Commentary on the Confession of 1967 and an Introduction to the Book of Confessions* (Philadelphia: The Westminster Press, 1968). Dowey was chairman of the original drafting committee.
108. Some of the titles include "UPUSA: A Creedless Church?," 14 December 1966, pp. 11ff.; "Confession or Concession?," in 26 April 1967, p. 15; "Is the UPUSA Christian?," 24 January 1968, pp. 7ff.; "That Galloping UPUSA," 23 March 1966, p. 12. In 1966, CP's counterpart in the UPUSA, the Presbyterian Lay Committee, had placed ads in 150 metropolitan American newspapers condemning the Confession for "undermining certain basics of our Christian faith." *PJ*, 12 January 1967, pp. 8ff.
109. Loetscher, *Brief History*, p. 165. The preface of the document itself says "This Confession is not a 'system of doctrine,' nor does it include all the traditional

topics of theology." *Journal of Presbyterian History* 61, no. 11 (Spring 1983): 186.

110. Loetscher, *Brief History*, p. 162. Part I was titled "God's Work of Reconciliation," Part II "The Ministry of Reconciliation," and Part III "The Fulfillment of Reconciliation."

111. James Daane, "Presbyterians Draft New Confession," *Christianity Today* 9 (23 October 1964): 38.

112. Previously the question had been whether the Scriptures were accepted as the only infallible rule of faith and practice.

113. Previously the vow had asked the ordinand to "receive and adopt" the confessions "as containing the system of doctrine taught in the Holy Scriptures." *PG*, March 1967, p. 43.

114. In addition to the dangers of losing the historic confessional base through union with the UPUSA or the adoption of another confession, there existed an increasing fear of being absorbed into COCU because COCU wanted organizational union before doctrinal agreement. *PJ*, 2 July 1969, p. 20.

115. In an article entitled "Go Along or Go Forth," William Hill of the PEF called for separation from the PCUS if a new confession similar to the 1967 Confession of the UPUSA is adopted, the PCUS merges with the UPUSA, or the PCUS merges with COCU. *PJ*, 8 October 1969, pp. 7-9.

116. During the 1960s, Rev. Donald B. Patterson, a missionary, had organized an informal prayer group that became known as the Presbyterian Ministers Prayer Fellowship. Other than holding prayer meetings on or about the time of Journal Day in North Carolina, the group did little except encourage one another to pray regularly. In August 1968, they elected their first officers, with Patterson as chairman and Morton H. Smith as recording secretary. Richards, *Birth of Presbyterian Church*, p. 77.

117. Almost without fail conservatives mention divergent attitudes toward the Bible as the root of all the liberal attitudes and therefore the divisions in the PCUS. See *PJ* editor L. Nelson Bell's "What are the Divisions?," *PJ*, 3 September 1969, p. 7.

118. Richards, *Birth of Presbyterian Church*, pp. 87-88; *PJ*, 8 October 1969, pp. 12-13.

119. Richards, *Birth of Presbyterian Church*, p. 88.

120. Ibid., p. 91. There were many accusations later that not all the signatories were PCUS ministers (*PJ*, 5 November 1969, p. 3), which the *Journal* responded to by printing their names (24 December 1969, p. 5).

121. Richards, *Birth of Presbyterian Church*, p. 88. *PO*, 12 February 1973, p. 6 called the PCU the ministerial arm of CP. Until 1973, PCU published *Contact*, when the periodical's name changed to *Continuing Toward*.

122. Liberals were very critical of this theological perspective of the declaration wherein signatories and other conservatives equated the Westminster Confessions with the "system of doctrine" taught in the Scriptures. A representative article of this type of criticism is by Vernon S. Broyles, "Is the PCUS problem 'Confessional Fundamentalism?'," *PO*, 11 September 1972, pp.

7ff. In opposition to this fundamentalism, Broyles, like the authors of the Auburn Affirmations, quoted the Westminster Confession.

123. Richards, *Birth of Presbyterian Church*, p. 93; *PJ*, 17 December 1969, p. 8.

124. *PJ*, 17 December 1969, p. 7; *PG*, November-December 1969, p. 126. Richards says that CP gave PCU "their valued support." *Birth of Presbyterian Church*, p. 113. Observers from other reformed denominations were also present.

125. *PG*, November-December 1969, p. 126. See Richards, *Birth of Presbyterian Church*, pp. 104-10, for the full text of Barker's speech. Another speaker, Dr. Strong, pastor of Trinity Church, Montgomery, predicted that the "liberal forces" would create a series of crises for the conservatives. Strong promised that no matter what the liberals do, "there will be a continuing Presbyterian Church." *PJ*, 17 December 1969, p. 7.

126. *PJ*, 15 March 1967, p. 20. Though not specifically indicated, the reference may be to CP and the Fellowship of Concern.

127. Ibid.

128. *PJ*, 28 January 1970, p. 5.

129. *PJ*, 12 February 1973, p. 6. For instance, they were opposed to COCU and UPUSA union if such unitive movements were not pursued on the basis of "Reformed faith and order." *PJ*, 4 November 1970, p. 24. The CFOP periodical was *The Open Letter. PJ*, 15 April 1970, p. 20.

130. Richard, *Birth of Presbyterian Church*, pp. 114-15. The regulars usually included W. J. (Jack) Williamson, an attorney from Greenville, Alabama, and secretary of CP; Kenneth S. Keyes, CP president; Roy LeCraw, former mayor of Atlanta and CP vice president.

131. The PCUS and UPUSA Boards of Education agreed to more cooperative ventures (*PJ*, 29 April 1970, p. 5), which eventually did lead to a union of the boards in 1971 (*PJ*, 10 March 1971, p. 6), well before denominational union was achieved in 1983. Loetscher, *Brief History*, p. 165. The Joint Committee of 24, established to discuss union between the PCUS and UPUSA, claimed that the union presbyteries were evidence of a de facto union that "already exists to such an extent that it would be impossible to extricate them." *Reformed World*, June 1970, p. 81; *PJ*, 11 February 1970, p. 4; 19 April 1970, p. 5.

132. *PJ*, 15 October 1969, p. 4.

133. G. Aiken Taylor explained the change on page 3 of the same issue. "In these critical days we want to make it perfectly clear that a new church is in the making and we don't mean COCU. God willing and enough Presbyterian types standing fast, a Reformed and evangelical witness greater than the generation has known will soon emerge."

134. Richards, *Birth of Presbyterian Church*, p. 122; *PJ*, 11 February 1970, p. 4.

135. Conservatives cringed at the thought of such an avowed ecumenist leading the denomination but complimented Benfield for the fairness with which he conducted affairs at the General Assembly. *PJ*, 1 July 1970, p. 3.

136. The talks were also expanded to include other reformed denominations. *PJ*, 8 July 1970, p. 16.

137. A parallel conservative proposal calling for a "provisional synod" to be set up as a "holding body" to receive congregations and presbyteries wishing to enter the proposed Church of Christ Uniting was defeated easily in a voice vote. *PJ*, 1 July 1970, p. 4.

138. *PJ*, 1 July 1970, p. 6. So many protests had been lodged against this restructuring plan released in the spring of 1970 that the Assembly felt it had no other choice. Despite the insistence of the committee responsible for drafting the plan that it was based on geography and demography rather than theological predispositions of the populations involved, many conservatives claimed that their voice would be lost. Others were just upset that traditional boundary lines were being redrawn. *PJ*, 15 April 1970, p. 9.

139. The General Assembly agreed with the committee responsible for considering the resolution that *Colloquy* "is a resource material compiled by Christians to help the Church better understand the world." *PJ*, 1 July 1970, p. 6.

140. Ibid., p. 7. Conservatives objected to abortion as a general principle, but they were particularly upset by the last of these justifying circumstances.

141. Ibid.

142. Ibid., p. 3.

143. *PJ*, 8 July 1970, p. 16; *PG*, September 1970, p. 49.

144. *PJ*, 19 August 1970, p. 4.

145. II Corinthians 6:17 "Wherefore come out from among them, and be ye separate, said the Lord, and touch not the unclean thing, and I will receive you." The entire text of Williamson's speech at Journal Day is in *PJ*, 16 September 1970, pp. 7-11.

146. Ibid., p. 8.

147. The text of this working model can be found in *PJ*, 11 November 1970, p. 7.

148. The reference was to the UPUSA's *Book of Confessions*, which had included the Westminster Confession as one among other confessions, the Confession of 1967 being one of those others. PCUS conservatives here asserted that they would not belittle Westminster as the UPUSA had done in their *Book of Confessions*, since for them Westminster was the paramount confession.

149. The PCUS approved women's ordination at the 1964 General Assembly.

150. The 1970 General Assembly gave youth delegates full voting privileges and set up a system whereby a certain quota of youth delegates was guaranteed for every Assembly. Conservatives felt that this measure endangered the office of the elder as the foundation stone of church government.

151. Other social matters also often mentioned in these resolutions include the 1970 abortion ruling, fighting hunger as a primary priority in the mission of the church, the support of Project Equality, and approval of the "new morality." *PJ*, 11 November 1970, pp. 7-8.

152. The conservatives had constitutional grounds to deny even considering a COCU proposal since union negotiations were to be considered only with those churches espousing reformed doctrine. The General Council, or year-round administrative and executive arm of the General Assembly, decided not to take

any action against the presbyteries passing these resolutions, though concern was voiced and action seriously considered. *PJ*, 2 December 1970, p. 5.

153. *PJ*, 10 February 1971 , p. 8.

154. Editor G. A. Taylor of *PJ* confirmed this dichotomy between clergy and laity in the denomination but his perspective was that, "Laymen are no longer following blindly." He was also critical of the ecclesiastical professionals such as the administrators, seminary teachers, and other paid workers for having an "overwhelming preference for social action while the church members indicated an overwhelming preference for evangelism. . . . Laymen must make their influence even more strongly felt." *PJ*, 10 February 1971, p. 14. The clergy-laity split had been noted as early as 1965 when Blake observed that at the General Assembly the clergy, generally better educated and more cosmopolitan, consistently voted liberal, while the laity voted conservative. See Howard Carson Blake, "Southern Presbyterians Sort Out the Issues," *Christianity Today* 9 (May 21, 1965): 41-43. Though this observation probably has some foundation, the clergy-laity split along liberal-conservative lines is more than offset by the emergence of the conservative clerical groups, the PEF, and the PCU.

155. With this provision in place, the seceding congregations would not have to worry about losing their property. This provision later developed into what was called the "escape clause."

156. The constitution demanded that all union plans receive the approval of three-quarters of the presbyteries. Conservatives had appealed earlier to the Permanent Judicial Commission's opinion of 1967, which affirmed this principle but seem to be willing to ignore it here. At this point most conservatives were more interested in leaving the denomination than in constitutional adherence. *PO*, 8 February 1971, p. 3.

157. This text appeared in the PCU publication *Contact*, April 1971. See also Richards, *Birth of Presbyterian Church*, pp. 141-42; *PJ*, 21 April 1971, p. 6; *PO*, 3 May 1971, p. 3.

158. *PJ*, 27 January 1971; 18 August 1971, p. 12; *PO*, 15 February 1971, p. 10; *PG*, Feb 1971, p. 32. By August of 1971, delegates to the NPRF meetings represented ten reformed denominations, while another two reformed denominations recognized the NPRF. *PJ*, 11 August 1971, pp. 4-5.

159. *PJ*, 28 April 1971, p. 4; 18 August 1971, p. 12; *PG*, April 1971, p. 60.

160. *PG*, April 1971, p. 60; *PJ*, 18 August 1971, p. 12.

161. *PG*, December 1971, p. 143.

162. *PJ*, 16 June 1971, p. 7; 19 February 1961, p. 12.

163. *PJ*, 19 February 1969, p. 6.

164. Conservative missionaries, increasingly unhappy with the social and liberal pronouncements of the Assembly, had been less than enthusiastic supporters of denominational directives, thereby alienating congregations from the BWM. As the national churches assumed more independence, the missionaries listened less to PCUS authorities, following rather the will of the conservative congregations

they had nourished. *PJ*, 7 May 1969, p. 6. *PJ* editor Taylor reflected conservative resentment to the increasing centralization of authority by the BWM when he called the directive an enforced "obedience to the BWM rather than the Gospel." *PJ*, 16 June 1971, p. 12.

165. *PJ*, 7 May 1969, p. 6.

166. After all other denominational agencies had received 100 percent of their budgeted receipts, direct gifts to the BWM were not subject to this equalization formula. *PJ*, 3 December 1969, p. 5. On another level, equalization meant that any donations made to the local church treasury were split proportionately among all the denominational causes. *PJ*, 16 June 1971, p. 7.

167. *PJ*, 14 May 1969, p. 9.

168. *PJ*, 3 December 1969, p. 5.

169. *PJ*, 20 May 1970, p. 7; 12 August 1971, p. 5; 16 June 1971, p. 7-8.

170. *PJ*, 16 June 1971, p. 9; 6 October 1971, pp. 10-11; 30 September 1970, p. 5; 28 October 1970, p. 6; 2 December 1970, p. 5.

171. ECOE officials claimed that they were only providing a "place to jump to" for evangelical missionaries, whose funding had been curtailed or even cut off by the BWM. *PJ*, 20 January 1971; 6 October 1971, p. 10.

172. *PJ*, 3 February 1971, p. 5; 17 March 1971, p. 6; *PO*, 29 March 1971, p. 3. The pertinent part of the 1941 statement condemned all appeals for money when they "carry a definitely implied questioning of the soundness and validity of the work done through our own agencies; and when the work for which appeal is made is one which parallels that of our benevolent agencies."

173. *PJ*, 17 February 1971, p. 4. These compromises were almost exactly what the conservatives had requested at their summit meeting with the liberals. *PO*, 12 July 1971, p. 3.

174. There were many reasons for this, including the fact that the UPUSA black caucus did not think the PCUS had progressed enough in race relations and, as a result, the UPUSA had already decided at its General Assembly of 1971 to postpone the union vote for one year. PCUS officials wanted to coordinate with the UPUSA as much as possible. As well, the restructuring timetable adopted would have been impossible without adjustments in the union timetable. *PO*, 1 March 1971, pp. 3-4; 17 May 1971, p. 3; 28 June 1971, p. 1; *PJ*, 17 February 1971, p. 4; 30 June 1971, p. 6. Editor Taylor of the *PJ* also argued that the liberals were cooling to the union plan because they were becoming aware that the result of UPUSA union would be a radical realignment of conservatives in a "continuing church" and liberals in a "union church" just as the NPRF had envisaged. *PJ*, 5 May 1971, p. 12.

175. The property issue had been a matter of contention for some time and became more important as the threats of schism escalated. No one questioned that the congregation had "beneficial ownership" of the property. However, because the presbytery usually had helped the congregation acquire its property, there was some question as to whether the congregation had to obtain the permission of the presbytery before making any major changes in the property (i.e., selling it)

as congregations were obliged to do in the UPUSA. Conservatives argued that the property belonged to the congregation even though this was not good Presbyterian thinking, as *The Presbyterian Outlook* gladly pointed out. 12 April 1971, pp. 4, 8; 3 May 1971, p. 8. The committee's ruling obviously favored those conservative congregations considering secession because it said that the "disposition of the property of a participating church rests in the will of the congregation of that church." However, the report also gave serious emphasis to the fact that a congregation "solemnly promises and covenants . . . to walk together . . . on principles of faith and order of the PCUS. . . . It [the congregation] is a part of an extended whole, living under the same ecumenical constitution and therefore subject to the inspection and control of the presbytery, whose business it is to see that the standards of doctrine and rules of discipline are adhered to by the particular Churches." *PO*, 7 June 1971, p. 10.

176. Civil courts had tried to decide this issue earlier with little success, as a series of court cases in Savannah dating back to 1968 demonstrated. *PJ*, 2 October 1968, p. 4; 12 February 1969, p. 4; 3 April 1969, p. 4; 28 January 1970, p. 4; 4 February 1970, p. 12. The result of this battle, confirmed here by the committee's report, was that ownership had to be decided on neutral legal principles. *PJ*, 18 February 1970, p. 5.

177. *PJ*, 30 June 1971, p. 4; *PO*, 12 July 1971, p. 9. The very existence of this dispute demonstrates that the perception that the conservative element was geographically limited may have some validity. However, the fact that neither side in the dispute could agree on which alignment was more favorable to conservative purposes indicates that the geographical alignment, if existent, was unclear.

178. This denunciation came from the wording of a minority report that was much more critical of the ECOE than the majority report. The majority report had asked the ECOE "to bring its policies and practices into conformity to the requisites of the standards of our Church and to a proper respect for the prerogatives of our Board of World Missions, desisting from activities which are directly destructive of those interests which properly belong to our board." All the majority report recommendations were included in the adopted resolution. *PJ*, 30 June 1971, p. 7; *PO*, 26 July 1971, p. 4.

179. *PG*, October 1971, p. 106.

180. *PJ*, 30 June 1971, p. 7. Conservatives did manage to change the resolution regarding Vietnam involvement so that no demands were made for unconditional withdrawal from the area. *PO*, 26 July 1971, p. 4.

181. *PJ*, 30 June 1971, p. 8; *PO*, 12 July 1971, p. 5.

182. *PO*, 28 June 1971, p. 3. Conservatives did agree that Ben Lacy Rose, whose chief opposition was the conservative candidate James Kennedy, handled Assembly affairs with great fairness. *PJ*, 23 June 1971, p. 3; 7 July 1971, p. 3. Conservatives were also disturbed by the deployment of the new official alcohol policy at the Assembly, which they charged liberated some to excess. *PJ*, 13 October 1971, p. 10.

183. *PJ*, 23 June 1971, p. 4; 30 June 1971, pp. 3, 4ff.; Richards, *Birth of Presbyterian Church*, p. xv.

184. *PJ*, 30 June 1971, p. 7.

185. *PO*, 12 July 1971, p. 8. Even this became a source of controversy as liberal PCUS moderator Rose added W. Jack Williamson of CP as PCUS representative while UPUSA moderator, Mrs. Stair, added E. Dowey, whose chief complaint with the proposal was that it conceded too much to the conservatives, especially in allowing conservative congregations not to join the union plan by exercising their rights under the escape clause. *PG*, October 1971, p. 106. Conservatives claimed that the obvious intent of the resolution was to get two conservatives on the Committee of 24, but that this had been intentionally overlooked by the UPUSA. *PJ*, 4 August 1971, p. 6; 25 August 1971, p. 3; 16 February 1972, p. 5. There is no question that the conservatives had a legitimate complaint here, though one could also argue that Stair enabled representation of a sizable portion of her constituency with her appointment of Dowey to a committee of moderates.

186. *PJ*, 7 July 1971, p. 14. See also E. R. Chandler, "Death Knell for Southern Presbyterians," *Christianity Today* 15 (2 July 1971): 31 and Chandler, "Massanetta Mandates," *Christianity Today* 15 (16 July 1971): 32.

187. *PJ*, 1 September 1971, p. 7.

188. *PJ*, 25 August 1971, p. 4; *PG*, October 1971, p. 106; Richards, *Birth of Presbyterian Church*, p. 171. *The Presbyterian Outlook* (20 September 1971, p. 3) claimed that the CFOP was also part of the Steering Committee, but there is no evidence to support this. In October, the CFOP officially announced that they would not be a part of the split (*PJ*, 25 October 1971, p. 5) and that they were seeking support for their position of remaining within the PCUS denomination and fighting for the conservative perspective from there. *PO*, 8 November 1971, p. 3.

189. Richards, *Birth of Presbyterian Church*, pp. 171-72.

190. Ibid., pp. 190-92; also *PO*, 12 June 1972, p. 3 (emphasis mine). C.O.F. stands for Confession of Faith with the section number following indicating its location; B.C.O. stands for Book of Church Order.

191. *PJ*, 20 October 1971, p. 5; *PO*, 21 February 1972, p. 4. Among the many questions that surfaced regarding the proposed continuing church was whether it was going to be national and racially inclusive. *PJ*, 3 November 1971, pp. 6-8. Though the first issue was handled with relative ease (a national church is a possible and desired future goal), the second seemed to cause a few more problems for conservative representatives. For instance, Ben Wilkinson, staff member for PEF, tried to emphasize at a meeting of conservative leaders in Atlanta that the new denomination would be racially inclusive and pleaded for help in facilitating contact between the Steering Committee and black pastors and elders interested in the continuing church. "We are not a racist group seeking to build a racist Church," he emphasized, though he also "acknowledged that participants in the movement would have different attitudes on the issue."

NOTES TO PAGES 33-35

Wilkinson added that "there was a determination that this [racism] would not be the 'primary' issue." *PJ*, 20 October 1971, p. 6.

192. *PJ*, 3 November 1971, p. 7. The ecumenical *Presbyterian Outlook* tended to highlight the property concern in its discussions, emphasizing the mercenary aspect of voting for a plan only to leave the church with the property. *PO*, 20 September 1971, p. 3.

193. Censured PCUS actions and pronouncements were listed on the back of the Declaration. *PJ*, 21 February 1972, p. 4.

194. *PO*, 21 February 1972, p. 4; *PO*, 6 March 1972, p. 4. Theological bases for such concepts of a pure church appeared regularly in the *PJ*. Francis A. Schaeffer was a regular contributor and his works are exemplary of the kind of thinking that demanded a church exercising its God-given discipline in order to maintain ecclesiastical purity. *PJ*, 16 February 1972, pp. 7-10.

195. *PO*, 21 February 1972, p. 4. PCUS officials reacted to the escalated separatist rhetoric with resignation. Ben Lacey Rose said that he hoped that all Presbyterians would remain in one denomination but he doubted that was possible. Stated clerk James Millard said, "Schisms have characterized Presbyterianism all through its history. This division has been developing for thirty years and it might even be healthy." *PO*, 6 September 1971, p. 3.

196. E. R. Chandler, "Conservative Fallout," *Christianity Today* 15 (24 September 1971): 42. Andrew Jumper of the CFOP said much the same thing when he spoke of the anticipated schism as a "violation of our ordination vows especially in light of the fact that no clear-cut issue of conscience is involved; thus any withdrawal plans are unjustifiably schismatic." *The Presbyterian Outlook* quoted CFOP representatives as wanting a "church within a church" wherein conservatives worked for their own programs within the diversity of the PCUS (8 November 1971, p. 3).

197. *PJ*, 1 September 1971, pp. 9, 12. Paul Settle, newly elected executive secretary of the PCU and Steering Committee member, made this the topic of his first written address to the readership of the *Presbyterian Journal*. See also *PJ*, 3 November 1971, pp. 7-10.

198. Richards, *Birth of Presbyterian Church*, p. 194. The overture was dated December 19, 1971.

199. *PJ*, 28 June 1972, p. 7.

200. *PJ*, 5 July 1972, p. 5. Bell was endorsed by the CFOP. *PO*, 24 April 1972, p. 3.

201. *PJ*, 28 June 1972, pp. 9-10.

202. *PJ*, 9 August 1972, p. 7; *PO*, 26 June 1972, p. 1.

203. *PJ*, 9 August 1972, p. 16. Nelson Bell also voiced his concern over many portions of the document and emphasized that this was not the final version. *Reformed World*, September-December 1972, p. 167. D. E. Kucharsky, "Southern Presbyterians: Bedrock Revision," *Christianity Today* 16 (15 September 1972): 51.

204. *PJ*, 30 August 1972, p. 10. Bell also criticized it, p. 6.

205. *PJ*, 28 June 1972, p. 7.
206. This was an interesting vote since the UPUSA, one of the founding members of COCU, had voted to withdraw from COCU just weeks before the PCUS General Assembly. *PJ*, 31 May 1972, p. 4; 7 June 1972, p. 4; *PG*, June-July 1972, p. 83.
207. *PJ*, 28 June 1972, p. 6.
208. Ibid., p. 11: A. H. Matthews, "Southern Presbyterians Elect Bell, Stay in COCU," *Christianity Today* 16 (7 July 1972): 34-35.
209. *PO*, 7 August 1972, p. 4.
210. The Committee of 24 discussing UPUSA/PCUS union had become the Committee of 32 because of the addition of "people unhappy with the plan" and minorities.
211. *PJ*, 23 August 1972, p. 4. The reason conservatives wanted the union proposal voted on immediately was that they felt they could help carry the vote toward a union plan that still included a constitutional escape clause. There were PCUS "radical ecumenists" who wanted the vote delayed so that the full resources of the church could be used to convince congregations to enter the union. *PJ*, 20 September 1972, p. 8; Richards, *Birth of Presbyterian Church*, pp. 202-3.
212. In all the conservative rhetoric, the "continuing" church was the old PCUS church and the "new" church was the one created by the union of the PCUS with the UPUSA.
213. *PJ*, 2 August 1972, p. 9. Williamson also acknowledged that conservatives were willing "to risk the loss of all property for the sake of the honor and integrity of the Church." *PJ*, 23 August 1972. p. 5. Because Williamson was a lawyer, his speeches made a very strong impression on his listeners, especially when he addressed legal problems such as the property decisions. Williamson speculated that despite the success of some congregations in Georgia to retain their property after leaving the denomination, property retention by a congregation wishing to leave the presbytery was probably not realistic unless the presbytery readily granted dismissal of a congregation with its property. This legal opinion was corroborated by the release of a factual paper in the fall of 1972 by the liberal Hanover presbytery of Virginia, which lost two congregations to conservative independence in 1971 after a protracted legal battle. The paper said that a congregation had "beneficial ownership" of property but that buying and selling decisions were subject to the veto of the presbytery. The paper also agreed with Williamson that other than the utilization of the escape clause, the only option guaranteeing a congregation retention of its property was willful dismissal by the presbytery. *PO*, 11 September 1972, p. 3.
214. *PJ*, 2 August 1972, p. 10.
215. Richards, *Birth of Presbyterian Church*, pp. 202-4.
216. *PJ*, 20 September 1972, pp. 9, 19-20; Richards, *Birth of Presbyterian Church*, p. 202-3.
217. The official name was Vanguard Presbytery, a Provisional Presbytery for Southern Presbyterian and Reformed Churches Uniting. *PJ*, 20 September

1972, p. 6; *PO*, 25 September 1972, p. 3; *PG*, October 1972, p. 125; Richards, *Birth of Presbyterian Church*, pp. 205-8.

218. Over fifty people attended, observing and encouraging, but only these sixteen who officially represented congregations became founding members that night. Richards, *Birth of Presbyterian Church*, p. 207; D. E. Kucharsky, "Schism Takes Shape," *Christianity Today* 17 (13 October 1972): 48-49.

219. By adopting the BCO as it existed before 1935, conservatives argued that they avoided copyright complications. Others also noted that by so doing, Vanguard excluded amended provisions allowing women elders and ministers. *PG*, October 1972, p. 125; *PO*, 4 December 1972, p. 3; *PJ*, 25 April 1973, p. 8.

220. Richards, *Birth of Presbyterian Church*, p. 207.

221. Todd Allen, "The Story Behind Vanguard Presbytery," *Contact*, no. 18, October 1972; Richards, *Birth of Presbyterian Church*, p. 208.

222. There were feelings in the Vanguard membership that cooperation with the Steering Committee could threaten the independence of the new presbytery. *PJ*, 20 September 1972, p. 6. *The Presbyterian Outlook* (25 September 1972, p. 3) implied that the Steering Committee was not happy about Vanguard's formation but the only quote they could produce was G. A. Taylor of the *Presbyterian Journal* saying that the group should organize as a fellowship and not as a church to prevent any hint of competition with the goals of the Steering Committee.

223. Morton H. Smith became an adviser to Vanguard and represented PCU at the constituting Assembly; PEF chairman, William Hill gave the evening address at the same Assembly. *PO*, 4 December 1972, p. 3; *PJ*, 29 November 1972, p. 6. John E. Richards of the Steering Committee had attended the organizational meeting in September as an observer. Richards, *Birth of Presbyterian Church*, p. 207. In the summer of 1974, Vanguard became a presbytery of the new National Presbyterian Church. *PJ*, 24 July 1974, p. 6.

224. The clause had read that a two-thirds majority vote by a congregation was sufficient procedure for a congregation to utilize the escape clause. The revision dictated two successive congregational meetings with the two-thirds majority necessary in both for an uncontested withdrawal. *PJ*, 21 February 1973, p. 4.

225. A number of presbyteries had studied the matter and found the escape clause unacceptable for the same reasons Dowey had outlined: namely, the method was not in keeping with the Presbyterian form of government. *PO*, 23 October 1972, p. 2. What was surprising about the PCUS recommendation was that it was made with so little extraordinary provocation and so late in the negotiating process, just four months before the union plan was to be taken to a vote. Conservatives had some justification for claiming that the move was one of expediency; PCUS authorities did not deny the accusation.

226. *PJ*, 21 February 1973, p. 4.

227. Ibid., p. 5; *PO*, 5 March 1973, p. 3; *PG*, March 73, p. 35.

228. *PJ*, 21 February 1973, p. 5; *PG*, March 1973, p. 35.

229. The militant sound of the name is derived from a river in the area. *PG*, March 1973, p. 35; *PJ*, 25 April 1973, p. 8.

230. The Steering Committee called "for the rebirth of the PCUS as it was originally constituted, committed to Biblical Presbyterianism and a theological stance faithful to the Westminster Confession." *PJ*, 28 February 1973, p. 5. *The Presbyterian Outlook* included an editorial that said the Steering Committee made this announcement in order to prevent more congregations from declaring independence as Vanguard and Warrior presbyteries had done. Such continued splintering would make it much more difficult to establish a "continuing church" at some future date. *PO*, 12 March 1973, pp. 4, 8.

231. Invitations were extended to all those who had already signed the "Declaration of Intent." *PJ*, 4 April 1973, p. 12; *PO*, 23 April 1973, p. 3.

232. Richards, *Birth of Presbyterian Church*, pp. 213-24.

233. Ibid., p. 225; also in *Contact*, March 1973. The publication of the Reaffirmations was part of a larger debate between those conservative groups demanding immediate separation and those wanting to continue to work for change from within. Moderator L. Nelson Bell and the CFOP are representative of the latter group, who pleaded for conservative patience in obtaining changes. *PJ*, 23 May 1973, pp. 11, 18-19. Robert Strong, "Why Some of Us are Not Leaving," *PJ*, 2 May 1973, pp. 11ff. On the other hand, those convinced that it was time to separate argued that the PCUS had already abandoned its historic doctrinal position by allowing, even espousing, nonbiblical doctrines such as evolution (*PJ*, 4 April 1973, p. 7; 23 May 1973, p. 9), by uniting already with the apostate UPUSA through union presbyteries (Ben Wilkinson, "De Facto Union," *PJ*, 4 April 1973, p. 8; O. Palmer Robertson, "Already Under a New Confession," *PG*, November 1972, p. 11), and by engaging in immoral activities such as the sponsoring of abortion programs (*PJ*, 4 April 1973, p. 7). They also predicted that it was only a matter of time before the PCUS officially changed its confessional position. This position was corroborated by the announcement in March 1973 that the presbyterial vote on the new confession would be delayed until 1975; again, a delay would allow the restructured, and presumably more liberal, presbyteries to decide the issue. *PJ*, 7 March 1973, p. 6; *PO*, 9 April 1973, p. 3.

234. Richards, *Birth of Presbyterian Church*, p. 227.

235. *PJ*, 6 June 1973, pp. 4-5. An abbreviated version of the address is in *PJ*, 13 June 1973, pp. 8ff.

236. Richards, *Birth of Presbyterian Church*, p. 251.

237. Ibid., p. 253.

238. Ibid., pp. 262, 264.

239. Williamson claimed that it was unlikely such a plan would be forthcoming; presbyteries would be weakened by those congregations who had already left; and restructuring would almost certainly quiet the conservative voices. Conservative questions and doubts were aired in a special gripe session and

many are quoted in *PJ*, 6 June 1973 p. 5; *PO*, 4 June 1973, p. 3; 11 June 1973, p. 8.
240. *PJ*, 6 June 1973, p. 1.
241. Ibid., pp. 4-5.
242. Ibid., p. 4; Richards, *Birth of Presbyterian Church*, p. 273.
243. *PJ*, 20 June 1973, p. 3.
244. *PJ*, 27 June 1973, p. 4; *PO*, 25 June 1973, p. 3.
245. *Reformed World*, December 1973, p. 376; *PO*, 25 June 1973, p. 3. In one of its first reports, this committee asserted that no one needed to leave the church because the "present tensions result from misunderstandings, exaggerations, and the ascription of general significance to isolated instances." This report was mailed to all ministers and clerks of sessions just about the time conservative representatives were preparing to hold the constituting assembly in Birmingham. D. E. Kucharsky, "I'm National: Join Me," *Christianity Today* 18 (4 January 1974): 52. The committee's second major report was not released until June 1974, when the results of its study belatedly indicated that many would leave the denomination if the PCUS joined the UPUSA or adopted a new confession. *PO*, 24 June 1974, p. 6. At the General Assembly of 1974, this "Unhappiness Committee" warned there would be further splits within the denomination unless "trouble spots" in four major areas were handled. Those major areas in order of importance were theology, polity, ecumenism, and policy. See Barrie Doyle, "Southern Presbyterians: Phasing Out Unhappiness," *Christianity Today* 18 (16 July 1974): 34-36.
246. *PJ*, 27 June 1973, pp. 4-5; *PO*, 25 June 1973, p. 3. In October 1973, just before the Constituting Assembly of the new denomination, this committee published and distributed guidelines intended for loyal minorities that wanted to keep the congregational property in the PCUS. The guidelines advised civil litigation if necessary. *PO*, 22 October 1973, p. 4.
247. *PJ*, 20 June 1973, p. 5; D. E. Kucharsky, "Presbyterians Confront Exodus," *Christianity Today* 17 (6 July 1973): 42; *PO*, 18 June 1973, p. 4. Kraemer was elected by acclamation not just because nobody else wanted the job but also because the conservatives had not fielded a candidate.
248. *PJ*, 27 June 1973, pp. 5-7; *PO*, 25 June 1973, p. 3.
249. *PJ*, 22 August 1973, p. 4. *The Presbyterian Outlook* disputed the calculations of conservative organizers that these two hundred congregations represented over forty thousand members. *PO*, 3 September 1973, p. 3.
250. Other requirements stated that one had to be a committed minister or elder from a congregation that had officially withdrawn from the PCUS. An elder for every five hundred in the congregation would be allowed to attend. *PJ*, 22 August 1973, pp. 4, 6. *PO* criticized this method of representation as congregational rather than presbyterial based, thereby vesting power in the congregations rather than the General Assembly (3 September 1973, p. 5). See the reply of the *PJ* editor in 19 December 1973, pp. 12-13.
251. *PJ*, 22 August 1973, p. 5.

252. *PJ*, 22 August 1973, p. 4; *PO*, 3 September 1973, p. 3; Richards, *Birth of Presbyterian Church*, pp. 281-82.

253. One of the first recommendations of this committee, subsequently adopted at the constituting assembly in December, was that the valuable work of the ECOE should be continued under the auspices of this committee. Richards, *Birth of Presbyterian Church*, p. 290.

254. For instance, the Committee on Administration was the subject of heated debate receiving approval only after its name had been changed from Administration Committee. Equalization of benevolences was not approved; instead the Committee on Administration was empowered only to recommend a budget to each of the other three committees. Regional synods were eliminated despite the fact that they were included in the 1933 Book of Church Order. *PJ*, 22 August 1973, p. 4; *PG*, August-September 1973, p. 98.

255. *PJ*, 22 August 1973, pp. 5-6; *PG*, August-September, 1973, p. 99. Because the organization was not yet a duly constituted church, the Advisory Convention decided not to appoint representatives to an NPRF-sponsored September meeting.

256. *PJ*, 19 December 1973, p. 4; *PG*, January 1974, p. 12. D. E. Kucharsky, "Birth of a Denomination," *Christianity Today* 18 (21 December 1973): 39-40. By January of 1974, the NPC was the third largest Presbyterian denomination in the United States. Kucharsky, "National," p. 52.

At its second General Assembly in 1974, the NPC changed its name to the Presbyterian Church in America because a local UPUSA church in Washington D.C., had already incorporated under the name National Presbyterian Church. Richards, *Birth of Presbyterian Church*, p. 348; *PG*, November 1974, p. 141; *PJ*, 18 September 1974, p. 3.

257. *PJ*, 19 December 1973, p. 5. Actually the whole of the constitution did not receive ratification until the third General Assembly in 1975. See *PJ*, 24 September 1975, p. 4. One of the main points of discussion in this section of the convention involved the inclusion of a statement on the miraculous gifts of the Spirit, which was obviously directed toward charismatics. The disputed paragraph said that the miraculous gifts of the Spirit associated with the ministry of the apostles in the New Testament "have long since ceased." Some thought that the reference was unduly critical while others wanted it stated clearly that "the apostolic office has ceased and the canon is closed." Time ran out on this debate so a special committee was appointed to study the matter. *PJ*, 19 December 1973, pp. 5-6; *PO*, 7 January 1974, p. 4. This indicates the difficulty even this "pure" young denomination had in establishing the form its acknowledged historic doctrine would take in the twentieth century.

258. *PJ*, 19 December 1973, p. 5. The title of this document reflects the NPC's claim to be the continuing southern Presbyterian church since it is the same title used by the Presbyterian church in the Confederate States of America when it was founded on December 4 (also!), 1861. Richards, *Birth of Presbyterian Church*, pp. 27ff., 425ff.

NOTES TO PAGES 42-43

259. The language here mirrors that used by Williamson in his keynote address at the Constituting Assembly. "But to understand this necessity which we feel God has laid upon us, one understands the principle that has motivated us. As an apologetic, we would lay this principle before the world. It is the practice of the principle of the purity of the visible church. In order that we might practice this principle, it has been necessary that we leave the visible church with which we have been associated. . . . Separation is merely the price we have had to pay for the principle." *Addresses Delivered During the First General Assembly of the Continuing Presbyterian Church* (Birmingham: Continuing Presbyterian Church, 1973), p. 6.

260. Further explanation was given later in "Message":

"We have called ourselves 'Continuing' Presbyterians because we seek to continue the faith of the founding fathers of that Church. Deviations in doctrine and practice from historic Presbyterian positions as evident in the Presbyterian Church US, result from accepting other sources of authority, and from making them coordinate or superior to the divine Word. A diluted theology, a gospel tending towards humanism, an unbiblical view of marriage and divorce, the ordination of women, financing of abortion on socio-economic grounds, and numerous other non-bible positions are all traceable to a different view of Scripture from that we hold and that which was held by the Southern Presbyterian forefathers. . . .

"When a denomination will not exercise discipline and its courts have become heterodox or disposed to tolerate error, the minority finds itself in the anomalous position of being submissive to a tolerant and erring majority. In order to proclaim the truth and to practice the discipline which they believe obedience to Christ requires, it then becomes necessary for them to separate. This is the exercise of discipline in reverse. It is how we view our separation." Richards, *Birth of Presbyterian Church*, p. 427.

261. Ibid., p. 426. This view of Scripture was reinforced in the ordination vows approved by this Assembly that asked the candidate for ministry: "Do you believe the Scripture of the Old and New Testaments to be the inerrant Word of God, the only infallible rule of faith and practice?" Kucharsky, "National," p. 52.

262. A resolution to this effect was also passed by the Assembly, stressing the desire "to have fellowship and communication with likeminded Christians," that is, those who believe in "the plenary verbal inspiration of Scripture, which Scriptures are inerrant in their original manuscripts; and have further reaffirmed their adherence to the Reformed faith as expressed in the Westminster Confession of Faith and Catechisms." From the resolution as quoted in *PG*, January 1974, p. 12. Advertisements were placed in various conservative newspapers announcing this ecumenical policy. *PG*, June-July 1974, p. 93.

263. Richards, *Birth of Presbyterian Church*, p. 428.

264. Ibid., p. 429. Donald Patterson of the PCU delivered a speech at the Constituting Assembly with a heavy emphasis on this theme. See *Addresses*, pp. 26ff.

265. Richards, *Birth of Presbyterian Church*, p. 430.
266. The geographical factor especially loses credence. As early as January 1974, the fledgling denomination was able to boast representative congregations in fourteen of the fifteen states in which the PCUS had congregations. See Kucharsky, "National," p. 52. Also see Dawson, "What about Heretics?," p. 514; E. T. Clark, "Non-Theological Factors in Religious Diversity," *Ecumenical Review* (July 1951).
267. The PCUS's own liberal Committee on Unhappiness warned the General Assembly in 1974 that foremost among the "trouble spots" that the denomination must concern itself were those related to theology.
268. Takayama, "Strains and Schisms," p. 317. Takayama suggests that the political and social nature of the split is demonstrated by the fact that the new denomination is characterized by an emphasis on congregationalism and "localism." However, Takayama has failed to put this congregationalist emphasis within the context of a group of congregations distrustful of a system of church government that they regarded as having stripped away their distinct theological emphases. When that context is remembered, the "political nature" of this schism as "seen in part in the constitution of the new denomination" is much less pronounced.
269. There is probably something valuable in Loetscher's observation that as the South moved increasingly into the mainstream of American national life in the twentieth century, the PCUS was influenced by the same forces of theological and social innovation. Consequently the differences between the northern and southern churches decreased noticeably and some PCUS church members felt that such social and theological change could not be tolerated. See *Brief History*, p. 123.

CHAPTER THREE

1. Carl Stramm Meyer, *A Brief Historical Sketch of the Lutheran Church-Missouri Synod* (St. Louis, Missouri: Concordia Publishing House, 1963), p. 7; also Meyer, ed., *Moving Frontiers: Readings in the History of the Lutheran Church-Missouri Synod* (St. Louis, Missouri: Concordia Publishing House, 1964), pp. 97ff.
2. Two works bring out the intensity of emotions at this betrayal. The first is a fictionalized work by Robert Koenig, *Except the Corn Die* (n.p.: Robert J. Koenig, publisher, 1975); the second was written by one of the betrayed, Edward Vehse, *The Stephanite Emigration to America* (Tuscon, Arizona: Marion R. Winkler, 1975).
3. Meyer, *Frontiers*, p. 140.
4. Ibid., p. 143. See also John W. Constable, "Of Congregational and Synodical Authority," *Concordia Theological Monthly* 43 (April 1972): 215-16.
5. Meyer, *Frontiers*, p. 143.

6. Richard Koenig, "What's Behind the Showdown in the LCMS? Church and Tradition in Collision," *Lutheran Forum* 6 (November 1972): 16.

7. Many conservatives quoted from the "Statement" to justify this inerrancy view: "If faith in John 3:16 and 1 John 1:7 is still found in one who denies the infallible divine authority of the scripture, that is an inconsistency which at any moment can turn into a damning inconsistency." Richard Koenig, "Showdown," p. 18.

8. Ibid., pp. 18-19. Pieper's definition of "unionism"—"church fellowship with adherents of false doctrine"—supports this distinction. The repercussions of this attitude are indicated by Theodore Graebner in "The Burden of Infallibility: A Study in the History of Dogma," *Concordia Historical Quarterly* 38 (1965): 88-99: "A passion for truth is tragically susceptible to becoming a passion to be right." See also Constable, "Authority," for a development of the relation between synodical authority and inerrancy; also Arthur Carl Piepkorn, "What Does Inerrancy Mean?," *Concordia Theological Monthly* 35 (September 1965): 588.

9. Richard Koenig, "Showdown," p. 20; Graebner, "Burden of Infallibility," p. 96.

10. Richard E. Koenig, "Missouri Turns Moderate: 1938-65," *Lutheran Forum* 7 (February 1973): 20.

11. Meyer, *Frontiers*, p. 418.

12. The Synodical Conference was an alliance of conservative Lutheran denominations formed in 1872 of which the Missouri Synod was the largest and at times the most ecumenically minded. At this point, it was the Norwegian and Wisconsin synods that objected to Missouri's involvement with the ALC. Richard Koenig, "Missouri Turns," p. 28.

13. Sunday schools, once considered wrong by synodical degree, increasingly replaced parochial schools as the system by which the laity educated their young.

14. The Troeltsch/Wach church/sect/denomination typology is used here. See Ernst Troeltsch, *The Social Teaching of the Christian Churches* (New York: Macmillan, 1931) and Joachim Wach, *Church, Denominations and Sect* (Evanston, Illinois: Seabury-Western Theological Seminary, 1946).

15. *Handbook of the Lutheran Church-Missouri Synod*, 1969, pp. 27-78.

16. Ibid., pp. 17-18, 28.

17. James E. Adams, *Preus of Missouri and the Great Lutheran Civil War* (New York: Harper & Row, Publishers, 1977), p. 166.

18. Frincke also argued that a significant aspect of that heterogeneity was the leadership of Jacob Preus, who was originally from a more conservative, isolationist denomination called the Little Norweigan Synod. From a transcript of a speech given March 10, 1974, St. Mark's Lutheran Church, Rochester, New York.

19. Tom Baker, *Watershed at the Rivergate* (Sturgis, Michigan, 1973), p. 4. Theophil W. Janzow, "Secularization in an Orthodox Denomination" (Ph.D. dissertation, University of Nebraska, 1970), p. 61.

20. John Warwick Montgomery, "The Last Days of the Late, Great Synod of Missouri," *Christianity Today* 16 (9 April 1971): 56.
21. Henceforth synodically adopted doctrinal statements were not to be "binding," though teachers and pastors were still expected to honor and uphold such documents. Constable, "Congregational Authority," p. 227.
22. *Proceedings of the Forty-sixth Regular Convention of the Lutheran Church—Missouri Synod*, Detroit, Michigan, June 1965, Resolution 2-03. The moderates in the Synod agreed with resolutions as conservative as the following: 2-27 that Jonah was a historical figure; 2-35 that Moses wrote the first five books of the Bible and that all of Isaiah was written by one eighth-century author. However, they would not agree that subscription to these beliefs was necessary for continued membership in the synod.
23. *The Lutheran Witness*, September 1969, p. 21.
24. The very name of this committee shows the close but tense relationship that existed for Missourians between correct theology and relations with other Christian bodies. Constable, "Congregational Authority," p. 214.
25. Altar and pulpit fellowship involves members of participating synods congregations being able to commune in the other synod, the easy transfer of membership from one synod to another, the approval of joint worship services and joint committee work, and calling of a pastor from one synod to another.
26. *Convention Proceedings, 1965*, pp. 478-80. For conservative thoughts on these matters that were finally put to paper, see "The Mission of the Christian Church in the World: A Review of the 1965 'Mission Affirmations' " in *Proceedings of the Fifty-first Regular Convention of the Lutheran Church-Missouri Synod*, Anaheim, California, July 4-11, 1975, pp. 471ff.

    In *Mission in the Making: The Missionary Enterprise among Missouri Synod Lutherans 1846-1963* (St. Louis, Missouri: Concordia Publishing House, 1964), F. Dean Lueking calls those who favored the "Affirmation," "evangelical confessionalists." Evangelistic confessionalists have a "strong sense of continuity with the past and present community of the Church Universal." The most distinctive feature of this group is its doctrine of the church wherein the visibility of the church is stressed, "with the church manifest in many churches in Christendom." Evangelistic confessionalists see the Lutheran confessions as a bridge to the rest of Christendom rather than a wall. "Doctrinal unity is circumscribed by the doctrine of salvation, the center of which is the doctrine of repentance and the remission of sins" (pp. 13-14). On the other hand, "scholastic confessionalists" see the Lutheran confessions from a seventeenth-century perspective where they are used to separate dissidents from participation in the visible congregation of those who possessed the truth of God in all its purity. "Those who refused to drop conflicting views on any of the wide range of doctrines considered essential by the scholastic confessionalists were relegated to the invisible church." The missionary task could be described as setting erring Christians right (pp. 16-17). For Lueking both groups existed in the Synod since its beginnings. Here the two groups are distinguished by the shorter "conservative" and "moderate" labels.

27. Marquart, *Anatomy of an Explosion*, pp. 91-92.
28. Adams, *Preus*, p. 131.
29. Ibid., p. 132.
30. Jacob Preus had already made something of a reputation for himself as a combative conservative at Concordia Seminary in Springfield just as the Synod was settling in to a more tolerant line of evangelical Lutheranism. When he was made acting president of Springfield Seminary in 1962, he managed to weed out moderate professors such as Richard Jungkuntz, Curtis Huber, and Bernard Kurzweg. As legalistic and arrogant as moderates later judged Jacob Preus to be, at this time what was most evident was the enthusiasm and energy of a brilliant young classics professor and administrator. To those who knew Preus, he was a jovial, "winsome" person who, at the height of the controversy, described himself as having "more faults than fleas on a dog." More important, despite his stature as president of one of the denominational seminaries, Preus was something of an unknown in Missourian circles, having joined the Synod after his ordination in the Little Norwegian Synod. Ibid., pp. 36, 207, 54ff. Much would be made of this "outsider" status in later analyses of the schism. See ibid., pp. 51-118; Richard E. Koenig, "Conservative Reaction: 1965-69" *Lutheran Forum* 7 (May 1973): 18-22.
31. Adams, *Preus*, p. 121. Marquart, *Anatomy of an Explosion*, pp. 94ff. *Affirm* was the periodical that gave this organization its voice in the Synod after March 1971 when it began publication.
32. Janzow speculates that because Christian charity dictated that no politicking would take place and because the election was held the first day of the convention, the incumbent was usually the only one with a high enough profile to win the election. "Secularization," pp. 164-65.
33. Ibid., p. 166.
34. Walter Wolbrecht, executive director of the Synod and Harms's right-hand man, took the opportunity while the first ballot was being counted to rail against the UPC for secular politicking. Preus replied that he had not directed any politicking and was not seeking office. *Proceedings of the Forty-eighth Regular Convention of the Lutheran Church-Missouri Synod*, Denver, Colorado, July 11-18, 1969, p. 20. In 1971, Wolbrecht's position was abolished by convention resolution. When the administration opened another position almost identical to Wolbrecht's old one, Wolbrecht was not considered for the post.
35. Adams, *Preus*, pp. 136-41.
36. Ibid., p. 142.
37. There was definitely an extensive moderate vote operating at the 1969 convention that seemed to become functional only after the presidential vote. For example, the moderate "A Review of the Question *What is a Doctrine?*," recommended for adoption by the 1967 convention, received approval at the 1969 convention. *Convention Workbook 1969*, p. 58; *Convention Proceedings, 1969*, p. 90. One also has to contend with the possibility that the election regarding ALC fellowship had been handled unfairly and that the vote was

swayed by the parliamentary procedures employed. Janzow, "Secularization," pp. 168-69.

38. Adams, *Preus*, p. 144.

39. Unless otherwise noted, all references to Concordia or Concordia Seminary refer to the institution in St. Louis, Missouri.

40. Marquart, *Anatomy of an Explosion*, p. 89.

41. Ibid., p. 92; Board of Control of Concordia Theological Seminary, *Exodus from Concordia: A Report on the 1974 Walkout* (St. Louis, Missouri: Concordia Seminary Publicity Office, 1977) pp. 8-9. When Harms asked for a clear rejection of liberal errors regarding biblical interpretation, Alfred Fuerbringer, president of Concordia, replied in April of 1966 that such an answer could not be formulated quickly; the matters were difficult ones not clearly discussed in the Scriptures or the Confessions, the only two documents that can be used as sources for doctrinal matters.

42. Originally *Lutheran News*, the *Christian News* was a weekly with an arch-conservative editorial slant. Herman Otten, *CN* editor, was a Missouri synod-trained preacher who did not receive certification at the end of his training at Concordia because of the virulent attacks he leveled against his teachers, whom he found much too liberal. A conservative congregation in New Haven called the energetic student, who continued his antifaculty attacks from the editor's desk of *CN*. The Missouri Synod gave no support to the publication though it was read by many Missourians because of its close scrutiny of synodical affairs.

43. Nominations were received from the congregations, synodical Board for Higher Education, and the seminary's Board of Control. The faculty made their selections from that list and then submitted their short list to a Board of Electors. In this way, the faculty would not have a president supervising them with whom they could not get along.

44. Adams, *Preus*, p. 168. Adams also called Tietjen a "zealous prophet," describing his stubbornness and earnestness in the face of great odds (p. 31).

45. "A Call to Openness and Trust," in Herman Otten, ed., *A Christian Handbook on Vital Issues: Christian News 1963-73* (New Haven, Missouri: Leader Publishing Company, 1973), pp. 760ff.

46. Ibid., p. 761.

47. The CTCR condemned "A Call to Openness" for not setting limits on diversity within a confessional church and emphasized the uniformity desired in the visible church. *Proceedings of the Forty-ninth Regular Convention of the Lutheran Church—Missouri Synod*, Milwaukee, Wisconsin, July 9-16, 1971, p. 37.

48. On January 27, 1970, Robert Preus, professor at Concordia Seminary and brother of the newly elected synodical president, wrote Tietjen describing the factions developing within the faculty. On March 12, 1970, the same Martin Scharlemann who had earlier questioned the accuracy of the total biblical record, met with Tietjen to alert him to theological irregularities within the exegetical department. When Tietjen did not act on his warnings, Scharlemann wrote Jacob Preus, in a letter dated April 9, 1970 requesting an inquiry. Since Scharlemann had sent Tietjen a copy of this letter, Tietjen called a meeting for

April 16 to discuss the letter. Scharlemann was not able to attend because of his duties as a military chaplain and there is some question as to whether he was given proper notice of the meeting. Board of Control, *Exodus*, pp. 22ff. and Danker, *No Room*, pp. 46ff. At the meeting, the faculty majority voted to censure the absent Scharlemann for his insubordination in writing the synodical president. Only three faculty dissented from this decision. *Exodus*, p. 23.

49. Board of Control, *Exodus*, p. 25; also see Danker, *No Room*, pp. 53-62.
50. *Convention Proceedings, 1971*, p. 51. To fortify this view of how doctrine is gleaned from Scripture, Preus quoted Walther: "The view prevailing at present, holding doctrines to be merely the results of historical movements, is of rationalistic origin" (p. 233).
51. Ibid., pp. 52, 119. Resolution 2-21 replaced a much stronger one that spoke of doctrinal resolutions being of "binding force." In the new resolution these "synodical statements were not to be given more or less status than they deserve."
52. Ibid., Resolution 2-35, p. 40.
53. Ibid., pp. 155-56. The onus was placed on individuals to take their dissent through a maze of synodical channels; the ultimate authority rested with the synodical convention. It was much easier to leave the Synod than pursue this route of dissent.
54. Ibid., Resolution 5-21, pp. 161-62. This resolution came after Preus railed against other proposed overtures that he thought demanded the "drastic reduction in the authority of the President's office" (p. 37).
55. Ibid., pp. 128-29.
56. Ibid., p. 56. The report was never submitted to the synodical membership because of its extended length. Simplification had been attempted with summaries and charts. However, as Danker reports, the faculty found these most unsatisfactory. Danker, *No Room*, pp. 65ff.
57. *Convention Proceedings, 1971*, p. 122.
58. Letter from Preus to the membership, 1 March 1972. See *Witness*, 16 March 1972, pp. 23ff.
59. Preus instructed Tietjen that Ehlen not be allowed to teach courses where he "would have the opportunity to advocate his higher critical views concerning Biblical interpretation." Ibid.
60. Ibid.
61. "God is therefore the true Author of every word of Scripture." Danker, *No Room*, p. 77.
62. "We believe, teach and confess that the authoritative Word for the church today is the *canonical* Word, not precanonical sources, forms or traditions." Ibid., p. 79.
63. "Since the Holy Scriptures are the Word of God, they contain no errors or contradictions but . . . are in all their parts and words the infallible truth . . . and *apparent* contradictions or discrepancies and problems . . . arise because of uncertainty over the original text." Ibid., p. 80.
64. Ibid., p. 82.

65. "Response of the Faculty of Concordia Seminary," 4 April 1972, in *Witness*, 30 April 1972, pp. 28-31.

66. His sincerity in maintaining this is open to question as the following quote from the same letter shows: "However that some of the antitheses touch on positions held by the St. Louis seminary professor is known to all." Ibid., p. 32.

67. In fact, more detailed critiques of Preus's statement did soon come from the faculty. See Danker, *No Room*, pp. 88-95ff.; Walter E. Keller, Kenneth F. Korby, Robert C. Schultz, and David G. Truemper, "A Review Essay of a Statement of Scriptural and Confessional Principles," *Cresset*, May and October 1973; Edward H. Schroeder, *Critique of President Preus' Statement* (n.p.: n.d.).

68. *Report of the Synodical President to the Lutheran Church-Missouri Synod (In compliance with Resolution 2-28 of the Forty-ninth Regular Convention of the Synod)* (Concordia Publishing House, September 1, 1972), p. 21.

69. Ibid., pp. 24, 87. Among the doctrines in which the faculty majority were willing to tolerate deviations were: Christology, miracles, creation, fall of man, virgin birth of Christ, physical resurrection of Christ, presence of Christ in the Lord's Supper. The more obtuse issues regarding the third use of the law and role of women in the church are listed by Preus here as having clear description in Scripture; yet the faculty majority position allowed several interpretations.

70. Ibid., pp. 123ff., 129.

71. Ibid., pp. 147-48. Preus also condemned the Board of Control for being too concerned with procedure and not doing enough about the obvious divergent doctrinal stances of the faculty members. Since for Preus it was "abundantly clear that some professors at the seminary held views contrary to the established doctrinal position of the Synod," the next step for the Board was to determine which faculty were teaching false doctrines. Preus singled out Tietjen as the man that the board had to deal with first, for his failure "to exercise the supervision of the doctrine of the faculty as prescribed in the synodical handbook" (p. 146).

72. "Fact Finding or Fault Finding? An Analysis of President J. A. O. Preus' Investigation of Concordia Seminary" (St. Louis: Concordia Seminary, 8 September 1972), pp. 1-2.

73. Ibid., pp. 8-12.

74. Ibid., p. 35.

75. "A Joint Statement," *Witness*, 24 September 1972, p. 31. The continued acrimony between these two leaders was a contributing factor in the schismatic process. For instance, Preus is reported to have said as early as February 1973, "Tietjen must go!" Adams, *Preus*, p. 178. However, reducing the debate to this unpleasant relationship as some popular commentaries did (see "The Lutheran Pope," *Newsweek*, 23 July 1973, p. 50) is too simplistic given both the long history of the debate and the number of people involved.

76. *Witness*, 24 September 1972, p. 28.

77. *Faithful to Our Calling Faithful to Our Lord: An Affirmation in Two Parts by the Faculty of Concordia Seminary, St. Louis, Missouri* (n.p., though contributions are solicited to the seminary address at 801 De Mun Avenue), pp. 3, 24-27, 41. This type of "secularistic" thinking was the object of much criticism among

conservatives, who charged that the faculty was not teaching what the majority of the denomination believed. See Baker, *Watershed*, pp. 3-25, and compare Adams, *Preus*, p. 179, which corroborates to some extent the conservative argument.

78. Being "commended" or "corrected" were the only two options that the Board of Control had. *Convention Workbook for the 1973 Convention* (St. Louis, Missouri: Concordia Publishing House, 1973), p. 100.

79. In somewhat more dramatic tones, the headlines of the *Christian News* screamed "The War is On!" Danker, *No Room*, p. 106.

80. *Witness*, 5 August 1973, p. 301.

81. *A Christian Handbook*, pp. 1, 841. Otten proposed a new confessional Lutheran church that would develop a twentieth-century Formula of Concord (p. 145).

82. Otten-sponsored resolutions demanded: that the *Concordia Theological Monthly*, a respected journal by the St. Louis faculty, cease publication immediately because it allowed articles discussing the ordination of women; that fellowship with the ALC be suspended; the reaffirmation of biblical inerrancy; that actions be taken against those favoring gospelism; that Tietjen be fired immediately; and that Otten be admitted to the lists of Missouri Synod pastors. See *Convention Workbook, 1973*, "Resolutions."

83. Despite the strong opposition to Preus, there was also strong support for him in the synod. The only other candidate as visible as Preus in the four years prior to the convention was Oswald Hoffman, speaker of a popular denominational radio broadcast "The Lutheran Hour," who declined nomination. *Proceedings of the Fiftieth Regular Convention of the Lutheran Church-Missouri Synod, New Orleans, Louisiana, July 6-13, 1973*, p. 20.

84. To indicate the strength of the conservatives on the Board of Control after the elections, E. Otto, who was editor of *Affirm* when it campaigned against the St. Louis faculty with phrases like "Tietjen must go," became president of the Board of Control. Alfred Biel and Ed Weber were members of the floor committees who approved Resolution 3-12 condemning Tietjen. Other members of the committee had already written against Tietjen. *Affirm*, June A & B, 1973.

85. Danker, *No Room*, p. 121. Though Danker is an interested party, being one of the faculty majority opposing Preus's "Statement," a check of convention procedure and committee membership confirms his observation. It was not unusual for a president to want his people on the important committees. What was unusual about Preus's appointments was his stacking of the committees to the extent that there was little or no possibility of a moderate voice being heard. *Convention Proceedings, 1973*, pp. 48-54.

Douglas Johnson thinks there is a shift here in the LC-MS from informal, traditional, communal-like values to a politicized system where power is employed to achieve unity. See "Program Dissensus Between Denominational Grassroots and Leadership and its Consequences," in Scherer, *American Denominational Organization*, pp. 340ff. Adams agrees that the push toward authoritarianism was not typical of the LC-MS. "The LC-MS had always been authoritarian by ethnocentric instincts not by constitution." *Preus*, p. 26.

In the 24 December 1973 edition of *Missouri in Perspective*, none other than Jacob Preus is quoted as saying at the Council of Presidents meeting held November 26-28 that politics is a "way of life in the Missouri Synod . . . those who can't stand the heat, get out of the kitchen."

86. *Convention Proceedings, 1973*, pp. 112-14. The obvious implication here is that once a doctrinal statement had gone through the synodical process of proposal by an appointed synodical body (usually the Commission on Theology and Church Relations), discussion in the congregations, redrafting, and consideration by convention delegates, that doctrinal statement is in accord with the Scriptures and the Lutheran Confessions as per Article II of the constitution.

87. Ibid., p. 114.

88. Ibid., pp. 25, 31.

89. Ibid., p. 33.

90. Ibid., pp. 33, 34, 36, 41. The traditional standing rule had been that debate could be closed only after a two-thirds majority of the convention voted to close debate. Under the new standing rule, debate could be closed after only a simple majority voted to do so. This new rule was protested, so it was necessary for a synodical attorney to read a legal statement to the convention asserting that the convention was acting within parliamentary rules by changing the standing rules as it did.

91. Ibid., pp. 36-37.

92. Ibid., p. 139.

93. Ibid., p. 37.

94. These special rules for this resolution had been drawn up the night before to ensure the faculty a fair hearing. Ibid., p. 38.

95. "RESOLVED, That the synod repudiate that attitude toward Holy Scripture, particularly as regards its authority and clarity, which reduces to theological opinion or exegetical questions matters which are in fact clearly taught in Scripture (e.g., facticity of miracle accounts and their details: historicity of Adam and Eve as real persons; the fall of Adam and Eve into sin as a real event, to which original sin and its imputation upon all succeeding generations of mankind must be traced; the historicity of every detail in the life of Jesus as recorded by the evangelists; predictive prophecies in the Old Testament which are in fact Messianic; the doctrine of angels; the Jonah account, etc.) . . ." Ibid., p. 139.

96. Ibid.

97. Ibid., pp. 140-41.

98. Ibid., pp. 140-42.

99. Ibid.

100. Ibid., p. 47.

101. "A Declaration of Protest and Confession." Danker, *No Room*, pp. 149-52.

102. *Witness*, 7 October 1973, p. 413. The official complainants in the case were Pastors Buelow and Harnapp.
103. The faculty minority members included Ralph Bohlmann, Richard Klann, Robert Preus, Martin Scharlemann, and Lorenz Wunderlich. Their "Appeal" was summarized in *Witness*, 4 October 1973, p. 415.
104. The moderates forced to retire were H. Bouman, R. Caemmerer, A. Fuerbringer, A. C. Piepkorn, A. C. Repp, and Alfred von Rohr Sauer. Lorenz Wunderlich was the only conservative in this category. *Witness*, 19 November 1973, p. 476.
105. There were many other examples of such "flexing." For example, on September 26, 1973, the Board of Control received authority from the Board of Directors to investigate FLUTE (Fund for Lutheran Theological Education), a new organization founded by Tietjen, Bertram, Damm, and Krentz, all members of the faculty majority. Board of Control, *Exodus*, p. 76.
106. Montgomery, "Last Days," p. 56; Scherer, *American Denominational Organization*, p. 20.
107. "Report from Sub-Committee for Objectives and Structural Suggestions," 28 August 1973, p. 1.
108. *The Lutheran Witness*, 16 September 1973, p. 382.
109. Letter from ELIM Board of Directors to members of the LC-MS, 25 September 1973. A law firm was engaged to help those whose civil rights had been infringed on as a result of the New Orleans resolutions.
110. Its acronym (ELIM) recalled "a place of refreshment for the Children of Israel on their journey to the Promised Land, immediately following their stop at Marah, where they found only bitter water to drink." Ibid. *Missouri in Perspective* began publication in October 1973 also.
111. 2-12 "To Adopt Synodical Doctrinal Statements"; 3-01 "To Adopt 'A Statement' "; 3-09 "To Condemn the Faculty Majority"; 3-12A "To Deal With Dr. Tietjen."
112. "In the Name of Jesus Christ and for the Sake of the Gospel," ELIM Board of Directors to LC-MS dated 25 September 1973, p. 1. The reference to the synodical administration as a coercive papacy reinforced the notion that ELIM was defending true evangelical Christianity, as Luther had.
113. "Where Does This Lead Us?," ibid., pp. 3-4.
114. Ibid.
115. *Perspective*, 5 November 1973, p. 1. Or as Rudolph Ressmeyer, president of the Atlantic District and one of ELIM's chief organizers, said at the 1973 ELIM conference, only 4 percent of world Lutheranism is Missouri Synod Lutheran. His clear implication was that there were other orthodox Lutherans who were not Missourian, many of those may not share all the same beliefs with Missouri, and Missouri may actually be in error in some of those beliefs.
116. *Witness*, 16 September 1973, p. 383. The whole tone of this article can be summarized in one succinct quote by Preus: "Synod has spoken and we ought to listen."
117. *Witness*, 16 December 1973, p. 515.

118. Published as a pamphlet of the CTCR in March 1973 (also found in *Convention Workbook, 1975*, pp. 468-70).
119. This included discussing the problem with one's peers, then with one's supervisor of doctrine, and finally with the CTCR. "Principles," pp. 7-9.
120. Ibid., p. 4.
121. Ibid., pp. 7, 10-11.
122. Ibid., p. 4.
123. *Perspective*, 5 November 1973 , p. 6.
124. Board of Control, *Exodus*, pp. 77-78.
125. Danker, *No Room*, pp. 180-84.
126. "Evidence Presented by John Tietjen," February 1974, p. 1.
127. *Witness*, 27 January 1974, p. 25; 17 February 1974, p. 3. The role of Scharlemann is significant. Once considered a moderate, Scharlemann wholeheartedly supported the denominational authorities in the seminary dispute, especially after the cherished position of seminary president was originally awarded to Tietjen. Danker, *No Room*, p. 220.
128. In return for Tietjen's leaving the seminary, Goetting would be rehired, there would be a one-year moratorium on the removal of faculty, and all theological charges would be dropped. Ibid., pp. 196ff.
129. The official report of the Board of Control, *Exodus from Concordia*, explains the deal as an attempt by the seminary's director of communications, Larry Neeb, who was directly responsible to Tietjen, working with Victor Bryant in an attempt to avert a crisis. At no time was the board involved in the discussions (p. 100).
130. "Evidence" contained transcripts of his meetings with complainants Buelow and Harnapp and outlined how the synodical president and the complainants cooperated in bringing speedy action against him.
131. Danker, *No Room*, pp. 200-201.
132. Ibid., pp. 205ff.; Board of Control, *Exodus*, p. 102.
133. Board of Control, *Exodus*, pp. 105-6; Danker, *No Room*, p. 201.
134. Danker, *No Room*, pp. 251ff.
135. Ibid., p. 275.
136. Board of Control, *Exodus*, pp. 108ff.; Danker, *No Room*, pp. 281ff.; Adams, *Preus*, pp. 202ff.
137. "Appendix six" was a letter allegedly written to Scharlemann from 120 students agreeing with the recent actions of the Board of Control and providing instances of bullying and agnostic, false doctrine by the faculty majority. Scharlemann claimed to have the names of the students on file. Danker, *No Room*, pp. 290ff.; Board of Control, *Exodus*, pp. 110ff.
138. A good example of a conservative student's reaction is a letter from Gary Phelleps, dated February 11, 1974. The Board of Control's *Exodus* admitted that Scharlemann actually only screened the students to make sure they were well documented. Danker argues effectively that, if in fact there were any students, there were one or two only. *No Room*, pp. 300-302.

139. Ibid., p. 302. Most of the Fort Wayne student body that intended to become clergy usually went on to St. Louis.
140. Letter from faculty at Concordia Teachers College, 12 February 1974.
141. "Position Statement of Atlantic District," 2 February 1974.
142. Letter from English District president Hecht to English District congregations, 19 February 1974.
143. Danker, *No Room*, p. 305.
144. Board of Control, *Exodus*, pp. 111-12; Danker, *No Room*, pp. 311ff.; Adams, *Preus*, pp. 202ff.
145. Board of Control, *Exodus*, p. 113.
146. Ibid., pp. 114-15; Danker, *No Room*, pp. 311ff.
147. Ibid., p. 318; Board of Control, *Exodus*, p. 117; Adams, *Preus*, p. 202-3.
148. *Perspective*, 25 February 1974, p. 1. Seminex leaders were attempting to answer the conservative charge that the Concordia faculty, many of whom were educated at non-Lutheran graduate schools, were too "secular" and not "Lutheran" enough in their thinking.
149. The Concordia campus did not cease to exist as a result of this exodus. Approximately ten part-time faculty together with the four full-time faculty were able to handle the teaching load of eighty-two students for the third quarter of the 1973-74 academic year. In May 1974, thirty-seven men received their Master of Divinity degrees. Robert Preus took over as acting president after Scharlemann's resignation in April. Ralph Bohlmann, who helped Preus pen his "Statement," was installed as seminary president on May 20, 1975. In the fall of 1978, 21 more faculty were hired and 193 students enrolled. Board of Control, *Exodus*, p. 147.
150. *Convention Workbook, 1971*, pp. 1-21.
151. On the thirteen-member board, a majority of seven consistently voted conservatively while the remaining six voted moderately. *Workbook, 1973*, pp. 12-13.
152. The BFM majority wrote in their report to the 1973 convention, "there is a euphoria in ecumenism which seems incapable of discerning the spirits or of confessing the infallible Scriptural truths." Ibid., p. 11.
153. There were other discussions at New Orleans regarding missions indicating the conservative-moderate split. Resolution 1-06 reaffirming the church's mission goals as found in the "Mission Affirmations" was adopted without dissenting vote, though only after prolonged discussion. The Board of Missions was instructed not to supervise missionaries but to leave that to staff members. This may seem like an innocuous enough directive, except that it was trying to deal with unpublicized troubles brewing in the missions department. Other overtures calling for the mission staff to maintain scriptural and confessional loyalty also came to the attention of the convention; though not adopted, their discussion indicates controversy. *Convention Proceedings, 1973*, p. 132.
154. *Perspective*, 14 January 1974, p. 1. Campus ministers complained about the isolationism of the BFM. *Perspective*, 25 March 1974, p. 7. The president of the New Guinea church traveled to St. Louis to protest the too brief visitation of

a team sent by the BFM in October 1973, whose recommendations included delaying the independence of the New Guinea church. *Perspective*, 25 February 1974, p. 1. Veteran missionaries such as Roland Miller and Luther Engelbrecht also went to St. Louis to protest Mayer's firing. *Perspective*, 11 March 1974, p. 8. A letter sent from the mission staff to the synodical membership complained of unethical practices, the subversion of mission policy (meaning the "Affirmations"), and the arbitrary use of synodical power to gain objectives. *Perspective*, 11 February 1974, p. 1.

155. *Witness*, 17 March 1974, p. 24.

156. *Perspective*, 22 April 1974, p. 1; *Witness*, 28 April 1974, p. 1.

157. *Perspective*, 12 August 1974, p. 1.

158. "Minutes of Consultation of Missouri Synod-Related Lutheran Churches in Asia," July 15-19, 1974, p. 2. The delegates cited the fact that the investigative Mission Study Commission did not have one mission church representative among its five members, that decisions were being made in St. Louis without any consultation, and that they were not consulted regarding Mayer's termination.

159. Ibid., p. 3. See also Richard Mueller, *Mission Made Impossible: The Sources of Schism in the Lutheran Church-Missouri Synod Hong Kong and Macao Mission*, (St. Louis, Missouri: ELIM, 1976) for another example of the same type of dispute.

160. *Perspective*, 12 May 1975, p. 1.

161. Ibid., p. 1; *Proceedings, 1975*, p. 867.

162. Formed in May 1974, the agency was to establish new mission efforts that would follow the objectives of the "Affirmations." James Mayer was named its first Coordinator. *Perspective*, 20 May 1974, p. 8.

163. *Laymen's Analysis*, August 1974.

164. Informal conversations with preachers and missionaries in the field have indicated that many of them, removed from the scrutiny of St. Louis by sheer distance, continued to preach and cooperate as a moderate interpretation of the "Affirmations" dictated.

165. *Witness*, 17 February 1974, p. 10; *Perspective*, 28 February 1974, p. 8.

166. The official date of dismissal was October 12, 1974. *Perspective*, 7 October 1974, p. 1; 21 October 1974, p. 1; *Witness*, 6 October 1974, p. 22; 3 November 1974, p. 19.

167. *Witness*, 3 November 1974, p. 19; *Perspective*, 4 November 1974, p. 1.

168. *Witness*, 7 April 1974, p. 22.

169. *Report of the Advisory Committee on Doctrine and Conciliation* (St. Louis, Missouri: Concordia Publishing House, 1975).

170. The conservatives charged that the moderate position presented in the report was not truly representative of the spectrum of positions on the moderate side and that in fact most moderates had replaced the plain sense of Scripture with the rationalism of historical criticism. The moderates complained that by the

time the report was released, most of the issues had been decided by the Anaheim convention. Ibid., pp. 146-47.

171. Ibid., p. 140. The conservatives were quoting the Formula of Concord in making this charge.

172. Ibid., p. 140. By this time, however, even the moderates were willing to acknowledge that honest efforts at reconciliation were too late. The seeds of schism had already been planted.

173. *Forward in Mission: A Report on the Assembly of Evangelical Lutherans in Mission: August 26-28, 1974 in Chicago* (St. Louis, Missouri: ELIM, 1974), p. 17.

174. Four major topics were discussed: 1) the inspiration and inerrancy of Scriptures; 2) the relationship between the Gospel and Scripture; 3) the historical-critical method; and 4) the church under Scripture.

175. Even Preus agreed in "We Hope for Consensus," *Witness*, 27 April 1975, pp. 3, 19. Also see "Weekly News Update #16" from the Synod's Public Relations Office, 16 April 1975 and "Many Delegates Encouraged by Discussion of Issues at Theological Convocation," *Perspective*, 28 April 1975, p. 1.

The one negative aspect of the conservative evaluations was the charge that the moderates did not always state their position fully, preferring at times to hide behind a defence of silence on controversial items. If this is an accurate description of the moderate presence at the theological convocation, and there seems to be enough evidence from both sides of the dispute to substantiate this (see the references above), it supports my contention that the critical issue was what constitutes the church and how much diversity can be tolerated within that church. The moderates did not think they were being dishonest with their silence on the discussions of scriptural interpretation and did not see the differences as important enough to inhibit reconciliation efforts. Conversely, the conservatives wanted to explore every little difference between the two positions because the differences were judged substantial enough not to be tolerated within their concept of what constituted the church.

176. *The Documents of the Theological Convocation held at Concordia Seminary, St. Louis, April 14-18, 1975* (St. Louis: Concordia Publishing House, 1975), pp. 26-27. In elaborating, Bohlmann made it clear that his definition of Gospel was much more encompassing than that of the ELIMites in that it included all the teachings of Scripture that were expounded so explicitly in the Synod's doctrinal statements.

177. Ibid., pp. 34, 38 (emphasis mine).

178. *Forward in Mission*, pp. 20, 23. "They not only think it legitimate for the church to serve as a control and enforcement agency; they think it essential. And they are the enforcers." (p. 24). In "Authority in the Church or Who's in Charge Here Anyway?," a discussion paper issued by ELIM's Division of Communications and Interpretation in 1974, Richard Jungkuntz related thoughts like these to what the church really is.

179. *Forward in Mission*, p. 28. Even more explicit was the speech of Elwyn Ewald, ELIM's general manager. He emphasized that ELIM should not be trying to

decide whether to remain within the Missouri Synod. Rather, ELIM should be asking how its mission to the world can be fulfilled. The Synod will have to decide whether ELIM remains in the Synod (p. 31).

180. Ibid., Resolution 74-1, p. 3. The confessing movement designation was important in that it distinguished ELIM from an "interim church body" or a "church within a church."

181. Ibid., pp. 43-49.

182. Ibid., Resolution 74-12, pp. 7-8. "Limitations on Academic Freedom," issued to synodical schools by the synodical administration in 1974, instructed faculty to teach according to synodically accepted doctrinal statements. If they disagreed with those statements, they were to share their views with their peer group and then with the CTCR but at no time were they to teach contrary to the Synod's official statements (pp. 47-48).

183. There was concern that this document not have the same binding force as Preus's "Statement" did after New Orleans, so "Persuaded" was only "commended for study." See Resolution 74-11, p. 7.

184. Ibid., p. 41.

185. Ibid. (Emphasis mine.)

186. Ibid., p. 42. The assembly made its position clear later when it refused to play the role of interim church body, instead promising to provide support to those who felt compelled to establish a body separate from the Synod.

187. Ibid., Resolution 74-13, p. 8. Resolution 2-21 was "To Uphold Synodically Adopted Resolutions" and 2-12 was "To Adopt Doctrinal Statements."

188. Ibid; also *Perspective*, 9 September 1974, p. 1. Other assembly resolutions adopted indicate ELIM's mission goals. Financial and moral support was pledged for the ELIM publication *Mission in Perspective*, the mission agency Partners in Mission, the Program of Education for Responsible Christian Action (PERCA), and the "Mission Affirmations." Solidarity with the sister churches of Asia was declared and Seminex was pledged over $700,000.

189. These procedures usually involved an analysis of the graduate's training and an intense colloquy wherein his doctrinal purity was assured. *Witness*, 17 April 1974, p. 27. See also good summaries of this in *Convention Workbook, 1975*, pp. 239-43 and *Convention Proceedings, 1975*, pp. 125-26.

190. *Witness*, 19 May 1974, p. 20; *Perspective*, 20 May 1974, p. 1.

191. *Perspective*, 3 June 1974, p. 1; *Witness*, 16 June 1974, p. 24.

192. *Witness*, 3 June 1974, p. 4; 16 June 1974, p. 24.

193. *Witness*, 7 July 1974, p. 19.

194. Preus called this the constitutional crisis of the synod. *Convention Proceedings, 1975*, p. 59. It was at least that, since it rallied the districts and congregations to support the moderate district presidents.

The eight district presidents were: Dr. Herman Frincke of the Eastern District, Rev. Harold Hecht of the English District, Dr. Paul Jacobs of the California-Nevada District, Dr. Emil Jaech of the Northwestern District, Dr. Waldemar Meyer of the Colorado District, Dr. Hermann Neunaber of the

Southern Illinois district, Rev. Rudolph Ressmeyer of the Atlantic District, and Dr. Robert Riedel of the New England District.

195. This argument receives full development in Walter Ross, "My Congregation and Synod," a discussion paper distributed by ELIM's Division of Communications and Interpretation in 1974. Ross emphasized that the founding fathers, particularly Walther, regarded the Synod as an advisory body only; the congregations never surrendered their rights of autonomy.

196. This argument was strengthened when the eight district conventions supported the district presidents in their actions and approved the rights of congregations to call Seminex graduates. See *Witness*, 7 and 28 July 1974, for the reports of the districts.

197. The paper was entitled "The COP, the synodical president and the district presidents with special reference to their duties under the Constitution and Bylaws of the Synod." See also *Witness*, 6 October 1974, p. 20.

198. *Witness*, 16 March 1975, p. 24.

199. *Perspective*, 9 June 1975, p. 8.

200. Letter from C. T. Spitz to ELIM congregations, 26 December 1974. More immediate goals included the support of those in need as a result of the Synod's oppressive actions, the providing of a retirement/welfare program for workers, the training of professional leaders, and acting as a liaison with other Lutheran church bodies.

201. Advantages included the fact that people would have a better opportunity to think through the issues with an incorporation option. Also, incorporation would make a public statement that would signal synodical authorities to the seriousness of the protest.

202. Resolution 75-6 of "Minutes of Contingency Meeting of Lutherans February 7 & 8, 1975 at the O'Hare Inn, Des Plaines, Ill." See also *Perspective*, 24 February 1975, p. 8.

203. "Summary report of Meeting of Continuation Committee of Lutheran Church in Mission on March 7, 1975 at Chicago, Ill.," p. 2.

204. "Catechism on LCM," 25 April 1975.

205. "Minutes of the Meeting of the LCM Board of Directors, Chicago, May 25-26, 1975," p. 1.

206. "Weekly News Update," 16 October 1974; *Perspective*, 21 October 1974, p. 1; *Witness*, 3 November 1974, p. 19.

207. *Perspective*, 21 October 1974, p. 1. Tietjen also stated he would not appeal the decision, to "underscore the conviction that the structure of the Lutheran Church—Missouri Synod has become hopelessly corrupt and that the leadership of the present synodical administration is morally bankrupt."

208. *Witness*, 16 March 1975, p. 24; 15 June 1975, p. 20.

209. In a concluding paragraph, which must have caused the ELIM supporters to gloat more than a little, he stated, "Our concern for purity of doctrine makes us very defensive regarding language and expressions which are not in traditional words. Although this concern for purity of doctrine is commendable and essential for our integrity as a church of the Word (Cf. Matt. 28:20a and

John 8:31), it is lamentable that we 'talk past each other' and are often guilty of misinterpreting what brothers and sisters in Christ say." *Perspective*, 18 August 1975, p. 8.

210. *Affirm*, 1 July 1975.

211. In the 20 May 1974 issue of *Affirm*, the Anaheim convention was termed "crucial" and readers were encouraged to do what they could to ensure that conservative delegates were elected to the convention. On the ELIM side, Elwyn Ewald wrote a series of newsletters asking ELIM representatives to rank candidates for the delegacy positions in the various districts in terms of how moderate they were.

212. They stated that they would go after all the positions they could in the elections. Their theme would appeal to the evangelical crowd at Missouri as it was entitled "A Faithful Witness." They listed their concrete goals as missions, the supporting of synodical workers grievously wronged by the exclusivistic synodical position, and the demanding of repentance from the Missouri Synod for its past actions. *Perspective*, 26 May 1975, p. 5.

213. *Convention Workbook, 1975*, pp. 113-21.

214. Ibid., pp. 186-89. The English District was a nongeographical district of the LC-MS, consisting of English-speaking congregations, most of whom joined the Missouri Synod in 1911 because they felt a theological affinity with the Missourians. Throughout its history the English District was the most moderate arm of the Missouri Synod, with most of its adherents easily characterized as moderates. For instance, almost all of the overtures emanating from the English District for the 1973 convention sympathized with the faculty majority. The intent of New Orleans Resolution 4-41 had been obvious; assimilating the English District in 1973 would have made them a minority in the districts to which they would have been joined and effectively would have eliminated their voice from Synod affairs.

The English District held special meetings to consider its alternatives for the Anaheim convention. *Perspective*, 7 July 1975, p. 1. To make a point, the moderate Atlantic District also voted not to dissolve itself and asserted publicly, through its district president, that any synodical effort "shackling" them to "one, necessarily fallible, theological perspective" would be categorically rejected. *Perspective*, 12 May 1974, p. 1. The early concentration of moderate support on the eastern seaboard (over against conservative support in the Midwest) is demonstrated not only by the strong statements of the Atlantic District but also by the formation of a moderate group called East Coast Common Endeavor, which acted as an information service for the moderate cause.

215. They included a two-minute limit on speaking from the floor and a rule that no omnibus resolution referring all resolutions not covered by the convention to the Board of Directors would be considered. Thus, resolutions not acted upon by the Anaheim convention would die and need to be proposed again in order to be acted upon at future conventions. *Witness*, 26 January 1975, pp. 14-15.

216. *Witness*, 6 October 1974, p. 22.

217. *Convention Proceedings, 1975*, p. 58. While conceding that they were not exactly of the same mind as the conservatives, moderates would not have talked about two different theologies.
218. Ibid., p. 59.
219. Ibid.
220. This is very different from the description of church ELIM provided, which spoke of diversity in unity and learning from one another in the same synod. See especially "We are Persuaded," *Forward in Mission*, pp. 40-42.
221. *Convention Proceedings, 1975*, p. 58.
222. Ibid., pp. 122-24. This resolution received theoretical support from the adoption of Resolution 5-08, which gave the synodical or district convention the right to remove a district president from office by expelling him from membership in the Synod or by removing him from office. In practice, most of the districts supported the rebel presidents so there was little chance that this resolution would be invoked (p. 126).
223. Ibid., p. 34.
224. Ibid., p. 77.
225. Ibid., pp. 141-44.
226. Ibid., p. 94.
227. Ibid., p. 126.
228. Ibid., pp. 36-37, 96-99. Appropriately enough, following the adoption of this resolution, the delegates sang the hymn "I Walk in Danger All the Way."
229. Ibid., p. 94.
230. Ibid., pp. 94-95.
231. Ibid., pp. 95-96. This resolution also said that though such doctrinal statements as Preus's "Statement" could not be considered a requirement for admission to the Synod, the Synod could "beseech all its members to honor and uphold the doctrinal content of such synodically adopted statements"; for the professional church worker that meant teaching and preaching such doctrinal statements until they have been shown to be contrary to the Word of God.
232. Ibid., p. 127.
233. For example, it was under the purview of the CCM that the dissenting district presidents were condemned (Resolution 3-02A, pp. 132-34), that the Seminex graduates were declared ineligible for ordination (Resolution 5-05, pp. 125-26), and that definitions of clergy and teachers would be established (Resolution 5-23, p. 131).

Three very conservative documents, though not adopted, were presented by the CTCR in the Convention Workbook Appendix to be read by delegates. They were not adopted due to time constraints resulting from the haggling over the controversial resolutions. However, all three reinforce this idea of an exclusivistic church wherein total doctrinal conformity to synodical standards is expected for membership to begin or continue:

1) "A Lutheran Stance Towards Ecumenism" said that doctrinal agreement in all areas was necessary before fellowship could be practiced. As well, member congregations should not practice selective fellowship with non-Missourian

individuals or congregations out of consideration for those in the Synod who might be offended. *Workbook, 1975*, pp. 458-61 and *Proceedings, 1975*, Resolution 3-22, p. 104.

2) "The Mission of the Christian Church in the World, A Review of the 1965 Mission Affirmations" qualified the progressive aspects of the "Affirmations" regarding social action, cooperation with other churches, or dialogue with other world religions. After these qualifications there was little substance to the "Affirmations." Ibid., pp. 472-73 and Resolution 3-27, p. 105.

3) "The Inspiration of Scripture" argued that the inerrancy of Scriptures is to be accepted in everything about which the Scriptures speak, even when other sources appear to conflict with what the Scriptures say. Ibid., pp. 106, 454-58.

234. *Report on Third Assembly of Evangelical Lutherans in Mission, Christ Alive, Church Alive*, August 13-15, 1975, Chicago, Illinois (St. Louis: ELIM, 1975), pp. 9-11.

235. Ibid., pp. 16-20.

236. Ibid., p. 2.

237. Ibid., pp. 3, 4.

238. Ibid., pp. 5, 7. The second resolution is a significant departure from LC-MS policy since the Synod practices a fairly strict form of closed communion.

This assembly also voted to continue support for Seminex (Resolution 75-7, p. 6) and affirmed the rights of congregations to "call and ordain as ministers whomever they determine are qualified" (Resolution 75-8, p. 6).

The broader scope of the ELIM mission goal was indicated in Resolution 75-12, "Chile," which called for the support of humanitarian Lutheran Bishop Helmut Frenz and the actions of the American government in providing refuge to 400 Chileans (p. 7). This resolution also directed Partners in Mission to educate ELIM members regarding the struggle for justice in various parts of the world.

239. *Witness*, 14 September 1975, p. 21.

240. *Reporter*, 20 October 1975. By early 1976, this opportunity had been refused by the professors. *Witness*, 22 February 1976, p. 24; *Perspective*, 19 January 1976, p. 1.

241. Letter from Spitz to ELIM members and congregations, dated August 26, 1975.

242. *Perspective*, 29 September 1975, p. 1.

243. *Witness*, 5 October 1975, p. 23.

244. *Perspective*, 10 November 1975, p. 1.

245. *Witness*, 3 November 1975, p. 20; *Perspective*, 24 November 1975, p. 1.

246. *Perspective*, 24 November 1975, p. 1.

247. *Reporter*, 8 December 1975, p. 1.

248. "ELIM Cluster Meeting Minutes," 26-28 February 1976, p. 3. The Synod took these English District rumblings seriously as its Board of Directors discussed the constitutionality of such a move (*Reporter*, 9 February 1976, p. 1; *Witness*, 22 February 1976, p. 23) and the COP expressed concern about the large number

of congregations that had recently affiliated with the English District. *Perspective*, 1 March 1976, p. 1, 8.
249. "Cluster Meeting Minutes," 26-28 February 1976, p. 3.
250. Ibid., Appendix B. Invited to serve on the Council were the eight district presidents, four ELIM members designated by the National Board, two persons designated by the LCM Board and two persons designated by the National Council of Afro-American Lutherans (NCAAL).
251. ELIM "News Release," 28 February 1976, pp. 2-3.
252. Ibid., p. 3. Also "LCM Board of Directors Minutes of the Meeting, February 27, 1976," Resolution 1.
253. *Witness*, 25 April 1976, p. 22; *Reporter*, 12 April 1976, p. 7; *Perspective*, 12 April 1976, pp. 1, 3, 7.
254. There was lots of discussion as to why Preus had not fired the other four, especially since Neunaber said after the four dismissals that he had, in fact, ordained Seminex graduates since being told not to do so. *Reporter*, 22 March 1976, p. 5.
255. "Minutes of Coordinating Council, Second Meeting, O'Hare Hilton, Chicago, Illinois, April 14, 1976," p. 2; *Perspective*, 22 April 1976, p. 1; *Witness*, 16 May 1976, p. 22.
256. "Minutes of the Coordinating Council, Third Meeting, Executive Inn, St. Louis, May 26, 1976," p. 1. The AELC was officially incorporated in the state of Illinois on May 10, 1976 as a nonprofit corporation but there was little function for the corporation at this time. *Reporter*, 10 May 1976, p. 1; *Perspective*, 7 June 1976, pp. 1, 3.
257. *Convention Proceedings of 1976: The Forty-first Convention of the English District of the LC-MS June 17-20, 1976 at Concordia Teacher's College, River Forest, Ill.*, "President's Address," pp. 30-31.
258. Ibid., Resolutions 8-31 and 9-01, "Initiate a Process for Orderly and Peaceful Separation," pp. 55-56. *Reporter*, 28 June 1976, p. 1; *Perspective*, 5 July 1976, p. 1.
259. "Minutes of the Coordinating Council, Fourth meeting, Executive Inn, St. Louis, June 29-30, 1976," p. 2.
260. "Minutes of Meeting of Board of Directors of AELC, Executive Inn, St. Louis, June 30, 1976," p. 1.
261. *ELIM Annual Assembly Report, Chicago, Illinois, August 18-20, 1976*, p. 6.
262. "Minutes of the Fourth Annual Assembly of ELIM," p. 4.
263. Ibid., p. 5. ELIM continued as a "confessing voice of protest" within the synod. *Witness*, 19 September 1976, p. 2.
264. "Minutes of the Fourth Assembly," p. 5.
265. *Witness*, 29 August 1976, p. 24; *Reporter*, 23 August 1976, p. 1.
266. *Reporter*, 11 October 1976, p. 1.
267. Meyer of Colorado resigned on October 22, 1976. *Witness*, 21 November 1976, p. 1; *Reporter*, 1 November 1976, p. 1; *Perspective*, 8 November 1976, p. 11.
268. *Perspective*, 22 November 1976, p. 1. The five regional synods were the Pacific Coast, Southwest, Great Rivers, East Coast, and New England. Note the lack

of geographical localization. Obviously, the theological debate had assumed national proportions.

269. *Reporter*, 29 November 1976, p. 1. The largest was reported to be the English Synod.

270. AELC News Release, December 4, 1976, p. 1. Only four regional synods were represented: the Eastern, Great Rivers, Southwest, and Pacific. The English Synod was the fifth nongeographic synod. Also *Reporter*, 13 December 1976, p. 1; *Witness*, 16 January 1977, p. 24. Many of the congregations still held their Missouri Synod membership. *Witness*, 10 April 1977, p. 19. The synodical administration did not force them to decide until September 1977. *Witness*, February 1979, p. 26.

271. Keynote Address of First Convention of Association of Evangelical Lutheran Churches, December 3-4, 1976, p. 4.

272. "Minutes of the Founding Convention of the Association of Evangelical Lutheran Churches," 3-4 December 1976, Resolution 76-3, pp. 2-3.

273. For instance, the most recent action of the Synod in this regard was taken in 1971 in Milwaukee when Resolution 3-07 was adopted declining to pursue membership in the NCC and the WCC. *Convention Proceedings, 1971*, p. 131. Resolution 3-06 of the same convention declined to pursue membership in the LWF. Ibid.

274. *Handbook*, pp. 16, 17; AELC *Constitution*, pp. 1-2.

275. *Constitution*, p. 2. The first sentence shown here is identical to the corresponding synodical section; however, while the second AELC sentence gives any unspecified powers to the congregations, the Missourian sentence here reads: "Accordingly, no resolution of Synod imposing anything upon the individual congregation is of binding force if it is not in accordance with the Word of God or if it appears to be inexpedient as far as the condition of a congregation is concerned." *Handbook*, p. 18. Since the Synod determined what the Word of God said, the congregation effectively had power in name only. Bylaw 1.09b of the Synod's constitution supports that interpretation; it reads: "The Synod expects every member congregation to respect its resolutions and to consider them of binding force if they are in accordance with the Word of God" (p. 28).

276. "Minutes of the Founding Convention," p. 5. This was very much in line with another thrust of Kohn's keynote address: "It is our intention as a church body to give the people of the AELC opportunity to be involved in the study of theological issues, so that consensus on understanding the Scriptures, rather than voting power, shall be the deciding factor." "Our Church in Mission," p. 3. This position is in stark contrast with that of the Missouri Synod, which at the Milwaukee convention enforced its uniformity of practice on the issue with Resolution 2-04 "To Withhold Ordination of Women to the Pastoral Office," *Convention Proceedings, 1971*, pp. 114-15.

277. In his keynote address, Kohn felt compelled to address the charge: "Recently I heard it said that the AELC stands for nothing and falls for everything." "Church in Mission," p. 4.

278. *AELC Constitution*, Article XI, p. 2.
279. See Danker's argument in *No Room in the Brotherhood*.
280. This is in stark contrast with Preus's assertion that the Synod and its convention were the "highest authority." Also compare the CTCR's "Opinion on Dissenting Groups," which stated "when the majority has been determined, it must be respected."
281. "Preamble to Constitution and Bylaws of the Association of Evangelical Lutheran Churches," 1976, pp. 1-2.
282. Takayama, "Strains and Schisms," pp. 319-20.

CHAPTER FOUR

1. Stephen H. Applegate, "The Rise and Fall of the Thirty-Nine Articles: an Inquiry into the identity of the Protestant Episcopal Church in the United States of America," *Historical Magazine of the Protestant Episcopal Church* 50 (December 1981): 409-21.
2. C. Allison FitzSimons, "Towards an Historical Hermeneutic for Understanding the PECUSA," *Historical Magazine of the Protestant Episcopal Church* 48 (March 1979): 9-25.
3. Powel M. Dawley, *Chapters in Church History* (New York: The National Council of the Protestant Episcopal Church, 1950), pp. 213, 221, 224.
4. Episcopal Church became an alternate official name in 1967. See Constant H. Jacquet, Jr., *Yearbook of American and Canadian Churches, 1984* (Nashville: Abingdon Press, 1984), p. 51.
5. Article XI of the *Constitution and Canons for the Government of the Protestant Episcopal Church in the United States of America Otherwise Known as the Episcopal Church*, adopted in 1789 and amended in conventions since then, printed in *Journal for the General Convention of 1970* (n.p.: n.d.), pp. 9-10. Piepkorn, *Profiles in Belief*, 2: 225.
6. For a summary of the General Convention structure, see Bob Wallace, *General Convention of the Episcopal Church* (New York: Seabury Press, 1976). The Executive Council was known as the National Council until 1964, when the name was changed to avoid confusion with the National Council of Churches. *The Living Church*, 29 October 1978, p. 21.
7. Article I, Sections 3 and 4, *Constitution and Canons*, 1970, pp. 1-2.
8. "No action of either order shall pass in the affirmative unless it receives the majority of all votes cast and unless the sum of all the affirmative votes shall exceed the sum of the other votes by at least one whole vote." Article I, Section 4, ibid., p. 2. While some see this as a restriction of the democratic process, proponents of the system argue that serious matters will pass only with a large supporting vote and that the system preserves the structural basis of the denomination as a group of dioceses working together. *The Episcopalian*, November 1973, pp. 54-55.

9. FitzSimons speaks of the apostolic succession of bishops as the "esse" of the Episcopal Church. "Understanding the PECUSA," p. 18. William H. Petersen says, "It has been progressively disclosed that doctrine is *not* what unifies Episcopalians. Among Anglicans, doctrine is not so much a positive and prescriptive thing as it is an historical and disruptive aspect of tradition and the parameters of it." "Tensions of Anglican Identity in the PECUSA: An Interpretative Essay," *Historical Magazine of the Protestant Episcopal Church* 47 (December 1978): 432. See also Michael McFarlene Marrett, *The Lambeth Conferences and Women Priests: The Historical Background of the Conferences and Their Impact on the Episcopal Church in America* (Smithtown, New York: Exposition Press, 1981), p. 39. Wayne B. Williamson, *Growth and Decline in the Episcopal Church* (Pasadena: William Carey Library, 1979), pp. 12ff. supports this view. The adoption of the tolerant Lambeth Quadrilateral at the third Lambeth Conference in 1897 also demonstrates the very broad doctrinal boundaries of the Anglican communion. The Quadrilateral adopted the Bible, the Apostle's and Nicene creeds, the two sacraments of Baptism and the Lord's Supper, and the historic episcopate "locally adapted" as the signs of the Anglican communion. No other doctrinal requisites were established. Piepkorn, *Profiles in Belief*, p. 176.

10. Article VIII, *Constitution and Canons*, 1970, p. 7. The second part reads, "and I do solemnly endeavor to conform to the Doctrine, Discipline and Worship of the Protestant Episcopal Church in the United States of America."

11. Williamson, *Growth and Decline*, pp. 14, 19. Williamson states it succinctly when he titles Chapter 2 "Anglicanism is more a Loyalty than a Doctrinal Position."

12. Paul Seabury, "Trendier Than Thou: The Many Temptations of the Episcopal Church," *Harper's*, October 1978, p. 44; Williamson, *Growth and Decline*, p. 20. As the *Constitution and Canons*, 1970, state in Article X, pp. 8-9: "The Book of Common Prayer and Administration of the Sacraments and other Rites and Ceremonies of the Church, together with the Psalter or Psalms of David, the Form and Manner of Making, Ordaining, and Consecrating Bishops, Priests and Deacons . . . now established or hereafter amended by the authority of this church, shall be in use in all the Dioceses and Missionary Dioceses. . . . No alteration thereof or addition thereto shall be made unless the same shall be first proposed in one triennial meeting of the General Convention and . . . be adopted by the General Convention at its next succeeding triennial meeting by a majority of all Bishops . . . and by a majority of the clerical and lay deputies of the Dioceses entitled to representation in the House of Deputies."

13. Seabury, "Trendier than Thou," p. 40.

14. For example, neither Awakening stirred up the Episcopal masses. The satirical remark that the "Episcopal Church entered the West in a Pullman car" (Williamson, *Growth and Decline*, p. 24) seemed to characterize much of the evangelizing effort of the Episcopal Church right into the twentieth century. See also pp. 35ff.; Dawley, *Church History*, pp. 228ff.

15. Williamson, *Growth and Decline*, p. xi.

16. Seabury, "Trendier Than Thou," p. 39. For a contrasting opinion, see Earl H. Brill, "Episcopal Church: Conflict and Cohesion," *Christian Century* 95 (18 January 1978): 41-47.

17. Williamson, *Growth and Decline*, p. 141.

18. Piepkorn, *Profiles in Belief*, pp. 216ff.

19. Williamson, *Growth and Decline*, p. 3.

20. Piepkorn, *Profiles in Belief*, p. 213.

21. This is part of the thesis of Charles Y. Glock and Benjamin B. Ringer, *To Comfort and to Challenge* (Berkeley: University of California Press, 1967).

22. *The Living Church*, 29 October 1978, p. 23. See also E. R. Chandler and J. F. Politzer, "Episcopal Church Convention," *Christianity Today* 14 (6 November 1970): 43-44. The GCSP was initiated at the 1967 General Convention and disassembled in late 1973. A new social program was subsequently organized under the Mission Service and Strategy department. In this way some of the more extreme aspects of Hines's "empowerment" program were conveniently dropped. *The Living Church*, 18 November 1973, p. 6.

23. Piepkorn, *Profiles in Belief*, p. 211. E. R. Chandler, "Squirming in South Bend," *Christianity Today* 13 (26 September 1969): 42-44.

24. Piepkorn, *Profiles in Belief*, p. 212. In 1967, the FCT released a "Christian Affirmation: A Response to the Crisis in the Episcopal Church," which asked Episcopalians to divert funds away from the PECUSA because of its "support of seditious and revolutionary groups." E. R. Chandler, "Double Trouble . . . Cauldron Boiling," *Christianity Today* 14 (7 November 1969): 51.

25. Seabury, "Trendier Than Thou," p. 44; *The Living Church*, 29 October 1978, p. 23.

26. J. E. Wagner, "Whither Episcopalians?" *Christianity Today* 17 (10 November 1972): 18-19. The other formative factors were experience, revelation, tradition, culture, and reason. See also Piepkorn, *Profiles in Belief*, p. 158.

27. Piepkorn, *Profiles in Belief*, p. 212; *The Living Church*, 29 October 1978, p. 22.

28. Piepkorn, *Profiles in Belief*, p. 214; *The Episcopalian*, September 1973, p. 3.

29. *The Living Church*, 10 October 1976, p. 7.

30. The 1976 convention resolution condemned any legislation that denied or abridged the right of women to obtain abortions; the same legislation also condemned abortions of convenience. *The Living Church*, 24 October 1976, p. 6.

31. Marjorie Hyer develops this point in "How Not to Heal Wounds," *Christianity and Crisis* 37 (28 November 1977): 281-83.

32. Piepkorn, *Profiles in Belief*, pp. 253-54; *The Living Church*, 29 October 1978, p. 21; Donald S. Armentrout, *Episcopal Splinter Groups: A Study of Groups Which Have Left the Episcopal Church, 1873-1985* (Sewanee, Tennessee: The University of the South, 1985), pp. 8-12. Dees also opposed the "socialism" of the Episcopal Church and espoused a political conservatism that linked the "American Free Enterprise System and our Constitutional Republican Form of Government . . . to the survival of Christianity." Armentrout, p. 9.

33. Piepkorn, *Profiles in Belief*, p. 254-55; Armentrout, *Splinter Groups*, pp. 13-17.
34. Piepkorn, *Profiles in Belief*, p. 212.
35. Seabury, "Trendier Than Thou," p. 40.
36. Ahlstrom, *Religious History*, 1: 131. Piepkorn said, "One central feature of Anglican fellowship continues to be high regard for and use of the Book of Common Prayer." *Profiles in Belief*, p. 178.
37. Piepkorn, *Profiles in Belief*, p. 148; Ahlstrom, *Religious History*, pp. 448-49. There were other issues involved in this compromise. William White, one of the English ordained bishops, fought for and won lay representation at every level of church government, and Seabury protected the esteemed place of the episcopate by establishing a separate House of Bishops, whose approval on all church legislation was necessary for a law to be effective.
38. Piepkorn, *Profiles in Belief*, p. 226; *The Episcopalian*, September 1976, p. 33. See also John Wallace Suter and George Julius Cleaveland, *The American Book of Common Prayer, Its Origin and Development* (New York: Oxford University Press, 1949) for detailed descriptions of the revisions of 1892 and 1928.
39. *The Episcopalian*, September 1975, p. 12.
40. In 1928, the General Convention established the SLC as an official continuing committee of six members; by 1964 it consisted of twenty-three members. *The Living Church*, 7 September 1975, p. 5.
41. *Journal of the General Convention of the Protestant Episcopal Church in the United States of America*, Washington, D.C., September 17-27, 1967, pp. 480-82; *The Episcopalian*, March 1976, pp. 12-13.
42. *Journal of 1967*, p. 459.
43. *Journal of the General Convention of the Protestant Episcopal Church in the United States of America*, 1970, pp. 342-50; *The Episcopalian*, September 1975. p. 9.
44. The six have been characterized as "intellectual and literary snobs." *The Living Church*, 22 December 1974, p. 5. They were John M. Aden, Harold L. Weatherby, Walter Sullivan, and John Glass of the English faculty at Vanderbilt University; Howard Rhys and William Ralston of the University of the South; Rev. James Law of Chattanooga; and Andrew Lytle, editor of *The Sewanee Review*. *The Living Church*, 10 June 1973, p. 12.
45. *The Living Church*, 22 December 1974, p. 5.
46. *The Living Church*, 10 June 1973, p. 13.
47. Ibid.
48. Ibid.
49. *Journal of the General Convention of the Protestant Episcopal Church in the United States of America*, 1973.
50. *The Episcopalian*, September 1975, p. 9.
51. *The Episcopalian*, November 1973, p. 2; September 1975. p. 9; Piepkorn, *Profiles in Belief*, p. 226.
52. *The Episcopalian*, November 1973, p. 40. The 1973 General Convention spent a great deal of time debating the proposed confirmation revisions that virtually

eliminated the rite as a effective act. The convention also directed the addition of material to the proposed draft including prayers, thanksgiving, litanies, a new daily office, a revised psalter, dedication ceremonies for churches, and a new catechism.

53. *The Living Church*, 10 November 1974, p. 6.
54. *The Living Church*, 22 December 1974, p. 5. This softened perspective of the SPBCP was in evidence again in the spring of 1975 when the SPBCP claimed that they wanted change but not schism and that they would be quite happy to get continuous authorization for the 1928 Prayer book if they could not obtain a moratorium for the current revision process. See *The Episcopalian*, June 1975, p. 5 and *The Living Church*, 11 May 1975, p. 6.
55. *The Episcopalian*, March 1975, p. 3.
56. Standing Liturgical Commission, *The Draft Proposed Book of Common Prayer and Other Rites and Ceremonies of the Church* (New York: The Church Hymnal Corporation, 1976); *The Episcopalian*, March 1975, pp. 12-13.
57. *The Episcopalian*, February 1976, pp. 14-16.
58. For a detailed analysis of the *Proposed Book*, see Charles P. Price, *Introducing the Proposed Book of Common Prayer* (New York: Seabury Press, 1977). Piepkorn gives a concise summary of most of Price's observations, *Profiles in Belief*, pp. 227-32.
59. *The Episcopalian*, March 1976, p. 1; also *The Living Church*, 7 March 1976, p. 6. As with the 1928 version, the model for the services of the Eucharist was the Scottish communion service as found in the Scottish Prayer Book of 1637.
60. *The Episcopalian*, September 1975, p. 12.
61. Piepkorn, *Profiles in Belief*, p. 228.
62. *The Living Church*, 10 November 1974, p. 5; *The Episcopalian*, December 1974, p. 3; Piepkorn, *Profiles in Belief*, p. 229.
63. *The Episcopalian*, March 1976, pp. 12-13.
64. Sullivan is also quoted as saying that he would try to delay consideration of the *Proposed Book* until 1979 because the public relations work already accomplished by the SLC would be impossible to overcome at the 1976 General Convention.
65. *The Episcopalian*, September 1976, p. 33.
66. These advertisements asked for fifty thousand Episcopalians to come forward to "save the Prayer Book." *The Episcopalian*, April, June 1976, p. 28.
67. *The Living Church*, 7 September 1975, p. 6.
68. *The Episcopalian*, September 1975, p. 2.
69. Concerns voiced and resolved at the Prayer Book hearings immediately prior to the General Convention included: initiation rites that were worked into the confirmation service; concerns regarding the international consultation in English texts; the fact that there were so many options in the *Proposed Book*; the changes in the Eucharistic rites; Psalter changes; and the use of generic pronouns. *The Episcopalian*, October 1976, p. 1; Jean C. Lyles, "Episcopal

Agony over Ecclesiastical Disobedience," *Christian Century* 91 (4 September 1974): 812-14.

70. For example, when the House of Bishops realized that the House of Deputies was not going to relent in its insistence that the "filioque" be included in the Nicene Creed, they conceded the point and the historical anomaly remained. *The Episcopalian*, October 1976, p. 1.

71. Jean C. Lyles, "Common Prayer and an Uncommon Convention," *Christian Century* 93 (6 October 1976): 829-30.

72. *The Episcopalian*, September 1976, p. 33; *The Living Church*, 10 October 1976, p. 9.

73. *The Episcopalian*, October 1976, p. 1.

74. Piepkorn, *Profiles in Belief*, p. 217. American women activists received little support at this time from the international Anglican community. In 1948, the Lambeth Conference affirmed a 1930 resolution that the "Order of Deaconess is for women the one and only Order of the Ministry which we can recommend our branch of the Catholic Church to recognize and use." In 1966, a Commission of the Church of England issued a report entitled *Women and Holy Orders* that showed irreconcilable views within the church on this subject (p. 152).

75. The Lambeth Conference had recommended the ordination of women to the priesthood in 1968; however, because the Conference was only an advisory body, its counsels did not have to be followed, though there is little doubt that its directives were taken seriously. Marrett's *Lambeth Conferences* demonstrates the power of the Conference with reference to women's ordination in the Protestant Episcopal Church.

76. *The Living Church*, 28 October 1973, p. 7.

77. *The Episcopalian*, September 1974, p. 6. Traditionally the diaconate had been a one-year training program following seminary training and prior to ordination to the priesthood. Though the resolution explicitly denied that women could be ordained to the priesthood, it did hint of movement toward the idea of an ordained female priesthood with this concession of full membership in the diaconate.

78. The Anglican communions in Burma, New Zealand, and Canada had adopted in principle the ordination of women by November of 1974. Prior to the 1948 Lambeth Conference, South China had actually asked for "an experimental period of twenty years to see how it [women's ordination] would work." Piepkorn, *Profiles in Belief*, pp. 153-54.

79. *The Episcopalian*, November 1974, p. 18.

80. Piepkorn, *Profiles in Belief*, pp. 154-55. Lambeth said there are "no conclusive theological reasons for withholding ordination to the priesthood from women as such," as the Scriptures appeared divided on the issue. Lambeth also acknowledged that the authority of tradition based on "biological assumptions about the nature of woman and her relation to man . . . are considered unacceptable in the light of modern knowledge and biblical study and have been generally discarded today." Marrett, *Lambeth Conferences*, pp. 7ff.

81. *The Episcopalian*, September 1974, p. 6.
82. *The Living Church*, 15 April 1973, p. 6; *The Episcopalian*, March 1973, p. 3.
83. The Coalition for the Apostolic Ministry (CAM) ran advertisements in *The Episcopalian*, June 1973, p. 21 and *The Living Church*, 10 June 1973, p. 9.
84. Most active of those groups favoring women's ordination was the National Coalition for the Ordination of Women. See Edward R. Plowman, "Episcopalian Church: Women are Winners," *Christianity Today* 21 (8 October 1976): 48-52; also *The Episcopalian*, March 1975, p. 6; December 1975, p. 9; January 1976, p. 14. The coalition also warned that "the church is perilously close to schism if the issue of women's ordination is not dealt with justly, promptly and forthrightly." *The Living Church*, 9 March 1975, p. 6.

    Other groups that had campaigned for the ordination of women prior to the convention were Women's Ordination Now (WON), Priests for the Ordination of Women (POW), the Episcopal Women's Caucus, and the Anglican Women's Alliance. See *The Episcopalian*, September 1975, p. 8; *The Living Church*, 19 June 1973, p. 26.
85. *The Episcopalian*, November 1973, pp. 16-17; *The Living Church*, 28 October 1973, pp. 7-8; William A. Norgren, "Ecumenical Relations and Ordination of Women to the Priesthood of the Episcopal Church," *Mid-Stream* 16 (October 1977): 374-82. For a good summary of the arguments regarding women's ordination, see Paul K. Jewett, *The Ordination of Women: An Essay in the Office of Christian Ministry* (Grand Rapids: William B. Eerdmans Publishing Co., 1980).
86. Other matters to be considered included the remarriage laws, the controversial social action program (GCSP) of the retiring Bishop Hines, the revision of the Common Prayer Book, and continuing ecumenical relations with other denominations.
87. Hines had already made it clear he favored the ordination of women to the priesthood. *The Living Church*, 21 October 1973, p. 7.
88. Missouri was one of the leading conservative dioceses and Allin's chief opponent in the election was a chief proponent of women's ordination. *The Episcopalian*, November 1973, p. 1; *The Living Church*, 28 October 1973, p. 6; also C. A. Forbes, "Renewal on the Right," *Christianity Today* 18 (26 October 1973): 55-57.
89. *The Episcopalian*, December 1973, p. 21.
90. *The Episcopalian*, November 1973, p. 1; *The Living Church*, 28 October 1973, p. 7.
91. *The Episcopalian*, November 1973, p. 1.
92. Ibid., November 1973, pp. 23ff.
93. Especially after the Triennial Meeting of Women, meeting concurrently with the General Convention, approved women's ordination by a 2-1 margin. Ibid., p. 23.
94. Ibid., p. 56.

95. The very nub of the question was reflected in an exchange where the question "Is this democracy?" was answered "No, this is the Episcopal Church." Ibid., p. 54.
96. Other questions were related to this issue. Were individual dioceses to be subjected to the will of the majority without regard to the denomination's basis as an association of dioceses? Was the apostolic succession of the denomination, upon which the denomination had been founded, to receive reinterpretation as a result of the vote of the majority in the denomination? How were dioceses to react when they were not allowed to ordain those whom they felt were qualified to follow in the apostolic succession of the priestly calling, especially when the dioceses, not the General Convention, were responsible for calling priests?
97. Ibid., p. 2. Terwilliper and Holmes, eds., *To Be a Priest: Perspectives on Vocation and Ordination*, and Homes and Barnhouse, eds., *Male and Female*, were published as a result of these studies.
98. *The Episcopalian*, December 1973, p. 21.
99. In June of 1974, the dean of the Philadelphia Divinity School, Edward G. Harris, and the vice president of the House of Deputies, Charles V. Willie, called on bishops to begin ordaining women. *The Episcopalian*, September 1974, p. 6.
100. Ibid.
101. A similar set of circumstances obtained for Bishop R. Spears and Deacon Merrill Bittner later in the month.
102. *The Living Church*, 18 August 1974, p. 5.
103. *The Episcopalian*, September 1974, p. 6.
104. Bishop Hall had excused himself from the ordination ceremony, explaining that he withdrew in penitence though he praised the courage of the three who did participate. Ibid.
105. *The Living Church*, 18 August 1974, p. 5.
106. Established in 1937 "with the commitment to uphold the doctrine, discipline and worship of the Episcopal Church," the ACU had a vision of the PECUSA as a part of the universal Catholic church. "Membership is open to any baptized person who states his/her belief that Anglicanism must remain part of the Catholic and historic Church of Christ, believe *ex animo* (in its entirety, in its historic sense) the Nicene Creed, recognizes Baptism, Confirmation, Holy Eucharist, Penance, Holy Orders, Matrimony, and Unction as sacraments as expressed in the 1928 Book of Common Prayer." Canon Albert J. DuBois was ACU chairman. Armentrout, *Splinter Groups*, p. 25.
107. Founded in late 1972 by Rev. John L. Scott, Jr. for the purpose of campaigning against women's ordination, CAM described itself in an advertising blitz prior to the 1973 convention as "an independent voice for the Episcopal Church's clergy and laity who believe that ordination of women to the priesthood or episcopate is a question to be decided only after study, consultation and debate." *The Episcopalian*, June 1973, p. 31. CAM's "Declaration of Principle" was a set of proofs from Scripture, tradition, and doctrine demonstrating their vision of an apostolic ministry as intended for

males only. CAM continued to advertise and lobby until the 1976 convention, when it dissolved. Armentrout, *Splinter Groups*, pp. 22-23. Even at that most emotional time just before the 1976 General Convention, CAM urged all those opposing women's ordination to stay in the PECUSA. "It [the Minneapolis decision] will cause pain. There will be no winners; Christian charity demands there be no losers. . . .[We must] stay and work within the Church. Only thus can reconciliation be reached." *The Episcopalian*, May 1976, p. 8. The committee became known as the Coalition for Apostolic Ministry after 1973.

108. *The Episcopalian*, September 1974, p. 10. Mallary's speech of protest can be found in Armentrout, *Splinter Groups*, pp. 33-34, where he concludes with an exhortation not to "shatter the unity and peace of the Church."

109. *The Living Church*, 18 August 1974, p. 5.

110. *The Episcopalian*, September 1974, p. 10. Almost the entire 16 September 1974 issue of *Christianity and Crisis* is devoted to the Philadelphia ordinations.

111. *The Episcopalian*, October 1974, pp. 10, 11. There was some debate about Vogel's interpretation of the Jesuit Franz Josef van Beeck's definition of "validity." See *The Episcopalian*, November 1974, p. 5; *The Living Church*, 27 October 1974, p. 9, and 3 November 1974, p. 6.

112. *The Episcopalian*, September 1974, p. 7.

113. Ibid. Allin managed to convince those who had already brought charges against the ordaining bishops to drop those charges; however, others soon brought new charges.

114. The censuring resolution had originally been adopted by an overwhelming majority of 129 out of a possible 146 votes. Ibid., p. 1.

115. W. Stringfellow, "The Bishops at O'Hare: Mischief and a Mighty Curse," *Christianity and Crisis* 34 (16 September 1974): 195-96.

116. *The Living Church*, 15 September 1974, p. 5 and *The Episcopalian*, September 1974, p. 1.

117. *The Living Church*, 22 September 1974, p. 7. Charges also flew from the pens of conservatives and other denominational leaders against ordaining bishops. *The Episcopalian*, October 1974, pp. 1, 3, 7ff; November 1974, p. 5; *The Living Church*, 22 September 1974, p. 7; 27 October 1974, pp. 5, 9; 3 November 1974, p. 6.

118. C. A. Forbes, "When is a Priest not a Priest?" *Christianity Today* 18 (13 September 1974): 68-70. Allin's comments stand in stark contrast to those analyses of the controversy that claimed that the context of the debate was not theological but one of power struggles between a "clergy-ridden hierarchy" and progressively "democratic dioceses." See Betty Gray, "Episcopal Church: An Endangered Species," *Christian Century* 94 (16 November 1977): 1053; Betty Medsger, "Episcopal Ordinations: Where have the Liberal Bishops Gone?" *Christianity and Crisis* 35 (18 August 1975): p. 190-92.

119. *The Episcopalian*, October 1974, p. 3; *The Living Church*, 22 September 1974, p. 7. Several of the ordinands wrote back complaining that if Allin wanted to contact them, why had he not done so in person at the House of Bishops

meeting August 14-15. The ordinands had all been ignored at this meeting though their presence was obvious. *The Living Church*, 8 September 1974, p. 7.

120. The bishops decided against the idea of a special General Convention to be convened before 1976 simply because it would not allow for adequate discussion on such a controversial topic. *The Living Church*, 3 November 1974, p. 6; 17 November 1974, p. 7; *The Episcopalian*, December 1974, pp. 1, 16.

121. "Theology Committee Report," *The Episcopalian*, December 1974, p. 17.

122. *The Episcopalian*, November 1974, p. 1; *The Living Church*, 17 November 1974, p. 10.

123. *The Living Church*, 8 December 1974, p. 5; M. M. Schidler, "Alison Cheek's Achievement," *Christian Century* 91 (11 December 1974): 1165-66.

124. *The Living Church*, 29 December 1974, p. 5.

125. Edward R. Plowman, "Wendt Case: Women on Trial," *Christianity Today* 19 (23 May 1975): 55-57; Leon Howell, "A Godly Admonition: The Trial of William Wendt," *Christian Century* 92 (21 May 1975): 517-19.

126. *The Episcopalian*, August 1975, p. 3. The accounts of their trails and the issues involved can be followed in *The Episcopalian*, June 1975, p. 3; July 1975, p. 4; August 1975, p. 3; *The Living Church*, 23 May 1975, p. 5; 17 August 1975, p. 7; 4 January 1976, p. 5; 11 January 1976, p. 10.

127. For example, with the Eastern Orthodox (*The Living Church*, 6 April 1975, p. 7; 21 December 1975, p. 5; 7 March 1976, p. 6; 25 July 1976, p. 10), the Polish National Church, with whom the PECUSA had been enjoying intercommunion, and the Antiochian Orthodox Church in America (*The Living Church*, 22 September 1974, p. 7), and the Roman Catholics (*The Episcopalian*, December 1975, p. 9; *The Living Church*, 23 November 1975, p. 6; 6 January 1974, p. 7).

128. *The Episcopalian*, February 1975, p. 13.

129. As the bishops said: "The doctrinal question was not simply whether women should be ordained . . . but rather whether this Church's understanding of the *nature of the church* and the authority of the episcopate permits individual bishops, by appealing solely to their consciences, to usurp the proper function of other duly constituted authorities of this church" (emphasis mine). *The Episcopalian*, May 1975, p. 1.

130. For example, Hurt of Ohio said he would resign if the General Convention did not open the priesthood. *The Episcopalian*, March 1975, p. 6. Creighton of Washington said he would not ordain anybody, male or female, until after the 1976 convention, when he would either start ordaining both men and women (regardless of the convention decision) or stop ordaining altogether (if the decision did not favor women's ordination). *The Episcopalian*, May 1975, p. 9; *The Living Church*, 27 April 1975, p. 6. Retired Bishops Dewitt and Welles said they would not ordain any more women until after the 1976 convention but would do so after the convention even if a negative vote was recorded. *The Episcopalian*, September 1974, p. 11.

131. *The Episcopalian*, July 1975, p. 7.
132. *The Episcopalian*, November 1975, p. 1; *The Living Church*, 19 October 1975, p. 6; 26 October 1975, p. 8.
133. *The Episcopalian*, November 1975, p. 1.
134. After predicting that the 1976 convention would approve women's ordination, Allin is reported to have said, "If God can make me a Presiding Bishop, he can make women priests." *The Living Church*, 29 February 1976, p. 8; *The Episcopalian*, March 1976, p. 2.
135. *The Episcopalian*, May 1976, p. 8.
136. *The Living Church*, 10 October 1976, p. 6.
137. Ibid., p. 7. Other compromises included ordaining women by way of a constitutional amendment, which would mean that two successive conventions would have to approve the resolution.
138. *The Episcopalian*, October 1976, p. 1.
139. *The Living Church*, 10 October 1976, p. 7.
140. *The Episcopalian*, October 1976, p. 1. Though the status of the eleven already ordained was of some concern, it was finally decided after two days of debate and a reversal of an earlier decision, to proclaim "in a public event" that the ordinations had been regularized. This was considered a compromise in view of the more extreme option of reordaining the women yet again. John Raeside, "Episcopal Reconciliation in Minneapolis?" *Christianity and Crisis* 36 (18 October 1976): 232-34.
141. The sessional chairman had issued a plea immediately prior to the vote for restraint on an issue of such great controversy. *The Episcopalian*, October 1976, p. 1; *The Living Church*, 10 October 1976, p. 6.
142. Armentrout, *Splinter Groups*, p. 20.
143. *The Certain Trumpet* began publishing in 1972 because of concerns regarding liberal developments in the PECUSA. Ibid., p. 26.
144. Ibid., p. 24. These organizations included the ACU, which published the *American Church Union News*; the Society for Promoting and Encouraging the Arts and Knowledge of the Church (SPEAK), which published *The Anglican Digest*; The Canterbury Guild, which existed only in preparation for the 1973 General Convention; the Foundation for Christian Theology, which published *The Christian Challenge*; Council for the Faith (Canada), which published *Comment*; the SPBCP; *The Certain Trumpet*; the Congregation of St. Augustine; the Episcopal Guild for the Blind; the Episcopal Renaissance of Pennsylvania; Episcopalians United/Anglicans United and the Society for the Holy Cross (also known as the *Societas Sanctae Crucis* or SSC). Though *The Living Church* was listed as a member, it never took any official action to associate itself with the FCC; however, its editor, C. Simcox, was very active in the FCC. Other than those mentioned specifically by name in the text, none of the organizations/publications listed plays any significant role in the schismatic process other than as a member of the FCC. For brief descriptions of them, see Armentrout, *Splinter Groups*, pp. 25-32.

145. Ibid., p. 21; *The Christian Challenge*, November 1973, p. 1. It is important to note that the "tradition" is defined here in terms of theological doctrines and constructs, with an emphasis placed on preserving the "substance of the Faith."

146. *The Christian Challenge*, November 1973, p. 1; Armentrout, *Splinter Groups*, p. 21.

147. Armentrout, *Splinter Groups*, p. 22; *The Christian Challenge*, November 1973, p. 28.

148. Armentrout, *Splinter Groups*, pp. 34-35.

149. *The Living Church*, 10 August 1975, p. 6.

150. *The Living Church*, 21 September 1975, p. 6; *The Episcopalian*, November 1975, p. 6.

151. *The Living Church*, 15 February 1976, p. 7; 28 March 1976, p. 6; "News Item," *Christianity Today* (18 June 1976): 137.

152. Armentrout, *Splinter Groups*, pp. 35-37.

153. "A Call to Episcopalians to Pray and Be Steadfast," ibid., p. 38; *The Christian Challenge*, September 1976, p. 4.

154. *The Christian Challenge*, November 1976, p. 1.

155. Armentrout, *Splinter Groups*, p. 41; also "Episcopal Fight Continues," *The Christian Century*, 22 December 1976, p. 11.

156. *The Living Church*, 5 December 1976, p. 8. At the close of the Nashville meeting, the FCC released a statement that said in part "that defection from true doctrine in the Episcopal Church is related both in cause and effect to defection from the moral principles which our Lord taught. It [the FCC] calls, therefore, not only for the structural implementation of a continuing church but for a renewal of spiritual life and a reassertion of moral principles." Ibid. Advertisements for the FCC congress read, "You are Invited to *A Congress* called by The Fellowship of Concerned Churchmen to continue the Catholic and Apostolic faith of Episcopalians in America AND to establish a church structure to that end." *The Living Church*, 15 May 1977, p. 5.

157. See Armentrout, *Splinter Groups*, p. 41; *The Living Church*, 6 March 1977, p. 6; 17 April 1977, p. 6; 15 May 1977, p. 10, for a listing of some of these "independents."

158. *The Episcopalian*, November 1977, p. 11 (Emphasis mine.) The ECM seemed to be one of the more positive movements. They insisted they were not just *against* things like women's ordination but were interested in *affirming* things like authority, ministry, spirituality, and morality.

159. Armentrout, *Splinter Groups*, pp. 44-45; *The Episcopalian*, August 1977, p. 8; *The Living Church*, 31 July 1977, p. 6.

160. *The Episcopalian*, October 1975, p. 8.

161. *The Living Church*, 10 October 1976, p. 7.

162. *The Living Church*, 6 February 1977, p. 5; *The Episcopalian*, March 1977, p. 1; Edward R. Plowman, "A Veteran Out: A Lesbian In," *Christianity Today* 21 (4 February 1977): 55-56.

163. *The Episcopalian*, March 1977, pp. 1, 15.

164. *The Living Church*, 27 February 1977, pp. 9-10.
165. *The Living Church*, 13 February 1977, p. 5; 6 March 1977, pp. 10-11. Conservatives protested even louder when the Commission for Ministry for the diocese of Ohio recommended homosexual marriage and ordination in late 1977. *The Living Church*, 6 November 1977, p. 6.
166. Armentrout, *Splinter Groups*, p. 43; *The Living Church*, 5 June 1977, p. 7.
167. *The Episcopalian*, September 1977, p. 3. See also *The Living Church*, 15 March 1977, p. 5; 15 May 1977, p. 5.
168. *The Living Church*, 9 October 1977, p. 7.
169. Ibid.
170. The discussions centered on complaints about the General Convention Special Program, the lack of sound theology in the seminaries, the toleration of liberal theology as espoused by Bishop Pike, Prayer Book revision, and women's ordination. The last two were described as the "straws that broke the camel's back." *The Living Church*, 16 October 1977, p. 9.
171. *The Living Church*, 9 October 1977, pp. 7-8. See also "Episcopal Spirit of St. Louis," *Christianity Today* 22 (7 October 1977): 60-61, which gave estimates for the new body ranging from 50,000 to 500,000 members, terming it probably the largest schism in Episcopal history.
172. Armentrout, *Splinter Groups*, Appendix I, p. 2.
173. This sentence is part of the section titled "The Dissolution of Anglican and Episcopal Church Structure." Ibid., Appendix I, p. 1.
174. Ibid.
175. Ibid., Appendix I, pp. 2-4. Only those priests having "true religion" were allowed to celebrate the Eucharist in St. Louis, though all were able to partake, even Presiding Bishop Allin, who attended ("I am here because I am concerned") without recognition by the Congress. *The Living Church*, 9 October 1977, p. 7. There were many at the Congress who did not share this vision of a church in which all truth had been revealed. In his reflections on the St. Louis Congress, the liberal bishop of Kentucky, David Reed, wrote: "I am convinced that the very nature of the church as the body of Christ require that we continue in communion with each other and make sure that the church to which we belong is big enough for all Christian people, however we might disagree on specific issues." *The Living Church*, 16 October 1977, pp. 9, 15.
176. Armentrout, *Splinter Groups*, Appendix I, pp. 3-4.
177. *The Episcopalian*, November 1977, p. 1; *The Living Church*, 30 October 1977, p. 5. See also Kenneth A. Briggs, "Episcopal Bishops Eke Out a Fragile Peace," *Christian Century* 94 (2 November 1977): 996-97. Briggs reported that Allin had said his ideas would not interfere with his office, but he refused to ordain women or participate in the consecration of a female bishop. Allin was criticized repeatedly for this stand, which allowed him to "violate the canons of the Church." See Betty Gray, "Episcopal Church," pp. 1052-53. Others saw this as an effort at reconciliation with the conservatives. If it was, Hyer is correct in her evaluation, "In his quest for the lost sheep, Presiding Bishop Allin may have scattered the ninety and nine." "How Not to Heal Wounds," pp. 281-83.

178. "We avoid any kind of pressure which might lead a fellow Christian to contravene his or her conscience; for it is evil for anyone to do what is believed to be wrong, whether that belief be right or mistaken. . . . In the light of all this and in keeping with our intention at Minneapolis, we affirm that no Bishop, Priest, Deacon or Lay person should be coerced or penalized in any manner, nor suffer any canonical disabilities as a result of his or her conscientious objection to or support of the 65th General Convention's action with regard to the ordination of women to the priesthood or episcopate." *The Living Church*, 6 November 1977, p. 11.

179. Ibid., p. 12.

180. They were the nongeographical dioceses of Christ the King and Holy Trinity, and the geographical dioceses of the Southeast, Midwest, and Mid-Atlantic States. Armentrout, *Splinter Groups*, p. 45.

181. This name was substituted for the Protestant Episcopal Church. *The Living Church*, 19 February 1978, p. 6; "Breakaway Bishops," *Christianity Today* 22 (24 February 1978): 44-46; Virginia Culver, "Anglican Secessionists Consecrate Four Bishops," *Christian Century* 95 (15 February 1978): 149-51.

182. This is based on church declarations since the Council of Nicea, A.D. 325, where three consecrators are specified. The FCC anticipated this argument and after the ceremony distributed a memo arguing that this was not mandatory and that other citations indicated only two bishops (or even one) as adequate for consecration. *The Living Church*, 19 February 1978, p. 6; 30 April 1978, pp. 14-15.

183. Charles F. Boynton, retired Suffragan Bishop of New York, was supposed to attend but could not because of illness. Bishop Mark Pae of the Korean Anglican Church had been forbidden to participate by the Archbishop of Canterbury but is supposed to have sent a letter endorsing Doren's consecration. However, this letter-sending later became a topic of some dispute since Richard Ostling, religious editor for *Time* magazine, reported he had talked with Pae, who denied ever sending his consent. *The Living Church*, 19 March 1978, p. 5; Armentrout, *Splinter Groups*, p. 46; "Episcopal Problems with Documentation," *Christianity Today* 22 (10 March 1978): 68ff.; *Time*, 13 February 1978, p. 36. It was also disputed whether the Philippine Independent Church had authorized Pagtakhan to participate in the consecrations. Armentrout, *Splinter Groups*, p. 46 and Appendix II; also *The Living Church*, 26 March 1978, p. 7.

184. *The Episcopalian*, March 1978, p. 1.

185. *The Living Church*, 19 February 1978, p. 6. Coggan's position was repeated in a letter from Allin to his fellow bishops dated February 6, 1978: "The Archbishop of Canterbury and I—both in prior conversations and lately by telephone—agree that the new ecclesiastical body is not in communion with the See of Canterbury nor in communion with this Province of the Anglican Communion." *The Episcopalian*, March 1978, p. 6; *The Living Church*, 5 March 1978, p. 6. Coggan also left no illusions regarding his feelings for the new group when he did not invite newly consecrated Bishops Watterson or Mote to

the 1978 Lambeth Conference even though both of them were in England at the time. Armentrout, *Splinter Groups*, p. 47. Watterson and Mote would have been disappointed at Lambeth Palace because 1978 was the year the Lambeth Conference approved in principle the ordination of women. For a full discussion of the Lambeth Conference, women's ordination, and the relation of the two to the PECUSA, see Marrett, *Lambeth Conferences*.

186. *The Living Church*, 12 November 1978, p. 11; Armentrout, *Splinter Groups*, p. 48.
187. *The Living Church*, 12 November 1978, p. 11.
188. Armentrout, *Splinter Groups*, p. 48; *The Living Church*, 12 November 1978, p. 11. In this way, the authority of the bishops was solidly entrenched in the structure of the emerging ACC. As Rev. G. Rutler said, "You always have the hotheads. The revolutionaries want to chop off the king's head; but the power has been clearly established in the hands of the bishops now." See also Ruthanne Garlock, "New Denomination is Born in Controversy," *Christianity Today* 23 (17 November 1978): 40-42, who quotes C. Simcox of the FCC. Simcox maintained that the root issue was the struggle between "high" and "low" churchmanship. The Southwestern district wanted to give less power to the bishops and more to the laity, but in the end the "high" churchmen of the ACC prevailed. As a result, Simcox said he was reappraising his decision to leave the PECUSA.
189. Armentrout, *Splinter Groups*, pp. 48, 52.
190. The ratifications were as follows: January 6, 1979, the Mid-Atlantic with Doren elected bishop; February 23-24, 1979, the Resurrection with William Francis Burns elected bishop; April 28, 1979, the Midwest with Bishop Lewis elected. The fifth diocese to ratify the constitution was Holy Trinity with Mote elected bishop. Ibid., pp. 48-49.
191. Ibid., p. 49.
192. Bishops Morse of Christ the King and Watterson of the Southeast were among the four who were originally ordained in Denver in January 1978. Thus of the original four ACC bishops, two decided not to join the new denomination. Ibid., pp. 48-49.
193. As Bishop Watterson of the Southeastern diocese said, "To associate oneself with that constitution is, in fact, to deny the Catholic Faith and Catholic Church." *The Living Church*, 29 July 1979, p. 5.
194. Armentrout, *Splinter Groups*, pp. 52-63, outlines concisely the progressive splintering of the continuing Anglican church.
195. In 1985 the ACC had 6,500 members. Even if all the post-1976 groups combined their membership totals, they would number only 15,000 members despite predictions that ranged between 75,000 and 100,000. See also *Time*, 13 February 1978, p. 36.
196. Armentrout, *Splinter Groups*, pp. 63, 67.
197. Bishop Robert S. Morse of the ACNA said at the St. Louis Congress: "We will in fifty years be the *only* Episcopal Church in the United States." *Time*, 13 February 1978, p. 36.

CHAPTER FIVE

1. Gustaaf Johannes Renier, *History, Its Purpose and Method* (London: George Allen and Unwin Ltd., 1956), p. 49. E. R. Elton agrees when he says the study of history is "legitimate in itself" as a task to understand the past and give it full honor. *The Practice of History* (New York: Thomas Y. Crowell Co., 1967), p. 47.
2. "The task of the historian is simply and exclusively to keep available for social use the knowledge of the past experiences of human societies. As soon as he tries to use the knowledge of these experiences for any purpose whatever apart from putting them into the story that makes them generally available, he ceases to be an historian." Renier, *History*, p. 222.
3. Ibid., p. 117.
4. Ibid. Edward Shils shares this same view of the relationship between the sociologist and historian. *The Calling of Sociology and Other Essays on the Pursuit of Learning* (Chicago: The University of Chicago Press, 1980), pp. 17-18, 30.
5. Neil Smelser, *Theory of Collective Behavior* (New York: The Free Press, 1965).
6. This stage sequence is not one in which the first stage brings about the second stage. Rather there is "a progression of increasing specificity such that the activation of each determines the scope and effectiveness of the next." Wilson calls this the "value added factor." Wilson, "Sociology of Schism," p. 19. The six determinants are only listed in Wilson's article on p. 5 and explained briefly by way of example on pp. 15ff. They are described in much greater detail in Smelser, *Collective Behavior*, pp. 14-20.
7. Smelser, *Collective Behavior*, p. 15. In her study of social conflict, Jessie Bernard made the same suggestion. "The implication is that there may be characteristics inherent in group structure itself which facilitate the breakdown of systems when costs, and therefore conflicts, are involved." "The Sociological Study of Conflict," in Jessie Bernard, ed., *The Nature of Conflict* (Paris: UNESCO, 1957), p. 74.
8. Smelser, *Collective Behavior*, p. 15.
9. Ibid., p. 17. Wilson admits that he has omitted the determinant of generalized belief from Smelser's scheme, but feels justified in doing so. I do not think Wilson has proven his case. In fact, Wilson has not omitted this determinant, since his summary paragraph at the conclusion of his article refers "to a time before the generalized belief has become current," that is, a time before the precipitating factor. Wilson, "Sociology of Schism," p. 19.
10. Smelser, *Collective Behavior*, p. 16.
11. All forms of social control are activated only after the "collective episode" has begun to materialize. Ibid., p. 17.
12. Wilson, "Sociology of Schism," p. 5. The similarities between Wilson's perennial values and Edward Shils's concept of "tradition" are striking. "The ramification

of a religious tradition into sectarian tendencies—it is called 'splitting' in radical political circles—leaves each of the branches claiming to be the true bearer of the tradition while denying the rightfulness of the claims of the other. . . . The members who leave the main line as a result of expulsion or withdrawal are treated as deviants. It is likely that both are deviants in the sense that both have deviated from the tradition which they originally received." *Tradition*, pp. 280-81.

13. Wilson, "Sociology of Schism," p. 5.
14. Takayama, "Strains and Schisms," pp. 299-300. From this we know that Takayama's major contributions will be to the beginning stages of the schismatic process.
15. Ibid., p. 302. Takayama expects that most denominations choose a "compromise strategy" but they may also choose an "inspirational strategy" depending on the extent of the disagreement regarding the objectives and their priority.
16. Ibid.
17. Takayama quotes O'Dea heavily here. "To affect the lives of men, the original religious message must be stated in terms that have relevance to the everyday activities and concerns of people. Moreover, to preserve the import of the message, it must be protected against interpretations which would transform it in ways conflicting with its inner ethos. . . . This process of definition and concretization is at the same time a relativization of the religious and ethical message—a rendering of it relevant to the new circumstances of life of the religious group—and therefore involves the risk of making everyday and prosaic what was originally a call to the extraordinary." Thomas F. O'Dea, *The Sociology of Religion* (Englewood Cliffs, New Jersey: Prentice-Hall, Inc., 1966), p. 94.
18. Takayama, "Strains and Schisms," pp. 309-10.
19. Ibid., pp. 311, 313. Takayama quotes Charles Y. Glock and Rodney Stark, *Religion and Society in Tension* (Chicago: Rand McNally, 1965), chapter 9, to demonstrate how the church not only informs the values of the larger culture but also can be informed by that larger culture. Glock and Stark maintained that the ability merely to reflect cultural symbols was the only option left to the churches as their capacity to regenerate value symbols had been lost.
20. As listed above, Takayama's factors include the nature of the religious tradition, the type of religious leadership, the internal strains, the social characteristics of its members, and the secular interests involved.
21. At first glance, one might argue that the LC-MS dispute was an exception to this generalization. But in fact Preus's "Statement" was a method of enforcing a "static" interpretation of Lutheran confessions, hermeneutics, and belief. His opposition on the moderate side viewed the Book of Concord as a historical document that had to be interpreted to the modern age, not enshrined as a literalistic idol.
22. At least four of the district presidents might argue that their summary firing by Preus was in fact a legislative shift in the authority structure, as Preus effectively was taking power from the congregations and districts and vesting it in the

office of the synodical president. However, this is a difficult constitutional question, made even more confusing by the ambiguous wording of the denomination's constituting articles. What is not difficult to see is that any ambiguity during Preus's presidency was interpreted in favor of a general rule that centralized power in the office of the synodical president.

23. Lewis Coser, *The Functions of Social Conflict* (New York: The Free Press, 1956), pp. 31, 48. "Far from being necessarily dysfunctional, a certain degree of conflict is an essential element in group formation and the persistence of group life."

24. Ibid., pp. 70ff. Support for this proposition can be found in David Moberg, *The Church as a Social Institution: The Sociology of American Religion*, rev. ed., (Grand Rapids, Michigan: Baker Book House, 1984), pp. 276ff. Moberg finds that few conflicts are as severe as those between groups similar doctrinally, historically, and organizationally; he cites the recent disputes among the Baptists as an example.

25. Coser, *Social Conflict*, p. 71.

26. Ibid., p. 103. David Moberg, "Theological Position and Institutional Characteristics of Protestant Congregations: An Exploratory Study," *Scientific Study of Religion* 9 (Spring 1970), supports Coser here. Moberg more bluntly concludes that theological position is related to institutional characteristics.

Liston Pope, *Millhands and Preachers* (New Haven: Yale University Press, 1942) also could be marshaled as support for this church-sect typology. As well, Arnold M. Rose, "Voluntary Associations under Conditions of Competition and Conflict," *Social Forces* 34 (December 1955): 159-63, draws interesting parallels. Where there is a persecution complex operating, participation in the groups increased, as did cohesiveness of the group and pursuit of the group's goals.

27. As Coser says, sects lack a "safety valve" for their conflict. *Social Conflict*, pp. 39ff.

28. Ibid., pp. 72-73. Coser follows Weber and Troeltsch in this sect-church dichotomy. See Max Weber, *Essays in Sociology*, trans. Hans Heinrich Gerth and C. Wright Mills (New York: Oxford University Press, 1946) and Troeltsch, *Social Teaching of Christian Churches*.

29. "What threatens equilibrium of structure is not conflict as such, but the rigidity itself which permits hostilities to accumulate and to be channelled along one major line of cleavage once they break out in conflict." Coser, *Social Conflict*, p. 157. See also Lewis Coser, *Continuities in the Study of Social Conflict* (New York: The Free Press, 1967), p. 29. James S. Coleman, "Social Cleavage and Religious Conflict," *Journal of Social Issues* 12 (1956): 44-56, provides the same kind of argument when discussing cross-pressures within and between individuals.

30. Coser, *Social Conflict*, p. 151 (emphasis mine).

31. Ibid., p. 80.

32. Ibid., pp. 151-52 (emphasis mine). The ultimate in the disruption of the structure would be a schism.

33. Ibid., p. 118.
34. Ibid., p. 114.
35. Ibid., pp. 117-18.
36. It should be noted that Wilson's observation that a schismatic group will have its origins in allegations that the main group has departed from the movement's original values holds true even in the LC-MS if the schismatic group is identified as the conservative majority. After all, it was the conservative majority that asserted that those who could no longer agree with the denominational position should leave. Hence, in all three instances the schismatic group was the conservative group, which was concerned that the original values of the movement were being compromised.
37. Dodd, Cragg, and Ellul, *Social and Cultural Factors*, p. 1.
38. Ibid.; H. Richard Niebuhr, *The Social Sources of Denominationalism* (New York: Henry Holt, Inc., 1929); Clark, "Non-Theological Factors," pp. 347ff.; Dawson, "What about Heretics?," pp. 513-16.
39. Richard Weaver, *Ideas Have Consequences* (Chicago: University of Chicago Press, 1948).

Bibliography

CHAPTER ONE

Brinton, Crane. *The Anatomy of Revolution*. Rev. ed. New York: Vintage Books, 1938.

Clark, E. T. "Non-Theological Factors in Religious Diversity" *Ecumenical Review* (July 1951): 347.

Constant, H. Jaquet, Jr. *Yearbook of American and Canadian Churches: 1984*. Nashville: Abingdon Press, 1984.

Rusch, William G. *Ecumenism—A Movement Toward Church Unity*. Philadelphia: Fortress Press, 1985.

Scherer, Ross P., ed. *American Denominational Organization*. Pasadena, California: William Carey Library, 1980.

Shils, Edward. *Tradition*. Chicago: University of Chicago Press, 1981.

Stark, Rodney, and William Sims Bainbridge. *The Future of Religion: Secularization, Revival and Cult Formation*. Berkeley: University of California Press, 1985.

Takayama, K. Peter. "Strains, Conflicts and Schisms in Protestant Denominations." In Scherer, *American Denominational Organization*, pp. 298-329.

Wilson, John. "The Sociology of Schism." In *A Sociological Yearbook of Religion in Britain*. Vol. 4, edited by Michael Hill, pp. 1-19. London: SCM Press, 1971.

CHAPTER TWO

Primary Sources

Addresses Delivered During the First General Assembly of the Continuing Presbyterian Church. Montgomery, Alabama: The Continuing Presbyterian Church, 1973.

The Constitution of the United Presbyterian Church in the United States of America: Part I The Book of Confessions. 2d ed. Philadelphia: Office of the General Assembly of the United Presbyterian Church in the United States of America, 1970.

Leith, John H. *Creeds of the Churches: A Reader in Christian Doctrine from the Bible to the Present.* 3rd ed. Atlanta: John Knox Press, 1982.

Presbyterian Church in the US: The Confession of Faith. Richmond, Virginia: Board of Christian Education, 1965.

PCUS General Assembly Annual Reports.

PCUS General Assembly Minutes.

Smith, Morton H. *How is the Gold Become Dim: The Decline of the Presbyterian Church, U.S. as Reflected in Its Assembly Actions.* The Steering Committee for a Continuing Presbyterian Church, 1973.

Periodicals

Colloquy
Contact
Focus
The Presbyterian Guardian
The Presbyterian Journal
The Presbyterian Outlook
Presbyterian Record
Presbyterian Survey
Reformed World
Union Seminary Review

Secondary Sources

Ahlstrom, Sydney E. *A Religious History of the American People.* 2 vols. Garden City, New York: Image Books, 1975.

Anderson, J. F., Jr. "Time to Heal: A Southern Church Deals with Racism." *International Review of Missions* 59 (July 1970): 304-10.

Armstrong, Maurice W., Lefferts A. Loetscher, and Charles A. Anderson. *The Presbyterian Enterprise: Sources of American Presbyterian History.* Philadelphia: Westminster Press, 1956.

Bailey, Kenneth K. *Southern White Protestantism in the Twentieth Century.* New York: Harper & Row Publishers, 1964.

_____. "The Post-Civil War Racial Separations in Southern Protestantism: Another Look." *Church History* 46 (1977): 453-73.

Belz, Joel. "Remaking Missions." *Christianity Today* 22 (10 March 1978): 60-62.

Blake, Howard Carson. "Southern Presbyterians Sort Out the Issues." *Christianity Today* 9 (21 May 1965): 41-43.

Boice, James Montgomery. "United Presbyterianism: A Crisis of Confidence." *Christianity Today* 18 (26 July 1974): 18.

Briggs, Charles A. *American Presbyterianism: Its Origins and Early History.* New York: Charles Scribner's Sons, 1885.

Bromiley, Geoffrey W. "The 1967 Confession and Karl Barth." *Christianity Today* 10 (4 March 1966): 15-17.

Calhoun, Malcolm P. "Presbyterian Church, U.S., After Division and Silence, Its Ministers are Again Speaking against Racism." *Christianity and Crisis* 18 (1958): 24-26.

Chandler, E. R. "Death Knell for Southern Presbyterians." *Christianity Today* 15 (2 July 1971): 31.

_____. "Massanetta Mandates." *Christianity Today* 15 (16 July 1971): 32.

_____. "Conservative Fallout." *Christianity Today* 15 (24 September 1971): 42-43.

Cochrane, Arthur C. "Barmen and the Confession of 1967." *McCormick Quarterly* 19 (1966): 135-48.

_____. "The Confession of 1967, Ecumenism and COCU." *McCormick Quarterly* 22 (1969): 169-78.

"A Confession? In 1967?" *Christianity Today* 10 (17 December 1965): 36-37.

"Confession of 1967." *Journal of Presbyterian History* 61 (Spring 1983): 186-95. Most of this issue is dedicated to a discussion of the Confession of 1967.

Crane, William H. "Mission and Radical Obedience." *International Review of Missions* 54 (July 1965): 325-34.

Daane, James. "Presbyterian Church in the U.S., General Assembly." *Christianity Today* 7 (24 May 1963): 23-24.

_____. "Presbyterians, U.S. Nail the Door Open." *Christianity Today* 8 (22 May 1964): 35-37.

_____. "Presbyterians Draft New Confession." *Christianity Today* 9 (23 October 1964): 38.

Dornbusch, Sanford, and Roger D. Irle. "The Failure of Presbyterian Union." *American Journal of Sociology* 64 (January 1959): 352-55.

Dowey, Edward A., Jr. *A Commentary on the Confession of 1967 and an Introduction to the Book of Confessions*. Philadelphia: Westminister Press, 1968.

Doyle, Barrie. "Southern Presbyterians: Phasing Out Unhappiness." *Christianity Today* 18 (16 July 1974): 34-36.

"Ecumenical Showdown for Southern Presbyterians." *Christianity Today* 13 (14 March 1969): 36.

Encyclopaedia Britannica Book of the Year 1974. S. v. "Religion," by Helen Hemingway Benton.

Farrell, Frank. "New Presbyterian Confession." *Christianity Today* 9 (7 May 1965): 52-53.

Ferry, H. J. "Racism and Reunion: a Black Protest by F. J. Grinke." *Journal of Presbyterian History* 50 (Summer 1972): 77-88.

Forbes, Charles. "Southern Presbyterians: Issues in Limbo." *Christianity Today* 19 (18 July 1975): 32-33.

Fry, John R. *The Trivialization of the United Presbyterian Church*. New York: Harper & Row Publishers, 1967.

Gerstner, John H. "Church Historians Warns: Presbyterians are Demoting the Bible." *Christianity Today* 10 (3 December 1965): 11-14.

_____. "New Light on the Confession of 1967." *Christianity Today* 11 (9 December 1966): 4-6.

Harrell, David Edwin, Jr. *White Sects and Black Men in the Recent South*. Nashville: Vanderbilt University Press, 1971.

Hendry, George S. "Bible in the Confession of 1967." *Princeton Seminary Bulletin* 60 (October 1966): 21-24.

Henley, Wallace. "Southern Presbyterians: the Gap Widens." *Christianity Today* 13 (23 May 1969): 32-33.

"High Time for a Confession?" *Christianity Today* 9 (23 October 1964): 24-27.

Hill, Samuel S., Jr. *Southern Churches in Crisis*. New York: Holt, Rinehart and Winston, 1967.

_____. *Religion in the Southern States*. Macon, Georgia: Mercer University Press, 1983.

_____. *Encyclopedia of Religion in the South*. Macon, Georgia: Mercer University Press, 1984.

Hoge, Dean. *Division in the Protestant House*. Philadelphia: Westminster Press, 1976.

Jameson, Wallace N. *The United Presbyterian Story: A Centennial Study*. Geneva: Geneva Press, 1958.

Johnson, Thomas Cary. "The Presbyterian Church in the United States." *Journal of the Presbyterian Historical Society* 1 (1901): 74-79.

Kucharsky, D. E. "Southern Presbyterians: Bedrock Revision." *Christianity Today* 16 (15 September 1972): 51.

_____. "Schism Takes Shape." *Christianity Today* 17 (13 October 1972): 48-49.

_____. "Presbyterians Confront Exodus." *Christianity Today* 17 (6 July 1973): 42-43.

_____. "Birth of a Denomination." *Christianity Today* 18 (21 December 1973): 39-40.

_____. "I'm National: Join Me." *Christianity Today* 18 (4 January 1974): 52-53.

Lake, Benjamin J. *The Story of the Presbyterian Church in the U.S.A.* Philadelphia: Westminster Press, 1956.

Leitch, Addison H. "Scriptures as Creed." *Christianity Today* 10 (5 November 1965): 61-62.

Loetscher, Lefferts A. *The Broadening Church: A Study of Theological Issues in the Presbyterian Church since 1869*. Philadelphia: University of Pennsylvania Press, 1954.

_____. *A Brief History of the Presbyterians*. 4th ed. Philadelphia: Westminster Press, 1983.

Long, Abram Miller. "Do Presbyterians Need a New Confession." *Christianity Today* 10 (1 April 1966): 10-14.

_____. "Does the New Confession Alter the Spiritual Mission of the Church?" *Christianity Today* 10 (13 May 1966): 16-20.

Lytle, Harold H. "They are Taking My Church Away from Me." *Christianity Today* 11 (18 August 1967): 18-20.

McKay, Arthur R. "In Praise of Confessing Here and Now." *McCormick Quarterly* 19 (January 1966): 69-73.

McMillan, T. Morton. "As Schism Looms, Southern Presbyterians Reorganize." *Christian Century* 90 (1-8 August 1973): 785-86.

Maddex, Jack P. "From Theocracy to Spirituality: The Southern Presbyterian Reversal in Church and State." *Journal of Presbyterian History* 54 (Winter 1976): 438-57.

Matthews, A. H. "Southern Presbyterians Elect Bell, Stay in COCU." *Christianity Today* 16 (7 July 1972): 34-35.

_____. "Montreat World Missions Consultation." *Christianity Today* 7 (9 November 1962): 31-32.

_____. "Togetherness Tonic for Growing Pains." *Christianity Today* 20 (10 October 1975): 60-61.

_____. "Southern Presbyterians: Counting the Costs." *Christianity Today* 20 (13 February 1976): 59-60.

_____. "Southern Presbyterians: Changing Patterns." *Christianity Today* 20 (16 July 1976): 53-54.

"News from the Churches." *The Reformed and Presbyterian World* 29-33 (1967-1975). Published quarterly by the World Alliance of Reformed Churches and the International Congregational Council.

Nichols, James H. "New Presbyterian Confession of Faith: A Concise and Coherent Document." *Christianity and Crisis* 25 (17 May 1965): 108-11.

Parker, Harold M. "Southern Presbyterian Ecumenism: Six Successful Unions." *Journal of Presbyterian History* 56 (1978): 91-107.

_____. *Bibliography of Published Articles on American Presbyterianism 1901-1980*. Westport, Conn.: Greenwood Press, 1985.

Penfield, Janet Herbison. "Presbyterian Prognosis: Guarded." In *Where the Spirit Leads: American Denominations Today*, edited by Martin E. Marty, pp. 189-211. Atlanta: John Knox Press, 1980.

Piepkorn, Arthur C. *Profiles in Belief: The Religious Bodies of the United States and Canada*. Vol. 2, *Protestant Denominations*. San Francisco: Harper & Row, Publishers, Inc., 1978.

Posey, Lawton W. "Southern Presbyterian Dilemma." *Christian Century* 94 (16 February 1977): 142-45.

"Presbyterians Rally to the Westminster Confession." *Christianity Today* 10 (3 December 1965): 48-49.

Quirk, Charles E. "Origins of the Auburn Affirmation." *Journal of Presbyterian History* 43 (1965): 182-96.

Reimers, David M. "The Race Problem and Presbyterian Union." *Church History* 31 (1962): 213-15.

"Revised Creedal Formula Wins Presbyterian Approval." *Christianity Today* 10 (10 June 1966): 44-45.

Richards, John Edwards. *The Historical Birth of the Presbyterian Church in America*. Liberty Hill, South Carolina: Liberty Press, 1987.

Rogers, Cornish R. "Presbyterians Draw Closer Together." *Christian Century* 91 (31 July 1974): 742.

Shannon, Foster H. "Too Many Confessions." *Christianity Today* 10 (16 September 1966): 19-21.

Smart. James D. "Scripture and the Confession of 1967." *Theology Today* 23 (April 1966): 21-43.

_____. "Sermon on the Confession of 1967 and Karl Barth." *Union Seminary Quarterly Review* 24 (Summer 1969): 377-83.

Smylie, James H. "Ecclesiological Storm and Stress in Dixie." *Christian Century* 12 (13 March 1968): 321-25.

Stimson, Edward W. "Threat to United Presbyerians." *Christianity Today* 9 (9 April 1965): 17-23.

Street, T. Watson. *The Story of Southern Presbyterians*. Richmond: John Knox Press, 1960.

_____. "Southern Presbyterians and Evangelism." *Christianity Today* 5 (2 January 1961): 23-24.

Sweet, William Warren. *Religion on the American Frontier*. Vol. 2, *The Presbyterians: A Collection of Source Material*. New York: Cooper Square Publishers, Inc., 1964.

"Symposium: A Confessional Church." *McCormick Quarterly* 19 (January, 1966). Entire issue devoted to a discussion of the Confession of 1967 and what it meant to Presbyterianism in the United States.

Taylor, G. Aiken. "Presbyterian Church In America: In Quest of Name and Niche." *Christianity Today* 19 (11 October 1974): 48-49.

Thompson, Ernest Trice. "Is the Northern Church Theologically Sound?" *Union Seminary Review* 42 (1931): 100-133.

_____. "Presbyterians North and South: Efforts Toward Reunion (1870-1964)." *Journal of Presbyterian History* 43 (March 1965): 1-15.

211

_____. *Presbyterians in the South*. 3 vols. Richmond, Va: John Knox Press, 1973.

Wall, Howard. "Cautious Note for Southern Presbyterians." *Christian Century* 94 (20 July 1977): 646-47.

West, Charles C. "New Presbyterian Confession." *Christianity and Crisis* 26 (27 June 1966): 137-39.

Wilson, Charles R. *Religion in the South*. Jackson: University Press of Mississippi, 1985.

CHAPTER THREE

Primary Sources

Board of Control of Concordia Theological Seminary. *Exodus from Concordia: A Report on the 1974 Walkout*. St. Louis, Missouri: Concordia Seminary Publicity Office, 1977.

Board of Directors of the Lutheran Church in Mission. "Catechism on LCM." Maple Heights, Ohio: Lutheran Church in Mission, 26 April 1975.

Christ Alive Church Alive: A Report on the Assembly of Evangelical Lutherans in Mission. August 13-15, 1975 in Chicago. St. Louis, Missouri: ELIM, 1975.

Commission on Theology and Church Relations Reports:

"What is a Doctrine." 1964.

"The Charismatic Movement and Lutheran Theology." January 1972.

"Gospel and Scripture." CTCR response to "Faithful to our Calling." 1973.

"The Ministry in Relation to the Christian Church as seen on the basis of Holy Scriptures and the Lutheran Confessions." 1973.

"A Comparative Study of Varying Comtemporary Approaches to Biblical Interpretation." 1973.

"Guiding Principles for the use of 'A Statement of Scriptural and Confessional Principles' With Special Reference to the Expression of Dissent." November 1973.

"A Lutheran Stance Towards Ecumenism." November 1974.

"The Inspiration of Scripture." March 1975.

"The Mission of the Christian Church in the World: A Review of the 1965 Mission Affirmations." 1974.

"Policy Statement of Limitation of Academic Freedom." March 1974.

"Report on Dissent from 'A Statement of Scriptural and Confessional Principles' and Other Doctrinal Resolutions of the Lutheran Church-Missouri Synod." September 1974.

English District Special Convention Proceedings. "Christ Frees Christ Unites." 19 September 1975.

English District Forty-First Convention Proceedings. "In Necessary Things Unity, In Doubtful Things Freedom But in Everything Love." Concordia Teachers College, River Forest, Illinois, 17-20 June 1976.

"ELIM." 1974. Promotional pamphlet describing the goals and objectives of ELIM.

ELIM, Division of Communication and Interpretation:

Boss, Walter. "My Congregation and My Synod."

Jungkuntz, Richard. "Authority in the Church."

_____. "Whose Mission is it?"

Neuhaus, Richard. "Christ's Mission to the Whole Person."

Stuenkel, Omar. "What's Wrong with the Preus Statement."

ELIM. "The Future of LCMS Moderates after St. Louis," August 1979.

Faculty Majority/Seminex Faculty Statements:

"A Call to Openness and Trust." January 1970.

"Response of the Faculty of Concordia Seminary, St. Louis." April 4, 1972.

"A Declaration by the Faculty of Concordia Seminary in Response to the Report of the Synodical President." September 1972.

"Faithful to Our Calling, Faithful to our Lord: An Affirmation in Two Parts by The Faculty of Concordia Seminary." St. Louis, Missouri: Concordia Seminary, January 1973.

"A Declaration of Protest and Confession." July 24, 1973.

Forward in Mission: A Report on the Assembly of Evangelical Lutherans in Mission: August 26-28, 1974 in Chicago. St. Louis, Missouri: ELIM, 1974.

Handbook of the Lutheran Church-Missouri Synod. N.p.: 1969. With conditions and bylaws as amended by the Denver Convention.

Hecht, Harold. Letter to the membership of the English District. November 18, 1974.

_____. Letter to the membership of the English District. June 3, 1975. Regarding dissolution resolutions.

_____. Letter from president of newly formed English Synod to English District membership. 22 June 1976, 9 July 1976, 5 August 1976.

Keller, Walter E., Kenneth F. Korby, Robert C. Schultz, and David G. Truemper. "A Review Essay of a Statement of Scriptural and Confessional Principles." *Cressett* reprints, May and October 1973.

Lutheran Church-Missouri Synod *Convention Workbooks* and *Convention Proceedings*. St. Louis, Missouri: Concordia Publishing House, 1965-77.

"Minutes of Consultation of Missouri Synod-Related Lutheran Churches in Asia." Hong Kong, July 15-19, 1974.

"The Nature and Function of Holy Scripture." St. Louis, Missouri: Concordia Publishing House, 1975. Essays from the theological convocation held in St. Louis, Missouri, April 14-18, 1975.

Otten, Herman, ed. *A Christian Handbook on Vital Issues: Christian News 1963-73.* New Haven, Missouri: Leader Publishing Company, 1973.

Preus, Jacob. "A Statement of Scriptural and Confessional Principles." 1 March 1972.

_____. "From the Desk of the President: Brother to Brother." 4 April 1972.

_____. "Report of the Synodical President to the Lutheran Church-Missouri Synod (in compliance with Resolution 2-28 of the 49th Regular Convention of the Synod held at Milwaukee, Wisconsin, July 9-16, 1971)." 1 September 1972.

_____. "Message to the Church From the Office of the President The Lutheran Church-Missouri Synod." 28 January 1974.

_____. "A Report to the Church." 15 January 1975.

_____. Letters to synodical membership. 16 August 1975, 30 October 1975, 9 December 1975, 23 February 1976, 13 April 1976, 25 May 1976.

_____. Letter to English District membership. 17 June 1976.

Report of the Advisory Committee on Doctrine and Conciliation. St. Louis, Missouri: Concordia Publishing House, 1975.

"Report and Recommendations of the Special Hymnal Review Committee." St. Louis, Missouri: Concordia Publishing House, 1978.

Repp, Arthur C. "Statement of Dissent in Regard to Res. 3-01 of 1973 Convention of LC-MS." N.p.: n.d.

Schroeder, Edward H. "Law-Gospel Reductionism in the History of the Lutheran Church-Missouri Synod." *Concordia Theological Monthly* 43 (April 1972): 232-47.

_____. *Critique of President Preus' Statement.* N.p.: n.d.

Scharlemann, Martin E. "Biblical Interpretation Today." *The Lutheran Scholar* 24 (April 1967): 15ff.

Tietjen, John. *Which Way to Lutheran Unity? A History of Efforts to Unite the Lutherans of America.* St. Louis, Missouri: Clayton Publishing House, 1966.

_____. "Fact Finding or Fault Finding? An Analysis of President J. A. O. Preus' Investigation of Concordia Seminary." St. Louis, Missouri: Concordia Seminary, 8 September 1972.

_____. "Evidence Presented by John Tietjen." St. Louis, Missouri: Concordia Seminary, February 1974.

_____. "Statement." 15 October 1974.

Periodicals

Affirm
Christian News
Concordia Historical Institute
Concordia Theological Monthly
Cross and Caduceus
Currents in Theology and Mission
ELIMletter (Canadian Production)
ELIM Newsletter
Info
Laymen's Analysis
The Lutheran Forum
The Lutheran Witness
Missouri in Perspective
Partners in Mission
The Reporter
Seminar
Seminary Newsletter
Seminex Bulletin
Together in Mission
Weekly News Update

Secondary Sources

Adams, James E. "Lutheran Church Missouri Synod—Dynamic Tensions of Sect and Church." *Christian Century* 88 (8 September 1971): 1058-62.

_____. *Preus of Missouri and the Great Lutheran Civil War.* New York: Harper & Row, Publishers, 1977.

Baker, Tom. *Watershed at the Rivergate.* Sturgis, Michigan, 1973.

Baumgartner, John H. *A Tree Grows in Missouri.* Milwaukee, Wisconsin: Agape Publishers Inc., 1975.

"The Bible: The Believer's Gain." *Time,* 30 December 1974, p. 24.

Braaten, Carl E., ed. *The New Church Debate.* Philadelphia: Fortress Press, 1983.

Bretscher, Paul G. *After the Purifying.* River Forest, Illinois: Lutheran Education Association, 1975.

_____. *The Sword of the Spirit.* St. Louis, Missouri: ELIM Books, 1979.

Caemmerer, Richard R., and Alfred O. Fuerbringer, eds. *Toward a More Excellent Ministry.* St. Louis, Missouri: Concordia Publishing House, 1964.

Christian Century. "From Concordia to Seminex: A Seminary in Exile."

Constable, John W. "Of Congregational and Synodical Authority." *Concordia Theological Monthly* 43 (April 1972): 212-31.

_____. "Rejoicing in Mercy: Unity in Diversity." *Concordia Theological Monthly* 44 (May 1973): 192-98.

Danker, Frederick W. *No Room in the Brotherhood: The Preus-Otten Purge of Missouri.* St. Louis, Missouri: Clayton Publishing Company, 1977.

Forster, Walter Otto. *Zion on the Mississippi; the settlement of the Saxon Lutherans in Mississippi 1839-41.* St. Louis, Missouri: Concordia Publishing House, 1953.

Franzmann, Martin H. "On Change in Theology." *Concordia Theological Monthly* 38 (January 1967): 5-9.

Graebner, Theodore. "The Burden of Infallibility: A Study in the History of Dogma." *Concordia Historical Quarterly* 38 (1965): 88-99.

Graebner, Theodore Conrad. *Our Pilgrim Fathers Story of Saxon Immigration of 1838.* St. Louis, Missouri: Concordia Publishing House, 1919.

Harms, Oliver R. "Beyond the One Hundred and Twenty-Fifth Anniversary." *Concordia Theological Monthly,* 43 (April 1972): 248-51.

Janzow, Theophil W. "Secularization in an Orthodox Denomination." Ph.D. dissertation, University of Nebraska, 1970.

Jewett, Robert. "The Gospel as Heresy: Concordia Seminary in Exile." *Christian Century* 91 (17 March 1974): 336-40.

Koenig, Richard E. "What's Behind the Showdown in the LCMS? Church and Tradition in Collision." *Lutheran Forum* 6 (November 1972): 16-20.

_____. "Missouri Turns Moderate: 1938-65." *Lutheran Forum* 7 (February 1973): 19-29.

_____. "Conservative Reaction: 1965-69." *Lutheran Forum* 7 (May 1973): 18-22.

Koenig, Robert J. *Except the Corn Die.* N.p.: Robert J. Koenig, 1975.

Kretzmann, Martin L. "That Word Mission." *Currents in Theology and Mission* 2 (June 1975): 126-31.

Lindsell, Harold. "Who is Right in the Missouri Synod Dispute?" *Christianity Today* 20 (11 April 1975): 17.

Lueker, E. I. "Doctrinal Emphases in the Missouri Synod." *Concordia Theological Monthly* 43 (April 1972): 198-211.

Lueking, F. Dean. *Mission in the Making: The Missionary Enterprise among Missouri Synod Lutherans 1846-1963.* St. Louis, Missouri: Concordia Publishing House, 1964.

Lueking, F. Dean, and Martin H. Franzmann. *Grace Under Pressure: The Way of Meekness in Ecumenical Relations.* St. Louis, Missouri: Concordia Publishing House, 1966.

"The Lutheran Pope." *Newsweek,* 23 July 1973, p. 50.

Manser, Nancy. "Lutheran Rift in Michigan." *The Detroit News,* 9 March 1974, p. 11a.

_____. "Lutheran Schism: Only the Beginning." *The Detroit News,* 11 August 1973, p. 13.

Marquart, Kurt. *Anatomy of an Explosion: Missouri in Lutheran Perspective.* Fort Wayne, Indiana: Concordia Theological Seminary Press, 1977.

Marty, Martin E. "Showdown in the Missouri Synod." *Christian Century* 89 (27 September 1972): 943-46.

Meyer, Carl Stramm. *A Brief Historical Sketch of the Lutheran Church-Missouri Synod.* St. Louis, Missouri: Concordia Publishing House, 1963.

_____, ed. *Moving Frontiers Readings in the History of the Lutheran Church-Missouri Synod.* St. Louis, Missouri: Concordia Publishing House, 1964.

_____. *Log Cabin to Luther Tower: Concordia Seminary during 125 Years Toward a More Excellent Ministry (1839-1964).* St. Louis, Missouri: Concordia Publishing House, 1965.

Meyer, Lawrence B., comp. and ed. *Missouri in Motion.* St. Louis, Missouri: Concordia Publishing House, 1969.

"Missouri Synod: The Showdown." *Christianity Today* 19 (17 February 1974): 45.

"Missouri Synod Furor: Lutheran Showdown." *Christianity Today* 17 (14 April 1972): 42.

Montgomery, John Warwick. "The Last Days of the Late, Great Synod of Missouri." *Christianity Today* 16 (9 April 1971): 56-57.

_____. "Last Judgement for Missouri." *Christianity Today* 18 (8 June 1973): 49-50.

Mueller, Richard. *Mission Made Impossible: The Sources of Schism in the LCMS Hong Kong and Macao Mission*. St. Louis, Missouri: ELIM, 1976.

Mundinger, Carl Solomon. *Government in the Missouri Synod: the Genesis of Decentralized Government in the Missouri Synod*. St. Louis, Missouri: Concordia Publishing House, 1947.

Neeb, Larry, "The Historical and Theological Dimensions of a Confessing Movement within the Lutheran Church-Missouri Synod." Doctorate of Ministry dissertation, Seminex, 1975.

Nelson, E. Clifford. *Lutheranism in North America 1914-1970*. Minneapolis, Minnesota: Augsburg Publishing House, 1972.

Piepkorn, Arthur Carl. "What Does Inerrancy Mean?" *Concordia Theological Monthly* 35 (September 1965): 588.

Plowman, Edward E. "Missouri Lutheran Showdown: The Battle of New Orleans." *Christianity Today* 18 (10 August 1973): 40-42.

_____. "The Misery of Missouri." *Christianity Today* 19 (10 May 1974): 46-48.

Rudnick, Milton L. *Fundamentalism and the Missouri Synod: A Historical Study of Their Interaction and Mutual Influence*. St. Louis, Missouri: Concordia Publishing House, 1966.

_____. "Fundamentalism and the Missouri Synod: A Historical Study of their Interaction and Mutual Influence." *Concordia Theological Monthly* 43 (April 1972): 252-57.

Scheidt, David L. "Recent Linguistic Transition in Lutheranism." *Lutheran Quarterly* 13 (February 1961): 34-46.

Tietjen, John. "The Gospel and the Theological Task." *Concordia Theological Monthly* 40 (June-August 1969): 114-23.

Vehse, Edward. *The Stephanite Emigration to America*. Tuscon, Arizona: Marion R. Winkler, 1975.

Weisheit, Eldon. *The Zeal of His House: Five Generations of LC-MS History (1847-1872)*. St. Louis, Missouri: Concordia Publishing House, 1973.

CHAPTER FOUR

Primary Sources

The Book of Common Prayer and Administration of the Sacraments and Other Rites and Ceremonies of the Church According to the Use of the Protestant Episcopal Church in the United States of America. New York: Oxford University Press, 1928.

Constitution and Canons of the Protestant Episcopal Church in the United States of America. In 1970 Journal of the General Convention. N.p.: n.d., appendix.

The Draft Proposed Book of Common Prayer and Administration of the Sacraments and Other Rites and Ceremonies of the Church according to the Use of the Protestant Episcopal Church in the United States of America. New York: Church Hymnal Corp., 1976.

Price, Charles P. Introducing the Proposed Book of Common Prayer. New York: Seabury Press, 1977.

Suter, John Wallace, and George Julius Cleaveland. The American Book of Common Prayer, Its Origin and Development. New York: Oxford University Press, 1949.

Journal of the General Convention of the Protestant Episcopal Church in the United States of America also known as the Episcopal Church in the United States. 1967, 1970, 1973, 1976, 1979.

Periodicals

The Christian Challenge
The Episcopalian
The Living Church

Secondary Sources

Applegate, Stephen H. "The Rise and Fall of the Thirty-Nine Articles: an Inquiry into the Identity of the Protestant Episcopal Church in the United States of America." Historical Magazine of the Protestant Episcopal Church 50 (December 1981): 409-21.

Armentrout, Donald S. *Episcopal Splinter Groups: A Study of Groups Which Have Left the Episcopal Church, 1873-1985*. Sewanee, Tennessee: University of the South, 1985.

"Breakaway Bishops." *Christianity Today* 22 (24 February 1978): 44-46.

Briggs, Kenneth A. "Episcopal Bishops Eke Out a Fragile Peace." *Christian Century* 94 (2 November 1977): 996-97.

Brill, Earl H. "Episcopal Church: Conflict and Cohesion." *Christian Century* 95 (18 January 1978): 41-47.

Carter, Howard. "In and Through the Impasses." *Christianity and Crisis* 34 (16 September 1974): 189-94.

Chandler, E. R. "Squirming in South Bend." *Christianity Today* 13 (26 September 1969): 42-44.

_____. "Double Trouble . . . Cauldron Boiling." *Christianity Today* 14 (7 November 1969): 51.

Chandler, E. R., and J. F. Politzer. "Episcopal Church Convention." *Christianity Today* 14 (6 November 1970): 43-44.

Constant, H. Jaquet, Jr. *Yearbook of American and Canadian Churches: 1984*. Nashville: Abingdon Press, 1984.

Culver, Virginia. "Anglican Secessionists Consecrate Four Bishops." *Christian Century* 95 (15 February 1978): 149-51.

Dawley, Powel M. *Chapters in Church History*. New York: National Council of the Protestant Episcopal Church, 1950.

"Episcopal Bishops: Dealing with Revolt." *Christianity Today* 22 (4 November 1977): 244-47

"Episcopal Problems with Documentation." *Christianity Today* 22 (10 March 1978): 68ff.

"Episcopal Spirit of St. Louis." *Christianity Today* 22 (7 October 1977): 60-61.

"Episcopalian Showdown Shaping Up." *Christianity Today* 20 (4 June 1976): 44-45.

FitzSimons, C. Allison. "Towards an Historical Heremeneutic for Understanding the PECUSA." *Historical Magazine of the Protestant Episcopal Church* 48 (March 1979): 9-25.

Forbes, C. A. "Renewal on the Right." *Christianity Today* 18 (26 October 1973): 55-57.

_____. "Evangelical Episcopalians: United and Moving." *Christianity Today* 18 (9 November 1973): 64-65.

_____. "Ordination of Women: Injured Episcopalian Peace?" *Christianity Today* 18 (16 August 1974): 39-40.

_____. "When is a Priest not a Priest?" *Christianity Today* 18 (13 September 1974): 68-70.

Frensdorff, Wesley. "Holy Orders and Ministry: Some Reflections." *Anglican Theological Review* 59 (July 1977): 279-94.

Garlock, Ruthanne. "New Denomination is Born in Controversy." *Christianity Today* 23 (17 November 1978): 40-42.

Glock, Charles Y., Benjamin B. Ringer, and Earl R. Babbie. *To Comfort and to Challenge*. Berkeley: University of California Press, 1967.

Gray, Betty. "Women Priests Now? Report on the Episcopal General Convention." *Christianity and Crisis* 33 (23 July 1973): 148-52.

_____. "Episcopal Church: An Endangered Species." *Christian Century* 94 (16 November 1977): 1052-53.

_____, and William Gray. "Mainline Disaffection and the European Connection." *Christian Century* 96 (24 January 1979): 77-79.

Gray, William B. "Standing in the Way of the Spirit." *Christian Century* 90 (12 September 1973): 876-77.

Howell, Leon. "A Godly Admonition: The Trial of William Wendt." *Christian Century* 92 (21 May 1975): 517-19.

Hyer, Marjorie. "How Not to Heal Wounds." *Christianity and Crisis* 37 (28 November 1977): 281-83.

Jewett, Paul K. *The Ordination of Women: An Essay in the Office of Christian Ministry*. Grand Rapids: William B. Eerdmans Publishing Co., 1980.

Krumm, John M. "Liberal Bishop Speaks." *Christianity and Crisis* 35 (29 September 1975): 228.

Lehman, Edward C., Jr. *Women Clergy in England: Sexism, Modern Consciousness and Church Viability*. Vol. 16 of *Studies in Religion and Society*. Lewiston: Edwin Mellen Press, 1985.

Lyles, Jean C. "Episcopal Agony over Ecclesiastical Disobedience." *Christian Century* 91 (4 September 1974): 812-14.

_____. "Episcopals: Wounded Healers." *Christian Century* 93 (29 September 1976): 803-4.

_____. "Common Prayer and an Uncommon Convention." *Christian Century* 93 (6 October 1976): 829-30.

Marrett, Michael McFarlene. *The Lambeth Conferences and Women Priests: The Historical Background of the Conferences and Their Impact on the*

Episcopal Church in America. Smithtown, New York: Exposition Press, 1981.

Medsger, Betty. "Episcopal Ordinations: Where have the Liberal Bishops Gone?" *Christianity and Crisis* 35 (18 August 1975): 188-92.

Noice, Elizabeth R. "Priesthood and Women: A Lay View." *Anglican Theological Review* 55 (January 1973): 53-62.

Norgren, William A. "Ecumenical Relations and Ordination of Women to the Priesthood of the Episcopal Church." *Mid-Stream* 16 (October 1977): 374-82.

"On the Philadelphia Ordinations." *Christianity and Crisis* 34 (16 September 1974): 187-89.

Petersen, William H. "Tensions of Anglican Identity in the PECUSA: An Interpretative Essay." *Historical Magazine of the Protestant Episcopal Church* 47 (December 1978): 427-52.

Piepkorn, Arthur C. *Profiles in Belief: The Religious Bodies of the United States and Canada.* Vol. 2, *Protestant Denominations.* San Francisco: Harper & Row, Publishers, Inc., 1978.

Pierce, Nathaniel W. "Divinity Amid the Dinosaurs." *Christian Century* 95 (18 January 1978): 56-58.

Plowman, Edward R. "Wendt Case: Women on Trial." *Christianity Today* 19 (23 May 1975): 55-57.

_____. "Episcopalian Church: Women are Winners." *Christianity Today* 21 (8 October 1976): 48-52.

_____. "A Vet Out: A Lesbian In." *Christianity Today* 21 (4 February 1977): 55-56.

Raeside, John. "Episcopal Reconciliation in Minneapolis?" *Christianity and Crisis* 36 (18 October 1976): 232-34.

Rehkopf, Charles F. "Reactions to Events of the 1960's and 1970's." *Historical Magazine of the Protestant Episcopal Church* 47 (December 1978): 453-62.

Rogers, C. "Episcopalian Convention: Thou Shalt Not Polarize." *Christian Century* 90 (24 October 1973): 1046-47.

Rutler, George. "Dissident Priest Reordained." *Christian Century* 98 (30 September 1981): 95-96.

Schidler, M. M. "Alison Cheek's Achievement." *Christian Century* 91 (11 December 1974): 1165-66.

Seabury, Paul. "Trendier Than Thou: The Many Temptations of the Episcopal Church." *Harper's*, October 1978, pp. 39-52.

Stringfellow, W. "Anarchy or Prophecy?" *Christianity and Crisis* 34 (16 September 1974): 197-99.

———. "The Bishops at O'Hare: Mischief and a Mighty Curse." *Christianity and Crisis* 34 (16 September 1974): 195-96.

Wagner, J. E. "Whither Episcopalians?" *Christianity Today* 17 (10 November 1972): 18-19.

Wallace, Bob. *General Convention of the Episcopal Church.* New York: Seabury Press, 1976.

Williamson, Wayne B. *Growth and Decline in the Episcopal Church.* Pasadena, Calif.: William Carey Library, 1979.

"Women Priests Rebuffed." *Christian Century* 91 (21 August 1974): 791.

Wright, J. Robert. "Documentation and Reflection: An Address in Favor of the Ordination of Women to the Priesthood." *Anglican Theological Review* 55 (January 1973): 68-72.

CHAPTER FIVE

Bateson, Gregory. *Man.* Cambridge: Cambridge University Press, 1930.

Bernard, Jessie. "The Sociological Study of Conflict." In *The Nature of Conflict.* Edited by the author. Paris: UNESCO, 1957. Pp. 33-117.

Borhek, James T., and Richard F. Curtes. *A Sociology of Belief.* New York: John Wiley & Sons, 1975.

Brinton, Crane. *The Anatomy of Revolution.* Rev. ed. New York: Vintage Books, 1938.

Cantor, Norman F., and Richard I. Schneider. *How to Study History.* Arlington Heights, Ill.: Harlan Davidson, Inc., 1967.

Clark, E. T. "Non-Theological Factors in Religious Diversity." *Ecumenical Review* (July 1951).

Coleman, James S. "Social Cleavage and Religious Conflict." *Journal of Social Issues* 12 (1956): 44-56.

Coleman, Richard J. *Issues of Theological Conflict: Evangelicals and Liberals.* Rev. ed. Grand Rapids, Michigan: William B. Eerdman Publishing Co., 1980.

Collingwood, R. G. *The Idea of History.* London: Oxford University Press, 1946.

Constant, H. Jaquet, Jr. *Yearbook of American and Canadian Churches: 1984.* Nashville: Abingdon Press, 1984.

Coser, Lewis A. *The Functions of Social Conflict*. New York: Free Press, 1956.

_____. *Continuities in the Study of Social Conflict*. New York: Free Press, 1967.

Dawson, Christopher. "What About Heretics? An Analysis of the Causes of Schism." *Commonweal* 36 (18 September 1942): 513-16.

Dodd, C. H., G. R. Cragg, and Jacques Ellul. *Social and Cultural Factors in Church Divisions*. New York: World Council of Churches, 1952.

Douglass, H. Paul. "Cultural Differences and Recent Religious Divisions." *Christendom* (Winter 1945): 89-105.

Dray, William H. *Philosophy of History*. Englewood Cliffs, N.J.: Prentice-Hall, Inc., 1964.

Dynes, Russell R. "Church-Sect Typology and Socio-Economic Status." *American Sociological Review* 20 (October 1955): 555-60.

Elton, E. R. *The Practice of History*. New York: Thomas Y. Crowell Co., 1967.

Firey, Walter. "Informal Organization and the Theory of Schism." *American Sociological Review* 13 (February 1948): 15-24.

Garrison, Winfred E. "Social and Cultural Factors in Our Divisions." *Ecumenical Review* (October 1952): 43-51.

Gaustad, Edwin S. *Dissent in American Religion*. Chicago: University of Chicago Press, 1973.

Hadden, Jeffrey K. *The Gathering Storm in the Churches: The Widening Gap Between Clergy and Laymen*. Garden City, New York: Doubleday, 1969.

Hill, Michael. *A Sociology of Religion*. New York: Basic Books, 1973.

Hoge, Dean R. *Division in the Protestant House*. Philadelphia: Westminster Press, 1976.

Hromadka, Josef. "Social and Cultural Factors in Our Divisions." *Ecumenical Review* (October 1952): 52-58.

Hutcheson, Richard G. *Mainline Churches and the Evangelicals*. Atlanta: John Knox Press, 1981.

Hutchison, William R. *The Modernist Impulse in American Protestantism*. Oxford: Oxford University Press, 1976.

James, J. "A Preliminary Study of the Size Determinant in Small Group Interaction." *American Sociological Review* 16 (1951): 474-77.

Jenkins, Daniel. "The Ecumenical Movement and its Non-Theological Factors." *Ecumenical Review* (July, 1951): 339-46.

Kane, J. J. "Protestant-Catholic Tensions." *American Sociological Review* 16 (1951): 663-72.

Kelley, Dean M. *Why Conservative Churches are Growing: A Study in the Sociology of Religion.* Rev. ed. San Francisco: Harper & Row, Publishers, 1977.

Kennedy, Renwick. "Why Churches Do Not Unite." *Christian Century* 69 (16 July 1952): 825-27.

Lee, Robert. *The Social Sources of Church Unity.* New York: Abingdon Press, 1960.

Lee, Robert E., and Martin E. Marty, eds. *Religion and Social Conflict.* New York: Oxford University Press, 1964.

Marbott, J. D. "Conflict of Ideologies." *Philosophy* 23 (July 1948): 195-207.

Marty, Martin E. *The Modern Schism: Three Paths to the Secular.* New York: Harper & Row, 1969.

_____. *The Righteous Empire: The Protestant Experience in America.* New York: Harper & Row, 1970.

_____. *Modern American Religion.* Vol. 1, *The Irony of It All, 1893-1919.* Chicago: University of Chicago Press, 1986.

Mead, Sidney. *The Lively Experiment The Shaping of Christianity in America.* New York: Harper & Row, 1976.

Moberg, David. "Theological Position and Institutional Characteristics of Protestant Congregations: An Exploratory Study." *Scientific Study of Religion* 9 (Spring 1970): 53-57.

_____. *The Church as a Social Institution: The Sociology of American Religion.* Rev. ed. Grand Rapids, Michigan: Baker Book House, 1984.

Niebuhr, H. Richard. *The Social Sources of Denominationalism.* New York: Henry Holt and Company, 1929.

Obendiek, H. *The Social and Culural Factors in Church Division.* London: SCM Press, 1953.

O'Dea, Thomas F. *The Sociology of Religion.* Englewood Cliffs, New Jersey: Prentice-Hall, Inc., 1966.

Pelikan, Jaroslav. *The Vindication of Tradition.* New Haven: Yale University Press, 1984.

Petersen, James C. "Comment: Church Polity and Denominational Democracy." *Sociological Analysis* 37 (1976): 81-82.

Pope, Liston. *Millhands and Preachers.* New Haven: Yale University Press, 1942.

Renier, Gustaaf Johannes. *History, Its Purpose and Method*. London: George Allen and Unwin Ltd., 1956.

Richey, Russell E. *Denominationalism*. Nashville: Abingdon Press, 1977.

Robert, General Henry M. *Robert's Rules of Order*. Newly revised. Glennview, Illinois: Scott, Foresman and Company, 1970.

Robertson, Roland, ed. *Sociology of Religion Selected Readings*. Middlesex, England: Penguin Books, 1969.

Rose, Arnold M. "Voluntary Associations under Conditions of Competition and Conflict." *Social Forces* 34 (December 1955): 159-63.

Scherer, Ross P., ed. *American Denominational Organization*. Pasadena, California: William Carey Library, 1980.

Shils, Edward. *The Calling of Sociology and Other Essays on the Pursuit of Learning*. Chicago: University of Chicago Press, 1980.

_____. *Tradition*. Chicago: University of Chicago Press, 1981.

Shils, Edward, and T. Parsons, eds. *Toward a General Theory of Action*. Cambridge, Mass.: Harvard University Press, 1951.

Simmel, Georg. *Conflict*. Trans. Kurt H. Wolff. New York: Free Press, 1955.

Smelser, Neil J. *Theory of Collective Behavior*. New York: Free Press, 1965.

Sperry, Willard. "The Non-Theological Factors in the Making and Unmaking of Church Union." *Faith and Order Paper 84*. Geneva: World Council of Churches, 1937.

Stark, Rodney, and William Sims Bainbridge. *The Future of Religion: Secularization, Revival and Cult Formation*. Berkeley: University of California Press, 1985.

Takayama, K. Peter. "Formal Polity and Change of Structures, Denominational Assemblies." *Sociological Analysis* 36 (1975): 17-28.

_____. "Reply." *Sociological Analysis* 37 (1976): 83-84.

_____. "Strains, Conflicts and Schisms in Protestant Denominations." In Scherer, *American Denominational Organization*, pp. 298-329.

Troeltsch, Ernst. *The Social Teaching of the Christian Churches*. New York: Macmillan, 1931.

Tubeville, Gus. "Religious Schism in the Methodist Church: A Sociological Analyses of the Pine Grove Case." *Rural Sociology* 14 (March 1949): 29-39.

Vrga, Djuro J., and F. J. Fahay. "The Relationship of Religious Practices and Beliefs to Schism." *Sociological Analysis* 31 (1970): 46-55.

Wach, Joachim. *Church, Denominations and Sect*. Evanston, Illinois: Seabury-Western Theological Seminary, 1946.

Weaver, Richard. *Ideas Have Consequences*. Chicago: University of Chicago Press, 1948.

Weber, Max. *Essays in Sociology*. Trans. Hans Heinrich Gerth and C. Wright Mills. New York: Oxford University Press, 1946.

Wilson, Bryan. "An Analysis of Sect Development." *American Sociological Review* 34 (February 1959): 3-15.

Wilson, John. "The Sociology of Schism." In *A Sociological Yearbook of Religion in Britain*. Vol. 4, edited by Michael Hill, pp. 1-19. London: SCM Press, 1971.

Yinger, J. Milton. *Religion, Society and the Individual: An Introduction to the Sociology of Religion*. New York: The Macmillan Co., 1957.

Zald, Mayer N. and Roberta Ash. "Social Movements Organizations: Growth, Decay and Change." *Social Forces* 44 (1966): 327-441.

Index

Some commonly used abbreviations in the Index

AELC   Association of Evangelical Lutheran Churches
BCP   Book of Common Prayer
ELIM   Evangelical Lutherans in Mission
LC-MS   Lutheran Church—Missouri Synod
PCUS   Presbyterian Church in the United States
PECUSA   Protestant Episcopal Church in the United States of America
UPUSA   United Presbyterian Church in the United States of America

abortion
  and the PCUS, 14, 25, 28, 30, 35, 40,
    160n233, 163n260
  and the PECUSA, 103, 121
Adams, James, 70
  *Preus of Missouri and the Great Lutheran
    Civil War*, 214
"Address by the General Assembly, 1861
  To all the Churches," 6
*Address Delivered During the First General
  Assembly of the Continuing Presbyterian
  Church* (Williamson), 163n259
Aden, John, 118, 188n44
Affirm, 51, 83, 167n31, 171n84, 180n211
Ahlstrom, Sydney
  *A Religious History of the American
    People*, 104
Alexander, Henry C., 143n35
Allen, Todd, 36-37
Allin, John, Presiding Bishop, 109, 111,
  112-116, 122, 193n113
  attends St. Louis Church Congress, 123
  chastised by Orthodox, 115
  offers to resign, 123

  repudiates communion with new church,
    198n185
  withdraws opposition to women's
    ordination, 117
American Church Union (ACU), 192n106
  and the FCC, 118, 195n144
  "Anglicans United." *See* "Episcopalians
    United"
  "Episcopalians United," 120
  protest "Philadelphia Eleven" ordination,
    113, 119
American Church Union News, 195n144
American Episcopal Church, 103
American Indian Movement, 102
American Lutheran Church (ALC)
  mentioned, 139n3
  "Common Confession of Faith" with
    LC-MS, 47
  fellowship with ELIM, 78
    and AELC, 94
  fellowship with LC-MS, 47, 49, 50-51,
    170n82
  New Orleans Convention (Resolution
    2-40), 62, 64
  Anaheim Convention (1975)

mentioned, 78, 84-87, 88
and ELIM, 84
Biblical interpretation, 85
church polity, 85
Concordia (St. Louis) faculty majority
    Resolution 3-03A, 87
district presidents
    Resolution 5-02A, 86, 91
doctrinal standards and tolerance, 85
    Resolution 3-04, 87
    Resolution 3-05, 87
    Resolution 5-09, 87
ELIM condemned
    Resolution 3-06, 87
English District, 84, 87, 180n214
mission
    Resolution 2-02, 74
parliamentary rules, 85
"President's Report," 85-86
Seminex graduates
    Resolution 5-02A, 86, 91
    Resolution 6-02, 87
Workbook, 84
*Anatomy of an Explosion: Missouri in
    Lutheran Perspective* (Marquart), 139n5
The Anatomy of Revolution (Brinton),
    140n13
Anglican Catholic Church
    "Affirmation of St. Louis," 125
    also called Holy, Catholic and Apostolic
        church, 124
    authority of bishops, 125
    "continuing Anglican Church," 125
    church polity, 125
    theological platform, 125-26
    controversy, 125
    five dioceses, 124
    formation, 124, 125
    high/low churchmanship, 199n188
    membership, 125
    place of Book of Common Prayer, 125
    See also Anglican Church in North
        America; Coalition for the Apostolic
        Ministry; Fellowship of Concerned
        Churchmen; Foundation for Christian
        Theology
Anglican Church in North America
    (ACNA), 118
    "Affirmation of St. Louis," 122, 125

constitutional assembly, 125
reason for forming, 122-23
See also Anglican Catholic Church;
    Fellowship of Concerned Churchmen
Anglican Consultative Council, 110
The Anglican Digest, 195n144
Anglican Orthodox Church of North
    America, 103
Anglicanism
    America, 99
    Burma, 190n78
    Canada, 99, 190n78
    New Zealand, 190n78
    South China, 190n78
    West Indies, 99
Anglicans United. *See* Episcopalians United
Antiochian Orthodox Church in America
    protests women's ordination, 115
    relations with PECUSA, 194n127
Apostolic succession, 99, 192n96
Armstrong, G. C., 143n35
Association of Evangelical Lutheran
    Churches (AELC), 88-97 passim
    mentioned, 139n3
    church polity, 92
    constitution, 91
    Coordinating Council for the Moderate
        Movement (CC), 90-93
        distinctive features, 95-97
        church polity, 95
        comparison with LC-MS, 95-96
        doctrinal standards, 96
        organization, 95
    district presidents dismissed, 91
    ecumenism, 94, 96
    English District support, 91
    founding convention, 94
    inclusiveness, 93
    Lutheran Contingency Conference, 81
    "Mission Affirmations" support, 94
    ordination of women
        Resolution 76-5, 95
    regional associations, 91, 94
    See also Concordia faculty majority;
        Evangelical Lutherans in Mission;
        John Tietjen; Lutheran Church in
        Mission; Seminex
Atkins, Stanley, 117
Auburn Affirmations, 16, 144n43, 151n122

Bailey, Kenneth K.
    Southern White Protestantism in the
        Twentieth Century, 8, 142n24
Balance Inc., 50, 51
Barker, Frank M., 23
Barrett, Ellen M., 122
Barth, Karl, 50
Beebe, L. Peter, 116
Behnken, John, 51
Belhaven College, 14
Bell, L. Nelson, 11, 18-19, 28, 34-35,
    146n72, 147n84, 160n233
Benfield, William A., 25, 26, 30, 151n135
Bertram, Robert, 70, 75, 173n105
Bible
    and the Continuing Presbyterian Church
        (National Presbyterian Church), 33,
        34, 37-38, 40-41, 163n260
    and the LC-MS, 46
    canonicity, 54
    historical critical method, 54, 55, 57,
        75, 77, 177n174
    inerrancy, 46, 50, 51, 75, 83, 171n82,
        177n174, 181n233
    infallibility, 49, 54
    inspiration, 51, 54, 75, 177n174
    "Inspiration of Scripture, The"
        182n233
    "Mission Affirmations," 72
    Scharlemann, Martin, 49
    scriptural interpretation, 49, 54, 55,
        64, 76, 84, 85
    verbal inspiration, 46, 49
    See also Anaheim Convention (1975);
        Jacob Preus's "A Statement of
        Scriptural and Confessional
        Principles;" LC-MS attempts at
        reconciliation
    and the PCUS
        criticism, 11, 143n35
        historical critical method, 11
        inerrancy, 11, 19, 20
        infallibility, 7, 22, 23, 150n113
        interpretation, 130, 150n117
        verbal inspiration, 8, 11, 20
    and the PECUSA, 101, 102
Biel, Alfred, 171n84
birth control
    and the PCUS, 16
Bittner, Merril, 192n101
Black Economic Development Committee,
    102
Bohlmann, Ralph, 75, 76, 173n103,
    175n149
Book of Common Prayer (BCP)
    American BCP, 99, 104
    foundational for Anglican Catholic
        Church, 125
    revised in 1928, 104
    1949 Prayer Book Studies, 105
    revision request (1964), 105
    The Draft Proposed Book of
        Common Prayer and Other Rites
        and Ceremonies of the Church,
        107
    adopted 1976, 109
    catechism, 107
    confirmation, 107
    historical documents, 107
    General Conventions of 1973 &
        1976, 106-108
    Plan of Revision, 105
    Standard Book of Common Prayer,
        109
    Standing Liturgical Commission,
        105-106
    Athanasian Creed, 104
    "Green Book," 105
    importance to Anglican faith, 100
    bonding factor, 101
    "expression" of Anglicanism, 104
    Liturgy of the Lord's Supper, 105
    revision as warrant for schism, 104, 126,
        197n170
    Scottish Prayer Book of 1637, 189n59
    See also Anglican Catholic Church;
        Anglican Church in North America;
        Fellowship of Concerned Churchmen;
        Protestant Episcopal Church in the
        U.S.A.; Society for the Preservation of
        the Book of Common Prayer;
        Standing Liturgical Commission
Book of Confessions (UPUSA), 152n148
Bouman, H., 173n104
Boynton, Charles F., 198n183
Branton, Peter, 28

Brief History of the Presbyterians, A
(Loetscher), 164n269A
Bright, John, 144n36
Brinton, Crane
The Anatomy of Revolution, 140n13
Bryant, Victor, 68, 174n129
Buelow, Pastor, 90, 173n102, 174n130
"The Burden of Infallibility: A Study in the
History of Dogma" (Graebner), 165n8
Burns, William Francis, 199n190

Caemmerer, Richard, 173n104
The Canterbury Guild, 195n144
capital punishment
and the PCUS, 12, 14, 145n51
Cartledge, Dr. Sam, 11
*A Conservative Introduction to the Old
Testament*, 144n36
The Certain Trumpet, 195n143
and the FCC, 118, 195n144
Chambers, Albert, 122, 124
Cheek, Alison, 112, 116
Christian Handbook of Vital Issues, A
(Otten), 58
The Christian Challenge, 195n144
and the FCC, 118
Prayer Book revisions, 108
The Christian News, 51, 58
Christianity and Crisis, 193n110
Church of Christ Uniting, 27, 152n137
church property
in the PCUS schism, 24, 26, 30, 33, 35,
38-40, 154n175, 155n176, 157n213
civil disobedience
and the PCUS, 14, 26
Civil War
and the PCUS, 6, 7
Clark, E. T., 139n9
clergy/laity split
in the LC-MS, 132
in the PCUS, 132, 153n154
in the PECUSA, 102, 132, 134,
193n118
Coalition for the Apostolic Ministry
(CAM), 192n107
"Declaration of Principle," 192n107
protest "Philadelphia Eleven" ordination,
113, 119

Coggan, Donald, 124
Colloquy, 25
Comment, 195n144
Committee of 24 (PCUS). *See*
PCUS—Joint Committee for Union
between the UPUSA and PCUS
Committee of 32. *See* PCUS—Joint
Committee for Union between the
UPUSA and PCUS
The Concerned Presbyterian, 19
Concerned Presbyterians, Inc. (CP), 19, 24,
26, 31, 35, 148n95, 150n121, 151n124
See also Continuing Church Committee
(CCC)
Concordia Seminary (Springfield), 167n30
Concordia Seminary (St. Louis), 51-57
Board of Control, 53, 54, 57, 58, 60,
61, 63, 64, 68-71, 75, 83, 168n43,
170n71
conservatives suspect teaching, 48, 49,
50
continues after departure of faculty
majority, 175n149
election of Tietjen, 51
student body
"A Student Resolution," 68
"Appendix 6," 69
Expanded Commission on Seminary
Concerns (ECSC), 68
moratorium, 70
Operation Outreach, 67
Students Concerned for Reconciliation
(SCRUG), 68
"With One Voice," 67-68
See also Concordia (St. Louis) faculty
majority; Concordia (St. Louis) faculty
minority; Seminex
Concordia Seminary (St. Louis) faculty
majority
"A Call to Openness and Trust," 52-53
"A Declaration by the Faculty of
Concordia Seminary in Response to
the 'Report of the Synodical
President,' " 57
"A Declaration of Protest and
Confession," 62
"Faithful to our Calling—Faithful to our
Lord," 57
Operation Outreach, 67

"Response of the Faculty of Concordia Seminary" to Preus's "Statement," 54, 170n65
suspended, 69, 71, 89
See also Anaheim Convention (1975); John Tietjen; LC-MS attempts at reconciliation; New Orleans Convention (1973); Seminex
Concordia Seminary (St. Louis) faculty minority, 63, 173n103
problem of Seminex graduates, 79-80
Concordia Senior College of Fort Wayne, 70
Concordia Teachers College (River Forest), 70
Concordia Theological Monthly, 171n82
Confession of 1967, 21, 149n107
The Confessional Lutheran, 47
Confessional subscription, 130
and the LC-MS, 134
and the PCUS, 134
Conflict (Simmel), 133
Congregation of St. Augustine, 195n144
Congregationalism
and the PCUS, 5
"Conservative Coalition" (PCUS), 24
"Call for Realignment of American Presbyterianism," 27
See also Concerned Presbyterians; Presbyterian Evangelistic Fellowship; Presbyterian Churchmen United; Covenant Fellowship of Presbyterians
Conservative Introduction to the Old Testament, A (Cartledge), 144n36
Consultation on Church Union (COCU)
and the PCUS, 17, 22, 24, 26, 30, 35, 150n114
and the UPUSA, 158n206
Contact, 150n121, 160n233
See also Continuing Forward
Continuing Church Committee (CCC), 150n93
See also Continuing Presbyterian Church
Continuing Forward, 150n121
Continuing Presbyterian Church (later known as National Presbyterian Church and Presbyterian Church in America)
mentioned, 38, 158n212

accused of congregationalism, 40, 161n250
Advisory Convention, 38-41
Book of Church Order, 36, 41, 42
Committee of 40, 39
Committee on Administration, 41
Committee on Christian Education and Publications, 41
Committee on Mission to the U.S., 41
Committee on Mission to the World, 41
Constituting General Assembly, 38-42
Convocation of Sessions, 38
"Declaration of Intent," 33, 160n231
Doctrinal Standards, 32-34, 38, 39, 40-42, 157n194, 163n260
ecumenical relations, 32, 35, 41
escape clause, 32-39, 159n224, 159n225
"Faith and Purpose," 32
"Message to All Churches of Jesus Christ Throughout the World," 42
origins, 34-35
Plan of Union, 32, 36, 39, 160n239
property issue, 33, 35, 38-40, 158n213
"Reaffirmations of 1973," 38, 39, 41
regionalism, 42, 156n191, 162n254
restructuring, 35, 38
spiritual mission, 38, 39, 42
Steering Committee, 32, 33, 37, 160n230
Vanguard Presbytery, 36-37
women, place of, 41, 159n219, 163n260
See also Bible; doctrinal standards; ecumenical relations; National Presbyterian Church; Presbyterian Church in America; race relations
Coordinating Council for the Moderate Movement. See Association of Evangelical Lutheran Churches
Corrigan, D., 112, 113
Coser, Lewis
appeal to a higher principle, 136
conflict
as dysfunctional, 134
as functional, 133-4
heightened in close relationships, 133
realistic and unrealistic, 133
heretical conflict, 133
ideological concerns, 134, 136
sects and churches, 134

doctrinal tolerance, 134
The Functions of Social Conflict, 133
Council for the Faith (Canada), 195n144
Covenant Fellowship of Presbyterians
(CFOP), 23-24, 156n188, 157n196,
160n233
"An Open Letter to the Church," 23
The Open Letter, 151n129
Creighton, Bishop, 116, 194n130
Cumberland Presbyterians, 143n29, 144n45

Damm, John, 71, 173n105
Dancing
and the LC-MS, 47
Danker, Frederick W., 139n5
Dawson, Christopher, 139n9
Dendy, Rev. H. B., 11, 18-19
Dendy, Moderator Marshall C., 17, 19
denominations, 129-31
Dewitt, R. L., 112, 113, 194n130
Diocese of San Francisco, 122
Diocese of the Holy Trinity, 122
divorce
and the PCUS, 12
and the PECUSA
remarriage, 103
doctrinal standards
and the AELC, 96
and the Anglican Church of North
America, 123
essential principles of belief, 123
"Nature of the church," 123, 197n175
and the Continuing Presbyterian Church
(National Presbyterian Church), 32-
34, 35-37, 38-42, 157n194, 163n260
and the LC-MS, 45-47, 130, 134,
166n26, 201n21
Article II, 59, 83
as a warrant for schism, 56, 76,
177n175
"A Review of the Question What is a
Doctrine?," 167n37
"A Statement of Scriptural and
Confessional Principles," 54
"Blue Book," 55-56
Board of Doctrinal Review, 53
doctrinal tolerance, 50, 52, 53, 54-56,
64, 66-67, 93, 166n26

among the Concordia faculty
majority, 54-56, 70
and the Atlantic District (LC-MS),
70
and the Concordia faculty majority,
59-61, 62-63, 76, 83, 87
"Limitation of Academic
Freedom," 77
and ELIM, 65, 66, 77-78, 93
and the Lutheran Church in
Mission, 82
false doctrine, 55, 83
freedom of the Gospel, 57, 86
"Guiding Principles for the Use of 'A
Statement'," 66-67
in missions, 72-75, 84
Lutheran Confessions, 56
"Opinion Regarding Dissenting
Groups," 53
precise doctrines, 52, 54, 55
third use of the law, 76
*Report of the Advisory Committee on
Doctrine and Conciliation*, 76,
176n169
resurrection of martyrs as
nonfundamental, 47
synodical stance, 49, 53, 59, 86,
166n21, 166n26, 181n233
See also Anaheim Convention (1975);
Bible and the LC-MS; "Mission
Affirmations;" New Orleans
Convention (1973)
and the PCUS, 5, 8, 10-13, 16, 130,
134, 144n43
as barrier to ecumenism, 17
as platform for Concerned
Presbyterians, 19, 22
as platform for Reformed Theological
Seminary, 20
as a problem in the Confession of
1967, 21
and the PECUSA, 186n9
Book of Common Prayer theology,
106, 189n69, 189n70
"comprehensiveness," 101
Lambeth Quadrilateral, 186n9
reason for schism, 123
secular humanism, 103
theological lack, 102, 108, 197n170

tolerance, 100-101, 186n9
unorthodoxy, 102-103
as a precipitating factor in schism, 137
tolerance, 130
Dodd, C. H., 139n9
Doren, C. Dale, 124, 199n190
Dowey, E., 37, 156n185
DuBois, Albert J., 118, 119, 192n106

East Coast Common Endeavor (ECCE),
180n215
Eastern Orthodoxy, 103, 115, 194n127
ecumenism, 1
and the Continuing Presbyterian Church,
32, 35, 41
and the LC-MS, 130, 134
"A Brief Statement of the Doctrinal
Position of the Evangelical Lutheran
Synod of Missouri, Ohio and Other
States," 46
"A Lutheran Stance Toward
Ecumenism," 181n233
altar and pulpit fellowship, 84, 89,
166n25
American Lutheran Church (ALC),
49, 50-51, 62, 64, 84
and ELIM, 89
and AELC, 94
Chicago Theses, 46
in missions, 74
Consultation of Asian Churches, 73-
74
"Mission Affirmations," 50, 72, 74,
84
Partners in Mission, 74
Lutheran council, 49
Jacob Preus's opposition, 50
"Statement of 44," 47
Synodical Conference, 47
Union Committee of 1925, 46
Walter Maier's position, 47
See also Anaheim Convention (1975);
New Orleans Convention (1973)
and the PCUS, 10, 11, 15-18, 130, 134,
147n77
Plan for Union with UPUSA, 16, 21,
25, 26, 30, 32, 36, 39, 151n131,
162n239

property issue, 24, 26, 30, 154n175,
155n176
"The Presbyterian Church in the
United States and Church Unity,"
17
union churches, 17, 24
union presbyteries, 21, 26, 149n102
and the PECUSA
dialogues, 233
The Draft Proposed Book of
Common Prayer and Other Rites
and Ceremonies of the Church,
107
Roman Catholic, 99, 194n127
women's ordination, 117, 194n127
Ehlen, Arlis, 54
Election Doctrine
in the PCUS, 9, 12, 143n29
at Reformed Theological Seminary, 20
Elliot, William M., 24
Engelbrecht, Luther, 176n154
Episcopal Charismatic Fellowship, 104
Episcopal Church, The. See Protestant
Episcopal Church in the United States of
America (PECUSA)
Episcopal Renaissance of Pennsylvania,
195n144
The Episcopalian
Prayer Book revisions, 107-108
optional ecclesiastical organization, 121
ordination of women, 108
Episcopalian Christ Church Cathedral, 70,
71
Episcopalians United/Anglicans United,
195n144
The Evangelical and Catholic Mission
(ECM), 121
Evangelical Lutheran Church in Canada
(ELCIC), 139n3
Evangelical Lutheran Church of America
(ELCA), 139n3
Evangelical Lutherans in Mission (ELIM)
"A Faithful Witness," 180n212
American Lutheran Church Fellowship,
78
Anaheim Convention (1975), 78, 84,
87-88, 180n211, 180n212
assembly in Chicago, 88
Board of Directors, 65, 173n109

chief emphases and function, 66, 88
church polity, 89, 91, 93
    Resolution 75-5, 89
    Resolution 75-13, 89
cluster organization, 89, 90
"Conference of Evangelical Lutherans,"
    65
doctrinal standards, 181n220
ecumenism
    Resolution 75-1 and 2, 88
    Resolution 75-5, 89
    Resolution 75-13, 89
formation, 65-67
"Here We Stand," 77
"In the Name of Jesus Christ and for the
    Sake of the Gospel," 65
Lutheran Church in America fellowship,
    78
mission goals, 178n188
    Resolution 75-1 and 2, 88
Missouri in Perspective, 178n188
recognizes Seminex, 78
social goals, 182n238
Second Assembly, 77
supports AELC resolutions (76-2, 76-3
    & 76-7), 93
"We are Persuaded," 75, 181n220
"Where Does This Lead Us?," 65
See also Anaheim Convention (1975);
    doctrinal standards and the LC-MS;
    ecumenism and the LC-MS
evolution, theory of
    and the PCUS, 12, 145n52, 160n233
Ewald, Elwyn, 65, 90, 177n179, 180n211
    Coordinating Council for Moderate
    Movement staff, 91
Executive Council of PECUSA, 100
    also called the National Council, 185n6

Faber, Dorothy, 108
    and the FCC, 118
Faith Forward—First Concerns (FF-FC),
    49, 50
Federal Council of Churches
    and the PCUS, 15-16, 146n75
Fellowship of Concerned Churchmen
    (FCC), 118-121
    "A Call to Anglican Integrity," 119

"An Open Letter to the Bishops of the
    Episcopal Church," 120
Book of Common Prayer, 120
"Catholicism," 124
"continuing Church movement," 121
dissent, 121
first Church Congress (St. Louis), 121,
    122
formation, 118
"Here We Stand" (Louisville
    Declaration), 119
"Hold Fast," 120-121
member organizations, 195n144
Minneapolis General Convention, 120
ordination of women, 120
theological platform, 118-119
See also Anglican Catholic Church;
    Anglican Church in North America;
    Faber, Dorothy; Foundation for
    Christian Theology; St. Louis Church
    Congress; The Christian Challenge;
    The Living Church
Fellowship of Concern (PCUS), 19,
    148n95
First Presbyterian Church of Macon,
    Georgia, 34
FitzSimons, C. Allison, "Towards an
    Historical Hermeneutic for
    Understanding the PECUSA," 186n9
Foundation for Christian Theology (FCT),
    102
    and the FCC, 195n144
    concerned with individual salvation, 103
    concerns regarding social action
    program, 102
    See also Fellowship of Concerned
    Churchmen
Frincke, Herman, 48, 91, 178n194
Fuerbringer, Alfred, 168n41, 173n104
The Functions of Social Conflict (Coser),
    133
Fund for Lutheran Theological Education
    (FLUTE), 173n105

George, James H., Jr., 103
Gerken, Otto, 83
Gillespie, Guy T., 14
Glass, John, 188n44

Glock, Charles Y. and Ringer, Benjamin B.
    To Comfort and to Challenge, 132
Goetting, Paul, 64, 68, 70
Graebner, Theodore
    "The Burden of Infallibility: A Study in
    the History of Dogma," 165n8
*Growth and Decline in the Episcopal
    Church* (Williamson), 101-102

Hall, C. F., 112, 192n104
Hanover Presbytery of Virginia, 158n213
Harms, Oliver, 49, 50, 51, 76
    defeat in 1969 re-election, 50-51
Harnapp, Pastor, 90, 172n102, 174n130
Harris, Edward G., 192n99
Harvey, Robert C., 125
Hecht, Harold, 89, 90, 91, 92, 178n194
Heyward, Carter, 116
Hill, Samuel
    Religion in the Southern States, 142n23
    Southern Churches in Crisis, 142n23
Hill, William E. Jr., 19, 24, 38, 150n115,
    159n223
Hines, John, 102, 111
    "The Historical and Theological Dimensions
    of a Confessing Movement within the
    Lutheran Church—Missouri Synod"
    (Neeb), 139n5
*The Historical Birth of the Presbyterian
    Church in America* (Richards), 139n5
History
    relationship to sociology, 127
History, Its Purpose and Method (Renier),
    127
Hoffman, Oswald, 171n83
How is the Gold Become Dim (Smith), 7
Huber, Curtis, 167n30
Hull, B.R., 114
Hurt, Bishop, 194n130

Inter-Religious Relations
    and the PCUS, 15, 21, 146n71

Jacobs, Paul, 88, 178n194
Jaech, Emil J., 86, 178n194

Joint Committee for Union between the
    UPUSA and PCUS (also known as the
    Committee of 24, 26 and 32), 24, 30,
    35, 37, 149n106, 151n131
Journal Day (PCUS), 19, 25, 31
Jumper, Andrew, 24, 157n196
Jungkuntz, Richard, 52, 167n30, 177n178

Kennedy, James, 155n182
Keyes, Kenneth, 19, 24, 151n130
Klann, Richard, 173n103
Klug, Eugene, 60
Kohn, William
    as ELIM official, 90
    AELC chairman, 93, 94
    "Our Church in Mission in Today's
    World," 94, 184n276, 184n277
    resignation from Board for Missions
    (LC-MS), 73, 74
Kraemer, Charles, 40
Kretzmann, Martin, 72
Kurzweg, Bernard, 167n30

Lambeth Conference, 110, 190n74,
    199n185
*The Lambeth Conferences and Women
    Priests: The Historical Background of the
    Conferences and Their Impact on the
    Episcopal Church in America* (Marrett),
    190n75
Lambeth Quadrilateral, 186n9
Laukhuff, Perry, 118, 122, 125
Law, James, 188n44
LeCraw, Roy, 151n130
life insurance
    and the LC-MS, 47
Lingle, Walter Lee, 143n31
The Living Church
    and the FCC, 195n144
    Prayer Book revisions, 108
Loetscher, Lefferts A.,
    A Brief History of the Presbyterians,
    164n269
Lueking, F. Dean, 166n26
    leader in ELIM, 65

Mission in the Making: The Missionary Enterprise among Missouri Synod Lutherans (1846-1963), 166n26
Lutheran Church in America (LCA), 78, 94, 139n3
Lutheran Church in Mission (LCM), 81-83, 88, 89, 183n250
"Catechism on L C M," 82
incorporation, 82

Lutheran Church—Missouri Synod (LC-MS), 45-97 passim
mentioned, 1, 3
American Lutheran Church (ALC)
Common Confession of Faith, 49
fellowship, 47, 49, 50-51
Americanization, 45, 47, 51, 64, 72, 96
Article II, 49, 53, 59, 77, 83
and schismatic theory
environmental change, 130
schismatic warrants, 135-36
appeal to higher principles, 137
basic assumptions questioned, 135-36
dysfunctional conflict, 135
doctrinal standards relaxed, 137
religious core threatened, 137-38
sect-like behavior, 134
shifts in the authority structure, 131-32
Article VIIIc, 66
Atlantic District, 70, 180n213
attempts at reconciliation, 75-76
authority of the president, 53
Board for Higher Education (BHE), 58, 61, 168n43
"Limitation of Academic Freedom," 77
Board for Missions (BFM), 72-74, 175n154
Mission Study Commission, 73-74, 176n158
resignation of Kohn, 72
Board of Directors, 48, 70, 75
Board of Doctrinal Review, 53
Book of Concord, 201n21
church polity, 46, 80-81, 83, 85, 88, 93
Article III, 85
Article VII definition, 46

comparison with AELC, 95
synod as advisory body, 48, 79-81
Commission on Constitutional Matters (CCM), 63, 70-71, 79-80, 83, 87-88, 94
"Opinion Regarding the Removal of District Presidents from Office," 81
Commission on Theology and Church Relations (CTCR), 49, 52, 59, 66-67, 75
"Guiding Principles for the Use of 'A Statement', " 66-67, 87
"Opinion on Dissenting Groups," 185n180
Committee on Theology and Church Relations, 132
constitution, 48, 66
conventions, synodical
1929 River Forest, Ill., 46
1965 Detroit, 49
1971 Milwaukee, 53, 64
doctrinal tolerance
"Opinion Regarding Dissenting Groups," 53
Resolution 2-21, 53, 78
faculty majority
Resolution 2-50, 53
Resolution 2-28, 53, 55
1967 New York, 50
1969 Denver, 50
"A Review of the Question What is a Doctrine?," 167n37
See also Anaheim Convention; New Orleans Convention
Council of Presidents (COP), 47, 57, 70, 75, 79-81, 182n248
"A Call to Face the Issues," 81
eight dissenting district presidents, 80-81, 86, 88, 90, 178n194, 183n250
four fired, 91
one resigned, 94
district presidents, 60, 86
English District, 70, 84-85, 87, 89-90, 180n213
district president H. Hecht, 89, 91, 178n194
supports AELC, 90-91
separates from LC-MS, 92

Lutheran Church—Missouri Synod (cont.)
  Fact Finding Committee (FFC), 52, 55, 56, 60
    See also Jacob Preus's "Blue Book"
  homogeneity, 48
  missions, 72-75
    Consultation of Asian Churches, 73
    India, 73
    New Guinea, 73, 175n154
    Philippines, 73
    resignation of Kohn, 73
      See also LC-MS—Board For Missions; "Mission Affirmations"
  organization, 47-48, 84
    comparison with AELC, 95
  Preus's "Statement," 131, 201n21
  parochial school system, 47
  "synod," 59
  women, place of, 49
  See also American Lutheran Church; Anaheim Convention (1975); Association of Evangelical Lutheran Churches; Bible; Concordia Seminary (St. Louis); Concordia (St. Louis) faculty majority; Dancing; Doctrinal Standards; Ecumenism; Preus, Jacob; Life Insurance; National Council of Churches; New Orleans Convention (1973); Scouting; Synodical Conference; Synodical Conventions; Takayama, K. Peter; Tietjen, John; Unions; Universalism; usury; Walther, Carl Ferdinand; women; World Council of Churches

Lutheran Contingency Conference, 81
Lutheran Council in the USA, 52, 94
The Lutheran News, 49, 168n42
The Lutheran Witness, 58, 66, 68, 75, 80, 89, 171n80
Lutheran World Federation, 94
Lynn, R. Matthew, 20
Lytle, Andrew, 188n44

Macquarrie, John, 103
Maier, Walter, 47

Mallary, Dewitt, 113, 193n108
Marquart, Kurt, 139n5
Marrett, Michael McFarlene
  The Lambeth Conferences and Women Priests: The Historical Background of the Conferences and Their Impact on the Episcopal Church in America, 190n75
Mayer, James, 73, 74, 176n154, 176n162
McKeludy, A.J., 143n31
Meyer, Waldemar, 178n194, 183n267
Millard, James, 157n195
Miller, Roland, 176n154
"Mission Affirmations"
  mentioned, 72-75, 84
  adopted, 49
  AELC's endorsement, 94
  author, 72
  Consultation of Asian Churches, 72
  doctrinal tolerance, 72, 84
  ecumenical, 50, 72
  ELIM's endorsement, 178n188
  firing of James Mayer, 72
  indigenous churches, 72, 73
  "The Mission of the Christian Church in the World: A Review of the 1965 'Mission Affirmations', " 166n26, 181n233
  Partners in Mission, 74
  Mission in the Making: The Missionary Enterprise among Missouri Synod Lutherans (1846-1963) (Lueking), 166n26
  Missouri in Perspective, 65, 84, 178n188
Montgomery, John W., 49
Moore, Paul, 122
Morse, Robert S., 124, 199n192, 199n197
Mote, James O., 124, 199n190

National Council of Afro-American Lutherans (NCAAL), 183n250
National Council of Churches (NCC)
  and the AELC, 94
  and the Continuing Presbyterian Church, 38
  and the LC-MS, 94
  and the PCUS, 14, 16, 28, 29, 30, 35, 146n75
  and the PECUSA, 103, 125

National Presbyterian and Reformed
Fellowship (NPRF)
mentioned, 162n255
formation and stated goals, 27
National Presbyterian Church (NPC), 40,
159n223, 162n256
See also Presbyterian Church in America
(PCA)
Gifts of the Spirit, 162n257
"Message to All Churches of Jesus Christ
Throughout the World," 42
Neeb, Larry, 139n5, 174n129
Neunaber, Herman, 60, 178n194, 183n253
New Orleans Convention (1973)
mentioned, 58-62, 64, 65
aftermath, 62-64
ALC fellowship
Resolution 2-40, 62
doctrinal standards and tolerance
Resolution 2-12, 59, 78
Resolution 3-01, 59
faculty majority
Resolution 3-09, 60, 69, 71
missions, 72, 175n153
"Mission Affirmations," 72
parliamentary rules, 172n90, 172n94
protests, 60
Tietjen, John
Resolution 3-12, 61
Resolution 3-12A, 62
New School Presbyterians, 5, 11
*No Room in the Brotherhood: The Preus-
Otten Purge of Missouri* (Danker), 139n5

O'Dea, Thomas F.
The Sociology of Religion, 201n17
Ogilby, Bishop, 112, 113
Old School Presbyterians, 5
The Open Letter, 151n129
Orthodox Presbyterian Church, 36
Osborn, Charles, 113, 120
Ostling, Richard, 198n183
Otten, Herman, 168n42, 58
A Christian Handbook of Vital Issues, 58
The Christian News, 51
Otto, E., 171n84

Pae, Mark, 198n183
Pagtakhan, Francisco J., 124, 198n183
Parsons, Donald, 113-114
Partners in Mission (PIM), 74, 178n188,
182n238
Patterson, Donald B., 23, 32, 150n116,
163n264
Petersen, William H., "Tensions of Anglican
Identity in the PECUSA: An
Interpretative Essay," 186n9.
Phelleps, Gary, 174n138
"Philadelphia Eleven," 112-116
actual ordination and protests, 113
authority of bishops, 114
conservative backlash, 115
House of Bishops discussions, 114
plans for, 112
"regularized," 195n140
"validity," 114
Pieper, Francis
"A Brief Statement of the Doctrinal
Position of the Evangelical Lutheran
Synod of Missouri, Ohio and Other
States," 46, 49
"unionism," 165n8
orthodox and heterodox definition, 46-
47
Piepkorn, A. C., 173n104
Pike, James, 103, 197n170
Pittenger, W. Norman, 100
Polish National Church, 194n127
Presbyterian Church in America (PCA),
162n256
See also National Presbyterian Church;
Continuing Presbyterian Church
Presbyterian Church in the Confederate
States
Constituting General Assembly (1861), 6

**Presbyterian Church in the United States
(PCUS)**, 5-43, passim
mentioned, 1, 3
Address by the General Assembly, 1861
To all the Churches, 6
Adopting Act of 1729, 5, 10
alcohol consumption, 25, 155n182
Board for World Missions (BWM), 14,
28-29, 147n76

Presbyterian Church in the United States (cont.)
  Board of Christian Education (PCUS), 14
  Board of Church Extension (PCUS), 14
    See also Board of National Ministries
  Book of Church Order, 26, 32, 158n190
  Board of National Ministries (PCUS), 14, 147n76
  clergy-laity split, 153n154
  Committee on Christian Relations, 14, 15
  Committee on Moral and Social Welfare, 13
  Committee on Unhappiness and Division in the Church, 40, 164n267
  congregationalism, 40
  "Conservative Coalition," 24
    See also Concerned Presbyterians; Presbyterian Evangelistic Fellowship; Presbyterian Churchmen United; Covenant Fellowship of Presbyterians
  Continuing Church Committee (CCC), 148n93
    See also Continuing Presbyterian Church
  doctrinal standards, 5, 8, 10-13, 16, 144n43
    as barrier to ecumenism, 17
    as platform for Concerned Presbyterians, 19, 22
    as platform for Reformed Theological Seminary, 20
    as a problem in the Confession of 1967, 21
  ecumenical relations, 10, 11, 15-18, 147n77
  plan for union with UPUSA, 16, 21, 25, 26, 30, 37, 151n131
  property issue, 24, 26, 30, 154n175, 155n176
  "The Presbyterian Church in the United States and Church Unity," 17
  union churches, 17, 24
  union presbyteries, 21, 26, 149n102
  equalization policy, 28

Executive Commission on Overseas Evangelism (ECOE)—PCUS, 20, 29, 30
form of government, 20
founding, 5
General Assemblies, 1861, 38; 1862, 15, 17; 1934, 11; 1939, 11; 1947, 11; 1950, 14; 1959, 12; 1961, 17; 1963, 12; 1964, 152n149; 1966, 12; 1968, 12, 17; 1969, 13, 17, 20-22, 28; 1970, 25; 1971, 29-31; 1972, 11, 34; 1973, 35, 39; 1974, 37; 1975, 35
General Synod (1716), 5
Holy Spirit, place of, 12
homogeneity, 8-9, 17, 143n28
Joint Committee for Union between the UPUSA and PCUS (also known as the Committee of 24, 26 and 32), 24, 30, 35, 37, 149n106, 151n131
"Meaning of Doctrinal Loyalty in the Ordination Vows," 11
Missions, 28-29, 30
  See also PCUS—Board for World Missions; Executive Commission on Overseas Evangelism (ECOE)
New School Presbyterians, 5, 11
Old School Presbyterians, 5
ordination of women, 12, 26
Permanent Committee on Christian Relations (PCUS), 14, 15
Plan of Union (1801) (PCUS), 5
polarization, 9-10, 143n28
presbyterial rule, 8, 16, 40
Presbyterian Church in the Confederate States, 6
Project Equality, 14, 145n67
property issue, 24, 26, 30, 39-40, 154n175, 155n176
regionalism, 5, 7-8, 30, 142n23, 147n75, 154n177
restructuring, 20, 25, 30, 35, 40
  and schismatic theory
  environmental change, 130
  schismatic warrants, 135-37
    appeal to higher principle, 137
    basic assumptions questioned, 135
    dysfunctional conflict, 135
    doctrinal standards relaxed, 137
    religious core threatened, 137-38

Presbyterian Church in the United States (cont.)
   sect-like behavior, 134
   shifts in authority structure, 131
   social issues, 9, 13, 30, 35, 40, 143n23, 152n151
   abortion. *See* Abortion and the PCUS
   child labor, 13
   "The Theological Basis for Christian Social Action," 15
   spiritual mission, 5-11, 13-15, 16, 20, 22, 38, 140n5, 141-142n18
   union presbyteries, 21, 26, 40
   youth voting privileges, 152n150
   See also abortion; Bible; birth control; capital punishment; church property in the PCUS schism; civil disobedience; Civil War; clergy-laity split; Congregationalism; Consultation on Church Union; divorce; doctrinal standards; ecumenism; evolution; Election Doctrine; evolution; Federal Council of Churches; Fellowship of Concern; Inter-Religious Relations; Journal Day; National Council of Churches; race relations; rationalism; Takayama, K. Peter; Universalism; vietnam involvement; Westminster Confession; women; World Council of Churches

Presbyterian Churchmen United (PCU), 24, 32, 150n121, 151n124, 159n223, 163n264
   "Declaration of Commitment," 22
   origins, 23
Presbyterian Evangelistic Fellowship (PEF), 19, 24, 29, 32, 156n191
   See also Executive Commission on Overseas Evangelism
The Presbyterian Journal, 14, 24, 34, 38, 159n222
   main editorial thrust, 17, 24, 148n87
   as supporting segregation, 26, 31, 145-46n63
Presbyterian Lay Committee, 149n108
Presbyterian Ministers Prayer Fellowship, 150n116

Presbyterians in the South (Thompson), 9, 142n19
The Presbyterian Outlook, 24, 156n188, 157n192, 157n196, 159n222, 160n230, 161n249, 161n250
The Presbyterian Standard, 143n31
The Presbyterian Survey, 14, 146n711
Preus, Jacob, 50, 165n18, 168n48, 172n85, 185n280
   and Concordia faculty majority, 69
   "A Joint Statement" (with J. Tietjen), 57, 170n75
   "A Message to the Church," 69
   "Blue Book," 55
   Ehlen affair, 54
   forms Fact Finding Committee, 52, 68
   New Orleans Convention (1973), 58-62
   "From the Desk of the President: Brother to Brother," 55, 57
   and ELIM, 89
   as member of Little Norwegian Synod, 167n30
   as president of the Springfield seminary, 167n30
   "A Statement of Scriptural and Confessional Principles," 54, 59
      See also Lutheran Church—Missouri Synod CTCR "Guiding Principles for the Use of 'A Statement' "
   condemns ELIM, 66
   elected synodical president, 51
   re-elected, 58
   "From the Desk of the President: Brother to Brother," 55, 57
   New Orleans Convention (1973), 58-62
   opposition to ecumenism, 51
   "President's Report," 85
   Seminex graduates refused, 80
Preus of Missouri and the Great Lutheran Civil War (Adams), 214
Preus, Robert, 50, 168n48, 173n103, 175n149
Program of Education for Responsible Christian Action (PERCA), 178n188
Project Equality, 14, 146n67

Protestant Episcopal Church in the United States of America (PECUSA) (The Episcopal Church), 99-118 passim
mentioned, 1, 3
also called Episcopal Church, 100, 185n4
and schismatic theory
  schismatic warrants, 135-37
    appeal to higher principle, 137
    basic assumptions questioned, 135-36
    dysfunctional conflict, 134
    doctrinal standards relaxed, 137
    religious core threatened, 137-38
    shifts in the authority structure, 131
  apostolic succession, 131
church polity, 115, 118, 123-24, 197n175
clergy, 102
  clergy-laity split, 102
  priesthood definition, 112
Committee on Theology, 113-114
Confirmation rite in PECUSA, 106, 188n52
constitution, 113, 116
declining membership, 101-102, 131
episcopate, 100, 115, 118
Executive Council of PECUSA, 100, 117
  also National Council, 185n6
founded, 99
General Conventions of the PECUSA, 100; 1789, 99; 1949, 104; 1964, 105; 1967, 105; 1970, 105, 110;
  Louisville (1973)
    election of Presiding Bishop, 111
    miscellaneous matters, 111, 191n86
    ordination of women, 110-112
    arguments for and against, 110
    groups campaigning, 191n84
    Prayer Book revision, 105, 106, 111
  Minneapolis (1976)
    homosexuality, 121-122
    ordination of women, 114, 115, 116-118
    approved, 117
    events leading to, 116-117, 120
    compromises attempted, 117
    convened, 117

  Prayer Book revision, 103, 106, 108, 189n64
  regional
    1785 & 1786, 99
    1979, 108
General Convention Special Program (GCSP), 102, 122
homosexuality, 103, 121
House of Bishops
  mentioned, 100, 132
  approval needed to validate church law, 188n37
  idea of church polity, 123-24
  ordination of women, 110, 113, 117
    approve women's ordination, 117
    Board of Inquiry, 117
    censure ordaining bishops, 117
    "Statement on Conscience," 123
  Prayer Book revisions, 106, 109, 190n70
House of Deputies
  mentioned, 100, 132
  ordination of women, 109, 115
    approve, 117
  Prayer Book revisions, 109, 190n70
integrity, 121
mission work, 101, 107
organization, 100, 112, 117
not a sect, 135
ordination of women, 131
"Philadelphia Eleven," 112-116
  See also "Philadelphia Eleven"
polarization, 100
Prayer Book revision, 131
Presiding Bishop, 100
province presidents, 113
social action, 102
Special Committee on Episcopal Theological Education, 102
See also abortion; Allin, John; Bible; Book of Common Prayer; clergy-laity split; divorce; doctrinal standards; ecumenism; General Conventions of PECUSA; House of Bishops; House of Deputies; Lambeth Conference; National Council of Churches; sexuality; Society for the Preservation of the Book of Common Prayer; Standing Liturgical Commission; *The*

Episcopalian; women; World Council of Churches

race relations
 and the Continuing Presbyterian Church, 156n191
 in the PCUS, 13-14, 16, 145n61, 145n63
 Black Manifesto, 14
 civil rights, 19, 142n26
 desegregation of schools, 14
 racial integration, 19, 28, 142n26, 147n79
 segregation, 145-46n63, 147n80
 slavery, 7, 13
 UPUSA differs, 30
Ralston, William, 188n44
Ramose, J. A., 113
Rationalism
 in the PCUS, 5
Read, Francis W., 118
Reed, David, 197n175
Reformed Church in America (RCA), 18, 146n86
Reformed Episcopal Church, 100
Reformed Presbyterian Church (Evangelical Synod), 36
Reformed Theological Seminary (RTS), 11, 20, 24
Religion in the Southern States (Hill), 142n23
Religious factors, 3
Religious History of the American People, A (Ahlstrom), 104
Renier, Gustaaf Johannes
 History, Its Purpose and Method, 127
Repp, Arthur, 68, 173n104
Ressmeyer, R. P. F., 91, 173n115, 178n194
Rhys, Howard, 188n44
Richards, John Edwards, 24, 34, 38, 139n5, 159n223
Riedel, Robert, 91, 178n194
Ringer, Benjamin B. and Glock, Charles Y.
 To Comfort and to Challenge, 132
Riverside Church (New York), 116
Robinson, James, 144n36

Rose, Ben Lacey, 155n182, 156n185, 157n195
Roth, Sam, 60, 66, 70, 88, 93
Rusch, William
 Ecumenism—A Movement Toward Church Unity, 1
Rutler, George, 113
 involved with formation of Anglican Catholic Church, 199n188
 protests "Philadelphia Eleven" ordination, 113

Scott, John L., 192n107
Schaeffer, Francis, 157n194
Scharlemann, Martin, 49, 168n48, 173n103
 acting president of Concordia Seminary (St. Louis), 68, 69
 "Appendix 6," 69, 174n137
Scherer, H., 83
schism
 theory of, 2-3, 127-138
Schleef, Roger, 88
Scouting
 and the LC-MS, 47
Seabury, Samuel, 99, 104
Seminex (Seminary-in-exile), 67-71
 Eden Seminary, 71
 faculty, 89
 founding, 71
 graduates, problem of, 71, 79-81, 84, 87, 182n238
 eight dissenting district presidents, 80-81, 86, 90, 178n194
 four fired, 91
 Joint Project for Theological Education, 71
 Lutheran School of Theology in Chicago, 71
 recognized by ELIM, 78, 178n188, 182n238
 St. Louis Divinity School, 71
 St. Louis University, 71
 See also Anaheim Convention (1975); Concordia (St. Louis) faculty majority; Concordia Seminary (St. Louis)
Settle, Paul, 157n197
sexuality
 and the PECUSA, 112

Shephard, Walter, 28
Shils, Edward, 140n10
  Tradition, 200n12
Simcox, C., 195n144, 199n188
Simmel, Georg
  Conflict, 133
Smelser, Neil
  Theory of Collective Behavior, 127
Smith, Morton H.
  mentioned, 24, 150n116,
  How is the Gold Become Dim, 7
  opposed to social action, 15
  organizer of the Continuing Presbyterian
    Church, 39-42, 159n223
  RTS lecturer, 20, 148n98
  supporting racial segregation, 14,
    146n64
Smith, William, 99
Societas Sanctae (Society for the Holy
    Cross), 195n144
Society for Promoting and Encouraging the
    Arts and Knowledge of the Church
    (SPEAK), 195n144
Society for the Holy Cross (*Societas
    Sanctae*), 195n144
Society for the Preservation of the Book of
    Common Prayer (SPBCP)
    and the FCC, 118, 195n144
    founded, 105
    growth, 106, 108
    protests, 106-108
    purposes, 105
Sociology, 4, 127
The Sociology of Religion (O'Dea), 201n17
"The Sociology of Schism" (Wilson), 127
Southern Churches in Crisis (Hill), 142n23
Southern Presbyterian Church. *See*
    Presbyterian Church in the United States
    (PCUS)
Southern Presbyterian Journal, 11, 16, 18,
    144n37
    censures the Confession of 1967, 21
    See also *The Presbyterian Journal*
*Southern White Protestantism in the
    Twentieth Century* (Bailey), 8, 142n24
Spears, R., 192n101
Spitz, Thomas 77, 81, 87, 88, 89, 90
Spong, John, 103
Spring, Gardiner, 6

St. Louis Church Congress, 121-122
  "Affirmation of St. Louis," 122, 125
  See also Fellowship of Concerned
    Churchmen
St. Louis Post-Dispatch, 70
Stair, Mrs.
  Moderator of UPUSA, 156n185
Standing Liturgical Commission (SLC)
  founding, 188n40
  revision of Prayer Book, 105
  appointment of Education and
    Communication Committee, 107
  General Convention of 1976, 108-109
  "Report on Trial Use," 106
  *The Draft Proposed Book of Common
    Prayer and Other Rites and
    Ceremonies of the Church*, 107
  adopted at 1976 General
    Convention, 109
  "Zebra" Book, 106
  Powell, 107
  Weil, 107
Stefan, Martin, 45
"Strains, Conflicts and Schisms in Protestant
    Denominations" (Takayama), 96, 127
Strong, Dr., 151n125
Sullivan, Walter, 107, 118, 188n44
Synodical Conference, 47, 165n12

Takayama, K. Peter
  mentioned, 1-2, 96, 127
  and the PCUS schism, 41, 142-43n27
  environmental changes, 128-30, 133
  environmental permeability, 128-30
  ideal/actual discrepancies, 129-31, 132
  ideological concern, 128
  internal strains, 128-30, 132-33
  shifts in the authority structure, 129, 131
  sociological model of schism, 1-2
  "Strains, Conflicts and Schisms in
    Protestant Denominations," 1-2
Taylor, G. Aiken, 11, 19, 24, 27, 31,
    147n75, 151n133, 153n164, 159n222
"Tensions of Anglican Identity in the
    PECUSA: An Interpretative Essay,"
    (Petersen), 186n9.
Theory of Collective Behavior (Smelser),
    127

Third World liberation, 102
Thompson, Ernest Trice
    as social activist, 13, 15, 145n61
    Presbyterians in the South, 9, 142n19
Thompson, William P., 37
Thornwell, James Henry, 5, 140n5
Tietjen, John
    as founding member of FLUTE,
        173n105
    as leader of Concordia faculty majority,
        52-53, 60-61, 63-64, 68-70, 168n48,
        169n57, 170n71
    as leader of ELIM, 65, 77
    as seminary president
        elected, 51
        expelled, 83
        fired, 83, 171n82
        suspended, 63, 68, 83
    "A Joint Statement" (with J. Preus), 57,
        170n75
    "Evidence presented by John Tietjen," 68
    "Fact Finding or Fault Finding? An
        Analysis of J.A.O. Preus' Investigation
        of Concordia Seminary" (also called
        the "Tietjen Report"), 56
    New Orleans Convention (1973)
        Resolution 3-12, 61
        Resolution 3-12A, 62
    Which Way to Lutheran Unity, 52
Tillich, Paul, 140n12
To Comfort and to Challenge (Glock and
    Ringer), 132
"Towards an Historical Hermeneutic for
    Understanding the PECUSA,"
    (FitzSimons), 186n9
Tradition, 129
    as important in religious schism, 2-3
Tradition (Shils), 200n12
Triennial Meeting of Women, 191n93

unions
    and the LC-MS, 47
United Planning Council (UPC)
    conservative arm of LC-MS, 50, 51
Universalism
    and the LC-MS, 50
    and the PCUS, 12
usury

    and the LC-MS, 47

Vanguard Presbytery, 36-37
    See also Continuing Presbyterian Church
Vietnam involvement
    for PCUS, 155n180
Vogel, Arthur, 113
"validity," 114
von Rohr Sauer, Alfred, 173n104
vote by orders, 100
    "divided vote," 111-112

Walther, Carl Ferdinand
    as first leader of LC-MS, 45
    "The False Arguments for the Modern
        Theory of Open Questions," 53
    Trinity Church in St. Louis, 46
Warrior Presbytery, 37
Watterson, Petter F., 124, 199n192,
    199n193
Weatherby, Harold, 118, 188n44
Weber, Edwin, 50, 171n84
Welles, E. R., 112, 113, 194n130
Wendt, William, 116
Werning, Waldo, 50, 72
Westminster Confession of Faith
    as confessional standard for the
        Continuing Presbyterian Church
        (National Presbyterian Church), 32,
        34, 36, 41, 42
    as confessional standard for PCUS, 5-6,
        9-12, 23, 32-33, 144n43
    revised, 13, 21, 26, 29-30, 35
    See also Book of Confessions
        (UPUSA)
Which Way to Lutheran Unity (Tietjen), 52
White, William, 99, 188n37
Wiederaenders, Roland, 61
Wilhelm III, King Frederick, 45
Wilkinson, Ben, 156n191
Williamson, W. Jack, 25, 31, 35, 36-42,
    151n130, 156n185
    *Address Delivered During the First
        General Assembly of the Continuing
        Presbyterian Church*, 163n259
Williamson, Wayne B.

Growth and Decline in the Episcopal Church, 101-102
Willie, Charles V., 113, 114, 192n99
Wilson, John
  mentioned, 127
  five determinant stages, 127
  mobilizing agent, 127, 136
  norms and values, 128-29, 132
  precipitating factor, 128, 136
  social control, 128
  sociological model of schism, 2-3
  "The Sociology of Schism," 2-3, 127
  structural conduciveness, 127, 129, 132-33
  structural strain, 127-30, 132-33
Winn, Albert C., 29
Wolbrecht, Walter, 167n34
women
  and the LC-MS
    ordination, 49, 184n27
  and the PCUS
    ordination, 12, 26
  and the PECUSA
    House of Deputies seating, 109-110
    Lambeth Conference, 190n74, 190n75
    ordination, 109-118
      Anglican Women's Alliance, 191n84
      arguments for and against, 110-111
      as warrant for schism, 104, 126, 197n170
      as grounds for new groups, 121
      bishop's authority, 114
      bishops demanding female ordination, 117
      Board of Inquiry established, 117
      debated in 1970ff, 110
      Episcopal Women's Caucus, 191n84
      Eucharist celebration, 116
      FCC, 120
      General Convention of 1973, 110
      House of Bishops approve idea, 110, 115
        disapprove "Philadelphia Eleven," 114, 115-116
      international approval, 110
      Minneapolis General Convention, 114
      National Coalition for the Ordination of Women, 191n84
      non-American ordinations, 110
      opposition groups organize, 117
      "Philadelphia Eleven" ordained, 112-116
        See also "Philadelphia Eleven"
      Priests for the Ordination of Women (POW), 191n84
      theological issues, 115, 117, 194n129
      Women's Ordination Now (WON), 191n84
      sexist language in BCP, 107
      See also Anglican Church in North America; Anglican Catholic Church; Cheek, Alison; Fellowship of Concerned Churchmen; Heyward, Carter
World Council of Churches (WCC)
  and the AELC, 94
  and the Continuing Presbyterian Church, 38
  and the LC-MS, 94
  and the PCUS, 16, 28, 29, 30, 35, 147n76
  and PECUSA, 125
Wunderlich, Lorenz, 173n103, 173n104

Chicago Studies in the History of American Religion

Editors

JERALD C. BRAUER & MARTIN E. MARTY

1. Ariel, Yaakov. *On Behalf of Israel: American Fundamentalist Attitudes toward Jews, Judaism, and Zionism, 1865-1945*
2. Bundy, James F. *Fall from Grace: Religion and the Communal Ideal in Two Suburban Villages, 1870-1917*
3. Butler, Jonathan M. *Softly and Tenderly Jesus is Calling: Heaven and Hell in American Revivalism, 1870-1920*
4. Dvorak, Katharine L. *An African-American Exodus: The Segregation of the Southern Churches*
5. Hardesty, Nancy A. *Your Daughters Shall Prophesy: Revivalism and Feminism in the Age of Finney*
6. Harding, Vincent. *A Certain Magnificence: Lyman Beecher and the Transformation of American Protestantism, 1775-1863*
7. Hewitt, Glenn A. *Regeneration and Morality: A Study of Charles Finney, Charles Hodge, John W. Nevin and Horace Bushnell*
8. Hillis, Bryan V. *Can Two Walk Together Unless They Be Agreed?: American Religious Schisms in the 1970s*
9. Jacobsen, Douglas G. *An Unprov'd Experiment: Religious Pluralism in Colonial New Jersey*
10. Kloos, John M., Jr. *A Sense of Deity: The Republican Spirituality of Dr. Benjamin Rush*

(continued, over)

11. Kountz, Peter. *Thomas Merton as Writer and Monk: A Cultural Study, 1915-1951*
12. Lagerquist, L. DeAne. *In America the Men Milk the Cows: Factors of Gender, Ethnicity, and Religion in the Americanization of Norwegian-American Women*
13. Markwell, Bernard Kent. *The Anglican Left: Radical Social Reformers in the Church of England and the Protestant Episcopal Church, 1846-1954*
14. Morris, William Sparkes. *The Young Jonathan Edwards: A Reconstruction*
15. Pellauer, Mary D. *Toward a Tradition of Feminist Theology: The Religious Social Thought of Elizabeth Cady Stanton, Susan B. Anthony, and Anna Howard Shaw*
16. Potash, P. Jeffrey. *Vermont's Burned-Over District: Patterns of Community Development and Religious Activity, 1761-1850*
17. Queen, Edward L., II. *In the South the Baptists are the Center of Gravity: Southern Baptists and Social Change, 1930-1980*
18. Schmidt, Jean Miller. *Souls or the Social Order: The Two-Party System in American Protestantism*
19. Shaw, Stephen J. *The Catholic Parish as a Way-Station of Ethnicity and Americanization: Chicago's Germans and Italians, 1903-1939*
20. Shepard, Robert S. *God's People in the Ivory Tower: Religion in the Early American University*
21. Snyder, Stephen H. *Lyman Beecher and his Children: The Transformation of a Religious Tradition*